RECENT RESEARCHES IN THE MUSIC OF THE MIDDLE AGES AND EARLY RENAISSANCE, 33

Early Medieval Chants from Nonantola

Part IV
Sequences

Edited by Lance W. Brunner

A-R Editions, Inc.
Madison

Early Medieval Chants from Nonantola

RECENT RESEARCHES IN THE MUSIC OF THE MIDDLE AGES AND EARLY RENAISSANCE
Charles Atkinson, general editor

Part I	Ordinary Chants and Tropes	vol. 30
Part II	Proper Chants and Tropes	vol. 31
Part III	Processional Chants	vol. 32
Part IV	Sequences	vol. 33

A-R Editions, Inc., Madison, Wisconsin 53717
© 1999 by A-R Editions, Inc.

All rights reserved. No part of this book may be reproduced or transmitted in any form by any electronic or mechanical means (including photocopying, recording, or information storage and retrieval) without permission in writing from the publisher.

The purchase of this work does not convey the right to perform it in public, nor to make a recording of it for any purpose. Such permission must be obtained in advance from the publisher.

A-R Editions is pleased to support scholars and performers in their use of *Recent Researches* material for study or performance. Subscribers to any of the *Recent Researches* series, as well as patrons of subscribing institutions, are invited to apply for information about our "Copyright Sharing Policy."

Printed in the United States of America

ISBN 0-89579-425-X
ISSN 0362-3572

♾ The paper used in this publication meets the minimum requirements of the American National Standard for Information Sciences—Permanence of Paper for Printed Library Materials, ANSI Z39.48-1984.

Contents

Preface   vii
   Acknowledgments   vii

Abbreviations   ix

Introduction to the Early Medieval Sequence   xi
   The Development of the Early Sequence   xi
   The Sequence in Italy   xiv
   The Nonantola Sequences   xvii
   Notes on Performance   xx
   Notes   xxii

Critical Apparatus   xxvii
   List of Manuscript Sigla   xxvii
   List of Works Cited   xxviii
   Editorial Methods   xxix
   Commentaries   xxx

Plates   lxxi

Sequences
   1. Christi hodiernae pangimini   1
   2. Natus ante saecula   4
   3. Hanc concordi   6
   4. Iohannes Iesu Christo   8
   5. Laus tibi Christe cui sapit   10
   6. Haec sunt sacra festa   12
   7. Laude mirandum   14
   8. Festa Christi   16
   9. Concentu parili   18
   10. Virginis venerandae   21
   11. Ecce vicit   22
   12. Clara gaudia   24
   13. Dic nobis   26
   14. Eia recolamus   28
   15. Sanctae crucis celebremus   30
   16. Laus tibi Christe patris   31

17. Summi triumphum 33
18. Rex omnipotens 35
19. Sancti spiritus assit 38
20. Alme mundi rex 41
21. Pretiosa sollemnitas 43
22. Petre summe 45
23. Sancti merita Benedicti 47
24. Candida contio melos 50
25. Laurenti David 51
26. Congaudant angelorum chori 53
27. Felix valde 55
28. Summa stirpe 56
29. Alma fulgens crux praeclara 58
30. Summi regis 60
31. Clare sanctorum senatus 62
32. Omnes sancti seraphin 63
33. Sacerdotem Christi Martinum 65
34. Deus in tua virtute 67
35. Ad templi huius limina 69
36. Benedicta semper sancta 71
37. Stans a longe 74
38. Laeta mente 75
39. O quam mira 76
40. Almiflua caelorum 77

Index: Alphabetical List of Sequences 79

Preface

Early Medieval Chant from Nonantola contains all the tropes, prosulae, Ordinary chants, sequences, and processional chants found in three troper-prosers from the northern Italian monastery of San Silvestro di Nonantola: Bologna, Biblioteca Universitaria 2824; Rome, Biblioteca Casanatense 1741; and Rome, Biblioteca Nazionale Centrale 1343. These related manuscripts, which represent the lion's share of complete medieval music books with diastematic Nonantolan notation, were presumably copied in the abbey's scriptorium between the late eleventh and early twelfth centuries. Together they provide a sense of the expanded repertory of chant performed at this northern Italian monastery during the period.

The present work is divided in a way that loosely parallels the organization of the manuscript sources, which is: (1) Ordinary chants by category; (2) fraction antiphons; (3) Proper tropes, prosulae, antiphons *ante evangelium*, and sequences by feast; (4) processional antiphons, responds, hymns, and litanies by occasion. (Complete inventories of the three Nonantolan tropes are found in the general introduction.) The first part of this edition contains all the chants for the Ordinary of the Mass with associated tropes and prosulae. The second contains all tropes and prosulae for the Mass Proper with their associated chants. The third includes *confractoria,* antiphons *ante evangelium,* and processional chants. The fourth contains the forty sequences of the Nonantolan repertory, including the earliest readable versions of a number of Notker's compositions. Within each category the chants are arranged according to their use during the yearly liturgical cycle. The reader will note the similarity of this plan to the *Beneventanum Troporum Corpus,* edited by John Boe and Alejandro Planchart, Recent Researches in the Music of the Middle Ages and Early Renaissance, vols. 16–28 (Madison, 1989–).

The general introduction outlines the development of Nonantola's chant repertory and describes the three manuscript sources in detail; it concludes with complete inventories. Each volume contains introductions to the individual repertories along with commentaries on the chants with Latin texts and English translations. Summary lists of manuscript sigla for the sources cited in the edition are found before the commentaries, along with a bibliography of works cited and a discussion of editorial methods. Transcriptions of the texts and music comprise the bulk of each volume. Finally, an alphabetical index of the contexts of the volume (individual trope verses or incipits of complete chants) is also included.

This edition is intended to meet the needs of a wide variety of users. Students of Romance philology and of medieval Latin may wish to consult manuscript spellings, which are generally retained. Significant text variants are also reported. Singers and conductors will find the translations supplied in the commentaries to be helpful. Musicologists and scholars of the liturgy can consult the readings and variants to compare them with other versions of the chants and tropes. It is also hoped that specialists will use the commentaries in the first and second volumes in their studies of chant transmission. Most important, the editors hope that these volumes will spark the interest of students, enabling them to study and perform the chants found in this edition.

James Borders

Acknowledgments

This edition has been a long time in the making. The transcriptions and variants were done in the early 1980s. Administrative assignments and unexpected career detours had this early work gathering dust on the shelves for too many years. I am very grateful to the editorial staff at A-R Editions for their consummate skills: a balance of wisdom and compassion allows them to nudge a project along with a firm but gentle hand. Allan Ho was very helpful early on in working with the critical apparatus in his days as a research assistant. More recently, Phil Todd and Kristen Stauffer have been a big help in proofreading the finished manuscript.

I had great fortune, through the support of a Fellowship from the American Scandinavian Foundation, to spend research time in Stockholm to work with members of *Corpus Troporum*. I'm very grateful for the generous help of Ritva Jacobsson, Gunilla Björkvall, and especially Gunilla Iversen. All helped early on with translations, but Gunilla Iversen has been largely responsible for bringing the translations into their final form, and I am most grateful for her skill and generosity.

James Borders began his work on the tropes and other chants in the first three volumes of this set well after I started, but finished in time for me to be able to stand on his shoulders in completing the fourth and final volume of the set. I am very grateful for his excellent scholarship in the earlier volumes, as well as his other published work, which has provided a firm foundation for this volume.

Chuck Atkinson has gone beyond his role as general editor of this series in offering encouragement and meticulous readings of different versions of the manuscript. His perceptive suggestions on points large and small have strengthened the work considerably. Since our days as graduate students began together, some thirty years ago now, he has served for me as a model of a scholar and teacher. Lori Kruckenberg was kind to offer a number of helpful suggestions for the introduction. I am also very grateful to Laszlo Dobszay and Janka Szendrei for making a fine recording with the Schola Hungarica of fifteen of the sequences that appear in this edition.

I am especially grateful to Calvin Bower, my mentor and friend for many years, who not only provided insightful suggestions and shared his elegant translations of many of the sequences texts published here, but who revealed another level of "being" with these pieces. His respect and devotion to the sequence in particular and medieval music in general helped open up ways for me to deepen my understanding and appreciation of this music.

Reflecting on these and other scholars in the field makes me very grateful, indeed. It is a blessing to be able to work with such fine and generous people. I've long marveled at how medieval chant still has such power to draw people together to study, sing, and listen to it, uniting us in that one voice. How good to be able to celebrate through this music!

Lance W. Brunner

Abbreviations

AH	*Analecta Hymnica Medii Aevi*. 55 vols. Edited by Clemens Blume, Guido Maria Dreves, and Henry Marriott Bannister. 1886–1922. Reprint. New York, 1961. (Numbers after the *AH* citation refer to the volume and *page*, not the number of the item.)
BTC I	*Beneventanum Troporum Corpus I. Tropes of the Proper of the Mass from Southern Italy, A. D. 1000–1250*. Edited by Alejandro Enrique Planchart. Recent Researches in the Music of the Middle Ages and Early Renaissance, vol. 16. Madison, 1994.
EMH	*Early Music History*.
JAMS	*Journal of the American Musicological Society*.
MGG[1]	*Die Musik in Geschichte und Gegenwart*. 17 vols. Edited by Friedrich Blume. Kassel and Basel, 1949–1978.
MGG[2]	*Die Musik in Geschichte und Gegenwart. Allgemeine Ezyclopädie der Musik*. 2d ed. Edited by Ludwig Finscher. Kassel and Basel, 1994– .
MQ	*The Musical Quarterly*.
New Grove	*The New Grove Dictionary of Music and Musicians*. 20 vols. Edited by Stanley Sadie. London, 1980.
PM	Palèographie musicale.
RISM	Répertoire International des Sources Musicales.

Introduction to the Early Medieval Sequence

The early Medieval sequence, from about 850 to the year 1000, "represented one of the most important kinds of music produced in the West—important because of its intrinsic musical values as well as its historical significance for the development of style in general."[1] In this statement, Richard Crocker summarized the remarkable achievement of the creators of the bold new song we call the sequence. This song was unlike any other music in the Mass, where it stood alongside older chants such as the Alleluia and the Gradual, which—although also elaborate and sophisticated—were from another stylistic world. The sequence was also distinct from most other categories of chant in that its texts were newly composed, rather than drawn verbatim from the psalms or other books of the Bible. The liturgical position of the sequence within the Latin Mass also remained stable throughout its history, following directly after the Alleluia and preceding the Gospel reading.[2]

Reconstructing the early history of the sequence remains problematic, given that only relatively few early documents have survived, making a detailed account of the genre's origin and early development elusive at best. The lack of evidence, however, has not deterred scholars from proposing a wide array of theories concerning early developments. Much of this speculation was based on assumptions about the morphology of the genre that cannot be reconciled with the historical evidence. Nevertheless, research over the past two generations has enabled scholars to reconstruct likely scenarios and to perceive patterns in the intricate web of relationships evident in the earliest surviving sources. The situation is far too complex to describe here in detail, but because of the intricate interrelationships between pieces from different places and times, a basic understanding of the early sequence is necessary in order to appreciate the place of the Nonantolan repertory in the history of the genre.[3] It should be pointed out that this essay addresses only the early sequence, sometimes referred to as those of the "first epoch," since the Nonantolan sequences are all from this early period. The "transitional" sequences of the eleventh century, which move from the prose-based lines of unequal length to the more regular rhyming stanzaic sequences of the twelfth century, lie outside the scope of this overview.[4]

The Development of the Early Sequence

Literary references attest to the existence of a musical entity called *sequentia* as early as the beginning of the ninth century, but the earliest surviving musical sources of any substance are about a hundred years removed, coming only from the tenth century, making it impossible to determine the exact form to which the term referred. The literary references, although sparse, provide important points of reference in the attempt to envisage the emergence of the genre and its early development.[5] The earliest use of the term is found in the Mount-Blandin Mass antiphonary, which is dated ca. 800 and lacks musical notation; the cue "cum sequentia" is found after six Alleluias.[6] The term *sequentia* is mentioned both by Amalarius of Metz (ca. 830) and in the fifth *Ordo Romanus* (second half of the ninth century), apparently referring to melismatic passages.[7] The earliest unequivocal reference to the use of sequentia with words (referred to as *prosa*) occurs in a conciliar canon from Meaux in 845, which sternly admonishes singers, on threat of dismissal, not to add words to the textless sequentia.[8] The most extensive discussion of the sequence from the ninth century is found in Notker Balbulus's well-known preface to his *Liber Hymnorum*, a collection of forty sequences thought to have been completed by ca. 880.[9] His account of how he discovered the sequence and set about writing his own texts provided scholars with enough evidence to reconstruct a great deal about the time, place, and form of the early repertory that would not have been possible without such testimony. These issues are discussed below, in conjunction with the formation of regional repertories. The literary references attest to the well-established presence of the sequence—in both melismatic and texted form—in the ninth century.

The earliest surviving sequences occur as isolated pieces or small groups of pieces in manuscripts or fragments from the end of the ninth and beginning of the tenth centuries.[10] Geographically scattered, these sources show that the genre had taken root and, as the literary references suggest, was known and preserved both in melismatic, or textless, versions and those with text. By the second half of the tenth century much larger collections were produced, now with musical notation. In southern France, for example, substantial anthologies containing up to 140 sequences have survived from this time.[11] By the early eleventh century, large collections from centers widely dispersed throughout the Latin West became increasingly more numerous and the repertories somewhat stable.[12]

Two distinct regional traditions, each with its own repertory, were already firmly established by the time of the earliest surviving manuscript collections at the beginning of the tenth century. The regions essentially corresponded to the partition of the Carolingian Empire into East and West Francia, established in the Treaty of Meersen (870). Surviving evidence from both regions reveals striking similarities (suggesting some type of exchange and shared tradition early on) and distinct differences (suggesting a strong sense of regional character and stylistic preference). In each of the two regions, one center assumes particular prominence: the monasteries of St. Gall, in East Francia, and St. Martial of Limoges, in the West. The abbey of St. Gall's prominence in the history of the early sequence owes primarily to Notker Balbulus, whose *Liber Hymnorum* formed the basis of the remarkably stable East-Frankish repertory.[13] Important sequence manuscripts were also produced in other East-Frankish centers, but their repertories essentially reflected that of St. Gall.

St. Martial, as far as we know, did not have a counterpart to Notker's creative genius. The musical prominence of the monastery rests rather on the strength of its library, which preserved the richest collection of Frankish chant (especially sequences and tropes) to have come down to us. A number of these manuscripts that found their way into the library, however, were from other centers in West Francia, Aquitaine in particular, and did not necessarily reflect the repertory of chant at St. Martial.[14] These sources have long attracted the attention of scholars because of the musical notation, which was the first to give clear enough indications of pitch relationships to allow for reasonably accurate transcriptions, and because of the extensive repertory transmitted in the manuscripts. The remaining manuscripts were acquired for the library from other centers in the region during the Middle Ages. Scarcity of early source material from other regions within West Francia, particularly in the North—an area considered of fundamental importance to the early history of the genre—has made it impossible either to identify composers or to locate the most important ninth-century centers of creativity in the West.

By the end of the tenth century the East- and West-Frankish traditions had about thirty melodies in common out of about 150 that were known throughout Europe.[15] Sequence melodies were usually identified by specific titles, although different titles were routinely assigned in the East and the West for the same melody, pointing to the independence of the two traditions. Some titles derive simply from the sequence text or Alleluia verse with which it was associated, such as "Fulgens praeclara" or "Dies sanctificatus."[16] Other melodies were given more colorful titles based on regions or places, such as "Occidentana" or "Romana," or even on musical instruments, such as the "Cithara" or "Tuba." The meanings of other titles, such as "Puella turbata," "Duo tres," or "Frigdola," still elude convincing explanations and have given rise to imaginative speculation as to the performance implications of the names and possible origins of the tunes.[17] A number of melodies became favorites, attracting new texts time and again. The tune called "Mater," for example, received around fifty different texts across all political and geographic boundaries in Europe.[18]

The use of the same or closely related melodies in both traditions suggests exchange early on. Indeed, the story Notker recounts in his preface to the *Liber Hymnorum* about how he came to discover and write his own sequences provides an example of such exchange between West and East.[19] Notker tells that in his youth a monk from Jumièges, fleeing from the Norman sack of his monastery, arrived at St. Gall with an antiphonary containing some sequences (referred to as, "versus ad sequentias");[20] Notker was taken with the idea, but found the quality of the texts so poor that he set out to write his own texts under the guidance of his teachers. If this little tale is reflective of early patterns of dissemination, then sequences were carried, perhaps originally from an origin in northern France, to new centers throughout the Frankish kingdom. St. Gall, with the young Notker on hand, happened to be a particularly fertile ground to receive such seeds sown.

Although Notker chronicled a very important point of contact and instance of exchange between the

West and the East, centers on opposite sides of the Rhine preferred distinctly different collections of texts, which they recorded and described in different ways as well.[21] West-Frankish sources generally presented the pieces in two ways: (1) melismatically, that is, music without the text, and (2) syllabically, that is, music and text together with a neume above each syllable. The melismatic version was called a *sequentia*, while the complete piece—text and music—was called a *prosa*, or *prosa ad sequentiam*. In a West-Frankish manuscript, the *prosae* and *sequentiae* were typically grouped together in separate sections referred to by modern scholars as a *prosarium* and a *sequentiarium*, respectively, both transmitting the same repertory but in different forms.[22] East-Frankish manuscripts, on the other hand, typically transmitted pieces with both text and music together; the music was usually written as melismas in the margins, and the entire piece was called a *sequentia*.[23] The various forms of transmitting melody and text have significant implications for performance and will be discussed below under "Notes on Performance." Scholars have tried in vain to align modern terminology with the West-Frankish sources themselves, since there are clear advantages in calling the texted version of the piece "prose," or *prosa*, and the untexted version *sequentia*, as will be discussed below. Force of habit has kept "sequence" the most commonly used term to describe the whole piece, while the Latin form *sequentia* is generally reserved for the textless version.[24] Nevertheless, since the medieval use of the term sequence was not consistent in early sources, terminology should be clarified in any discussion of the genre. Italian sources consistently use the term *sequentia* to refer to the piece with both melody and text.

Crocker used Notker as his central witness in identifying ninth-century West-Frankish sequences.[25] Since substantial manuscript documentation of sequences begins only in the tenth century, Crocker reasoned that if he could determine which sequences from the West were Notker's probable models, he could confirm their existence by 880, accepting Wolfram von den Steinen's dating. *The Early Medieval Sequence* provides a detailed account of his detective work, comparing multiple textings to melodies used in the West and East, in order to isolate at least a core of pieces that comprised the first generation of the West-Frankish repertory (ca. 850–80). Crocker went so far as to offer conjectural revisions of some of the West-Frankish sequences by stripping away what may have been tenth-century accretions.[26]

Crocker assumed that Notker's account of his first encounter with the genre and his early attempts at composition was accurate, that it reflected the general trend for transmission, and that it described, along with Notker's works themselves, the genesis of the bulk of the East-Frankish repertory. His working hypothesis was that Notker may simply have written new texts for the West-Frankish pieces that came to him from Jumièges without altering the melodies; thus, his sequences are a way of discovering the "original" form of both melody and text in the West-Frankish pieces. Although this hypothesis produced highly insightful analysis of both text and music, along with compelling speculation, subsequent research has begun to question the simplicity of the picture it paints. While it is certain that some pieces did move from region to region and across cultural and political boundaries, especially very early on, most pieces did not. The fundamentally different stylistic preferences between the West and East kept the traditions quite separate. So complete was the separation of the East- and West-Frankish sequence repertories, that Lori Kruckenberg has proposed the likelihood of a reception barrier (*Rezeptionsbarriere*) between the two traditions in the tenth and eleventh centuries.[27] The recognition of such divisions has important implications that have led scholars to refine or revise some of Crocker's findings.[28]

The Early Medieval Sequence is the most extensive and perceptive study of style in the early sequence to date, recent challenges to some of its assumptions notwithstanding. Crocker's analysis uncovered such a wide range of individual traits "as to render many generalities invalid."[29] Yet, as he also made clear, there are important shared stylistic traits that help define the genre and distinguish it markedly from other categories of chant. In the early repertory we can note two general types of pieces called sequence. The first, and by far most common type, has been referred to as the "standard-form" sequence, which is characterized by a formal process that has been called "progressive parallelism." Under this process, basically syllabically-set lines occurring as couplets, where pairs of iso-syllabic lines with ongoing text share the same melodic phrase. This form can be represented as *aa bb cc*, etc. Often single lines begin and close the piece, and internal singles are not uncommon in the early repertory as well. References to the sequence in the current introduction, unless otherwise qualified, are to the standard-form type. The second type of sequence has been called "aparallel," since it is not based on the musical repetition of phrases; it is discussed briefly below.

The sequence is radically different from the older Gregorian Mass Propers in that it employed new strategies that, while flexible, allowed levels of organization on a large scale, including movement toward climactic high points, a teleological orientation not possible within the stylistic constraints of the earlier chant. The musical repetition of the couplet structure serves as both a powerful organizing force and a means of expansion, emphasizing the musical phrases and thereby serving to clarify the overall structure built from these phrases. The melodic phrases have much sharper tonal focus on the final or co-final than the other Proper chants. This focus results from the use of standard and distinctive cadential formulas, as well as from the use of the disciplined and simplified melodic style that avoids ornamental flourishes, but is more shapely than the even-keeled reiteration associated with recitation tones. Sequence melodies usually span a broad ambitus, using a pitch set larger than that of any single mode; the melodies often include or exceed the combined ranges of authentic and plagal modes for a given final. Melodies are often constructed from recognizable motives or melodic formulas that are used freely to explore specific registers and tonal areas as the piece unfolds.[30]

The elevated "poetic-prose" of the texts provides continuity and a sense of progression within the repetitive melodic structure. Through its properties of sonority, prose rhythm, rhetoric, and articulation of grammatical distinctions, the text plays a critical role in determining the shape of the piece. The interaction of textual and musical structure—the way the syntax is aligned with and reinforces the musical phrases or, on occasion, reinterprets them into larger groupings in the overall design—is an essential aspect of the early sequence. The large-scale design or plan for each of the early melodies is unique in the way it combines phrases of different lengths into the whole. The most ambitious texts both utilized and helped project the overall plan. Because the plans are unique, they are like an individual fingerprint that makes it possible to identify the melody to which a text was sung, even if the text is transmitted without music, simply by matching the number of syllables with the number of notes in the phrases.[31] The simple syllabic setting and direct melodic motion organized around selected tonal centers, which allows us to perceive readily the large-scale form, represents one of the finest artistic achievements of the Carolingian period.

East- and West-Frankish traditions held a number of melodies in common, and in general shared a similar approach to melodic style. The most pronounced stylistic distinctions between the two traditions occur in the texts themselves and the ways they were set to the music. Notker preferred the elegant diction and vocabulary of classical and early Christian Latin prose, in particular that of the Church Fathers, frequently alluding to scriptural and hagiographic literature and often expressing subtle shades of meaning with refined syntax.[32] West-Frankish composers, on the other hand, seemed to value a more exuberant diction, what Crocker calls "the smoothing, homogenizing effects of alliteration and assonance," often at the expense of smooth, or even completely coherent, syntax.[33] Notker's texts represent fine poetry in their own right, while West-Frankish texts need to be sung to experience their full impact.[34] The difference is quite pronounced, making it easy to envisage Notker's disappointment with the West-Frankish texts from Jumiège, which, as his preface relates, became the goad for him to provide his own texts.

The so-called aparallel sequences form a very small group.[35] These sequences share neither the couplet structure nor length and design with the larger, standard-form sequences. Furthermore, musical phrases generally do not use the distinctive cadential patterns that clearly set off the phrases. Without the couplet structure, clearly articulated phrases, and strong tonal focus, the aparallel sequences resemble the discursive style of the jubilus.[36] Most of these sequences show a clearer relationship to specific Alleluias than do the standard-form sequences. Aparallel sequences have melodic incipits that are likely to match those of Alleluias they are paired with. In West-Frankish sources, aparallel sequences occur primarily during Advent and the Sundays after Pentecost, as well as during the Easter Vigil. In East-Frankish sources these sequences occur in the ferial masses of Easter week, as well as on the Sundays after the Octave of Easter. Some scholars have proposed that the aparallel sequences represented an earlier stage of development that led to the parallel, standard-form sequences.[37] This hypothesis is not supported by historical evidence, however. Both types of sequences existed side by side in the earliest manuscripts. In his extensive study of these pieces, Klaus Kohrs concluded that they represented another possibility within the broad scope of the genre, rather than an earlier stage of development.

By the end of the ninth century, the early sequence was already a very rich and complex genre. Even within the standard-form sequence, there was a range of compositional possibilities and stylistic options. When one considers the smaller samplings of aparallel sequences, the spectrum opens wider still. Although the evidence is too sparse to reconstruct with certainty how, when, and where the genre first appeared, we can imagine plausible scenarios. And by the late tenth century we have the documentary evidence of the range of creative activity that made the sequence, as Crocker has noted, "one of the most important kinds of music produced in the West."

The Sequence in Italy

The central developments in the formation of the early sequence took place, from all indications, north of the Alps, leaving Italy and other regions (such as England, Scandinavia, and central Europe) on the fringe of this activity. Yet these striking new pieces must have spread fairly quickly to areas on the periphery, radiating out in all directions from the intense activity at the center. Their impact must have also spawned local creativity, since we find in many outlying centers local counterparts to the received pieces: some in direct imitation or supplied with new texts to popular international melodies, others departing radically from the received forms and introducing their own stylistic preferences. These pieces rarely reached the same artistic levels as the greatest achievements from the center, but they reveal new possibilities and allow us to witness the broader stylistic spectrum explored in the genre throughout Europe. Regional and local repertories, as one might assume, developed their own character, revealed both by the way imported pieces were transmitted and in the new works created there.[38]

Scholarly investigation of regional traditions outside the major northern centers, particularly with respect to tropes and sequences, is a relatively recent development. Early research efforts were directed toward the restoration of the Gregorian Mass Propers and the Office, with little attention to the so-called accretions, which included tropes and sequences.[39] These focused on the earliest surviving sources and on those centers where the concentration of early manuscripts was high, as in St. Gall, St. Martial of Limoges, Laon, and Chartres.[40] Scholars who began studying tropes and sequences likewise focused their research on the earliest sources in an attempt to clarify the origins of the various genres.[41] Notker's artful sequence texts, in conjunction with the ambitious international melodies, were seen as the classical ideal in the early sequence, to which pieces from other regions did not fully compare.[42] The early West-Frankish sequences have found a champion in Richard Crocker, who extolled, more emphatically than any scholar previously, the artistic achievements of many of these pieces in their exuberant melodic play.[43] Only relatively recently have scholars begun studying sequences and tropes from the peripheral repertories outside the major Frankish centers.[44] Italian sequences, in particular, often seemed odd or clumsy by comparison, and the Italian manuscripts themselves unreliable sources for the transmission of Notker's and other northern sequences.[45] Much research on both sequence and trope in the last twenty-five years has focused on regional centers throughout Europe, revealing a more complete picture of these genres of medieval chant.[46]

The initial task in assessing the role of the history of early sequence in Italy has been in uncovering the surviving manuscripts and delineating the repertory. There are close to fifty known surviving manuscripts or fragments of manuscripts of Italian origin written before 1200 that contain sequences.[47] This includes a substantial group of manuscripts from southern Italy, particularly Benevento, as well as individual manuscripts and small groups of manuscripts from other centers in central and northern Italy.[48] Facsimiles of a number of Italian manuscripts containing sequences are now widely available.[49] Well over 250 different sequences are found in these manuscripts, representing a remarkably wide stylistic range.[50] One can speak of an Italian "repertory" only in a very general sense, for the surviving manuscripts written on Italian soil reflect a number of local repertories that are significantly diverse. Furthermore, we can assume that the surviving sources give us but an imperfect picture, since the loss of manuscripts in Italy and throughout Europe must have been enormous.[51] Nevertheless, however great the losses, however many threads of continuity that once tied local traditions together but are no longer visible, the surviving sources reveal clear patterns of diversity that were surely characteristic in the Middle Ages as well. If the intricate details of the fabric have largely disappeared, basic themes and outlines of major developments can still be perceived via the precious few remaining clues.

One obvious trait common to Italian sequence manuscripts is a reliance on pieces imported from northern centers to build local repertories. We find texts by Notker alongside those by West-Frankish poets, as well as a range of Italian texts and melodies. The diversity of local repertories is a result of the varying strengths of the difficult regional components and the selection of individual sequences for specific feasts. The result is a stylistic pluralism in most Italian sources that would have been inconceivable in either East- or West-Frankish sources, where the sequences remained within narrower and more consistent limits defined by both genre and style. It is not surprising that trope repertories show similar tendencies and often stylistically striking contrasts between Franco-Roman Propers and Italian tropes with entirely different melodic style, apparently preserving archaic pieces.[52]

In assigning regional origins, given the current state of our knowledge, the texts are easier to work with than the melodies, since texts generally remained within specific regions that suggest likely origins, while melodies are often widely dispersed across regions by the time of the earliest manuscript witnesses, thus making reasonable assessment of origin difficult, if not impossible.[53] In working with the Italian manuscripts, the most useful categories are: East Frankish, Italian (which can be further divided into north, south, and pan-Italian), West Frankish, and Romanic (which refers to the romance language zone of Italy and France, but can also extend to the British Isles). This final category is necessary for those texts that had equally strong distribution in both Italian and French (and occasionally English) manuscripts and where a more precise determination of origin is not possible.[54]

East-Frankish texts are very strongly represented in local Italian repertories. In a survey of eighteen Italian centers, 43 percent of texts on average are of East-Frankish origin (almost all of these found in St. Gall), 33 percent Italian, 13 percent West Frankish, and 11 percent Romanic.[55] The high percentages of East-Frankish sequence texts in Italian manuscripts is a result of the widespread adoption of relatively few texts (52), most of which are believed to be by Notker. There are over twice as many texts of Italian origin (112) in these sources, many of which enjoyed primarily local use, appearing in only a few manuscripts, whereas a popular piece such as Notker's *Sancti spiritus assit* is found in over thirty Italian manuscripts.[56]

Yet, within Italy, manuscript repertories differ widely with respect to the regional origins of their texts and the traditions they represent. For example, in the manuscript Padua, Seminario 697, 31 of the 36 sequences (or 86 percent) have texts of East-Frankish origin, with only four texts of West-Frankish origin and one from Italy.[57] On the other end of the spectrum are the manuscripts from southern Italy, where 55 percent of the texts are of Italian origin, most of these from southern Italy, with only roughly 17 percent of East-Frankish origin.[58] In the Novalese source Oxford, Bodleian, Douce 222, about 60 percent of the texts are either West Frankish or Romanic. At any given center the distribution of texts according to likely origin is a result of a number of variables, including geographic location, cultural and political ties with other centers, as well as local tastes and creative activity.

The nature of the Italian sequence tradition has several important implications about the way the material might best be approached, as well as the type of information we can expect to learn. First, the diversity of the tradition suggests that any significant study must proceed on the basis of repertories at specific centers or areas within Italy. Now that the overall terrain has been mapped, additional sources that may come to light can be placed easily within this broader picture. Second, the various regional components that comprise individual repertories invite us to look beyond the strictly stylistic considerations of text and music and explore the cultural and political forces once operating in individual centers that accounted for the unique formulation of their repertories. Third, the coexistence in the same manuscript of both imported and Italian works suggests comparative study of style between regions. Assessing the ways in which imported works were transmitted offers another perspective on the northern sequences. Furthermore, many Italian pieces convey a completely different picture of the genre. It is this juxtaposition of different stylistic worlds that makes the Italian tradition so fascinating and instructive.

Pluralism allowed sequences of widely different origins and styles to co-exist, side by side within the same manuscript. But more than just accommodating strange bedfellows (or so East- and West-Frankish pieces would be considered north of the Alps), it is the texts and melodies of Italian origin themselves that make Italy so unusual in the history of the genre. It is difficult to make generalizations about all texts of Italian origin, since they were produced in different centers and under very different circumstances—some texts are very good imitations of classical models, while others are as far removed from such models as one can imagine. One trait common to a number of texts is a tendency toward acclamation and passionate assertion.[59] A vivid example is the southern Italian text *Cantemus canticum*, which contains the following lines:[60]

4. O veneranda annuata pascha!
5. O gloriosa festa pretiosa!
6. In qua exsultant angelorum agmina: O pascha, O pascha, pascha iam sancta!
7. Chorus apostolorum est tripudians: O pascha, O pascha, pascha omnes te laudent!
8. Et nos de terris iubilemus: O pascha, O pascha, pascha iam clara facta!

4. O venerable annual pascha!
5. O glorious feast most precious!
6. In which the troupe of angels cries out: O pascha, O pascha, pascha now holy!
7. The chorus of apostoles is dancing with joy: O pascha, O pascha, pascha all sing your praises!
8. Let us on earth also sing in celebration: O pascha, O pascha, pascha now made glorious!

The editors of *Analecta Hymnica* compared *Cantemus canticum* unfavorably with the well-known East-Frankish sequence *Cantemus cuncti melodum*, which is also found in the Beneventan manuscripts. The texts do bear a certain resemblance, but they are from very different worlds. Ritva Jacobsson has shown how the Italian text is an unusual and original mixture of three popular *topoi*: a call to praise—reminiscent of many psalms—employing musical instruments; a veneration of the feast of Easter; and a central theological statement about Christ's incarnation through Mary (more commonly associated with Christmas than Easter).[61] *Summa solemnitas*, found in sources from

Benevento and Ravenna, is another example of a text with acclamatory phrases.[62]

Melodies of Italian origin also span a broad stylistic compass, including tunes that would not be out of place north of the Alps. There are, however, a number of pieces that are strikingly different from the popular melodies from the North. Kenneth Levy was one of the first to explore the implications of such stylistic disparity in his study of *Lux de luce*.[63] Levy showed that the sequence as transmitted in manuscripts from Ravenna preserved an ancient hexameter hymn text, as well as a musical procedure he termed "variation versus." The ambitus of the piece remains relatively narrow, unlike the full-blown northern melodies, which systematically explore a large range, emphasizing different tonal areas. Moreover, because a single melodic line is repeated with some variation, the lines are roughly similar in length, thus not creating the unique plan that distinguishes many northern sequence melodies.

The pan-Italian sequence *Alma fulgens crux praeclara* (no. 29 in this edition) is similar in style to *Lux de luce*. It is found in some fifteen manuscripts ranging in origin from Benevento in the south to Brescia in the north. Like *Lux de luce* the various lines are essentially elaborations of the same melodic profile, including an elaborate cadential pattern used throughout. A salient feature is its florid melodic line, which gives the piece a neumatic-melismatic character, rather than the more typical syllabic text setting. Bruno Stäblein viewed this phenomenon as a stylistic choice in which Italians preferred to emphasize the ornamental grace of a melodic line, rather than its structural dimensions, which requires more precise repetition within couplets and a more disciplined, syllabically-set melodic line.[64] Although *Alma fulgens crux praeclara* is an extreme example of departure from the principles adopted in most standard-form sequences, the tendency for such departures can be seen in a number of other works.[65]

Pieces like *Lux de luce* and *Alma fulgens crux praeclara* raise some fundamental issues pertinent to the Italian sequence tradition. The first generation of scholars to study the genre assumed that the Italians either did not fully understand the genre or were not up to the task of producing works comparable to many of those north of the Alps. Yet, clearly, there were other forces at work. The introduction in Italy of the sequence, as a new kind of piece, created an opportunity for singers to preserve older layers of chant or styles in a new guise, as the Franco-Roman chant from the north replaced the indigenous chant—as Levy maintained with *Lux de luce* and Planchart with the southern Italian tropes.[66] With these pieces there is no sense of the text "punctuating" the melodies, as Notker's skillful syllabic placement of the text accomplishes. Notker's texts help articulate the small groups of notes that fit together like a carefully wrought mosaic. In a piece like *Alma fulgens crux praeclara* the neumatic, ornamental texture suggests a continuously flowing melos, without clear motivic articulations within the phrases, nor strict adherence to parallelism between the halves of a couplet.

Another unusual product of the encounter of north and south is the complex of Easter sequences based on the famous trope text *Quem queritis mulieres*.[67] The sequence appears in ten manuscripts, most from southern Italy, where it seems to have originated, but it also appears in northern Italian manuscripts. The transmission is so complex that it is best to treat individual phrases like trope "elements," for they were handled with the same kind of freedom that marks individual lines of tropes, easily arranged in a variety of configurations from one version to the next.[68] This is in marked contrast to Notker's sequences, where the careful coordination between text and music, particularly the unique shapes and teleological orientation, precluded the kind of exchange of phrases found in trope elements. A striking feature of this complex is the restricted ambitus, where most melodic motion moves primarily within the fifth F–c. The formulaic character is similar to the variation-versus principle of *Lux de luce*. *Quem queritis mulieres* also exhibits the tendency toward ornamental expansion of the syllabic setting, as seen in *Alma fulgens crux praeclara*.

Whether one considers pieces like these Italian sequences a degeneration of a classical form or an expansion welcoming new possibilities, which included preserving older forms and styles in a new garb, it is clear that another set of principles and assumptions were operating in Italy. The unusual stylistic features of the Italian sequences may be summarized as follows: (1) ornamental expansion of syllabic units, often threatening the syllabic orientation of the music; (2) considerable variations in line lengths within the couplet and frequent departures in detail; (3) a structure, in some pieces, based on relatively equal line lengths, as in the variation-versus principle; (4) a reduction in the range or tonal space explored in a work; and (5) a softening of the profile of the melody, making phrases seem similar rather than sharply differentiated.

The Nonantolan Sequences

The Abbey of San Silvestro at Nonantola was one of the most important monastic centers in northern Italy during the Middle Ages. Its strategic location and political and spiritual importance made it a center of lively, if not always friendly, exchange between both the north and south, as well as the east and the west.[69] This exchange must have involved music and liturgy as well; the musical manuscripts include many chants from other geographical regions that imply different layers of influence over time.[70]

The repertory of sequences at Nonantola, like other Italian centers, is made up of pieces of diverse origin. Table 1 lists, in liturgical order, all of the forty known sequences from the abbey preserved in the three principal trope-sequence manuscripts.[71] The numbers of the sequences in table 1 correspond to their ordering in this edition. The repertory is comparatively small because, with rare exceptions, feasts are usually provided with only a single sequence, whereas the larger Italian repertories, like those from southern Italy or from Mantua (Verona 107), often have three or more sequences for major feasts. Furthermore, as the second column in the table shows, most pieces are preserved in all three manuscripts, suggesting that the repertory must have been fairly stable throughout most of the eleventh and twelfth centuries. In comparing the tropes from Nonantolan sources with those of Verona 107, Borders attributed the different sizes of the repertories as a reflection of the different functions of the manuscripts: Verona 107 was more of an "encyclopedic anthology," while the Nonantolan manuscripts reflect a working repertory, with the sources being essentially practical.[72] The sequences from both centers support this assertion about the manuscripts serving different functions.[73]

East-Frankish sequences, with 22 of the 40 texts, account for more than half the Nonantolan repertory; 15 of these texts have been ascribed to Notker (compared with 11 Italian, 3 West-Frankish, 3 Romanic, and 1 of unknown origin). The preponderance of East-Frankish pieces is not hard to understand, given the important cultural and political ties to East Francia. Borders has pointed to some of the important connections between regions in the general introduction to this edition.[74] To this, one might add Heinrich Pfaff's research on the lively commerce and travel that took place during the Middle Ages between northern Italy and the north through the Alpine passes.[75] The Sachsen emperors, for example, took a number of trips to Italy through the Septimer pass during the second half of the tenth century that have been documented. Pfaff referred to this period as Septimer's "Golden Age" (*Glanzzeit*), a time when travelers from the north poured into northern Italy, no doubt introducing some of their own culture and even songs to the sunny realms south of the Alps.[76] In the tenth century, the Ottonian emperors had a particularly strong influence at Nonantola and had control of the abbey until 1083.[77] Imperial influence was especially strong during the abbacy of Rudolph I, abbot of St. Silvester from 1002 to 1035.[78] Rudolph won renown for his enthusiastic acquisition of books for the abbey library. With such interchange it is not difficult to imagine why there is such a strong East-Frankish representation in the sequence repertory. Yet the trope repertory reminds us that this neat description of influences and transmission does not apply to other genres. Borders pointed out that with respect to Proper tropes Nonantolan sources had a greater affinity for West- than East-Frankish pieces. Indeed, each category of chant (i.e., tropes, sequences, prosulae) seems to have its own pattern of transmission.[79]

The Nonantolan manuscripts provide the earliest readable versions with clefs of some 22 East-Frankish sequences. Despite their early witness and careful execution, the Nonantolan sources have often been overlooked or dismissed by modern scholars. In his edition of Notker's sequence texts, for example, von den Steinen explicitly rejected manuscripts from the northern Italian centers of Ivrea, Mantua, Vercelli, Novelese, and Bobbio, because in his view the scribes either used third- or forth-hand copies for their work or, worse, they did not entirely grasp the sense of the texts.[80] He did not include Nonantola on his list of unreliable centers, but neither did he use these sources for his edition.

A comparison of the East-Frankish sequence texts transmitted in the Nonantolan manuscripts with those in von den Steinen's edition is revealing. The Nonantolan versions of Notker's texts are in fact very close to his critical editions. The variants are minor for the most part and do not affect the meaning or clarity of the text, as in a preference for the indicative mood over the subjunctive. None of the fourteen texts by Notker found in Rc 1741 requires emendation to make sense of the text.[81] The quality of the Latinity in this and the other two Nonantolan sources is very high. Several readings, in fact, offer more correct Latin or different theological nuances than those in von den Steinen's versions. Furthermore, very few of the variants found in the Nonantolan versions occur in the fifteen East-Frankish manuscripts he used to establish his critical edition. These variants apparently reflect a northern Italian, if not specifically Nonantolan, tradition that was distinct from the St. Gall and other East-Frankish centers. The difference between the Nonantolan and von den Steinen's versions of the East-Frankish texts by other poets is even stronger than with Notker's texts. Once again the Nonantolan readings provide a different perspective and, on occasion, better readings than the Northern sources. It seems unlikely that any of the Nonantolan variants provide the original version, even when the readings seem slightly better, although this possibility should not be ruled out; after all, since we know from the dedication that the original destination of the *Liber Hymnorum* was northern Italy (Vercelli). These texts as copied at Nonantola should be the basis of a more systematic investigation, which the present edition invites.

TABLE 1
The Repertory of Sequences at Nonantola

Incipit [AH citation]	MSS*	Feast	Origin of Text	Melody Title†
1. Christi hodiernae pangimini [53:25]	**Bu**	Christmas I	Italian (north)	"Christi hodiernae" (cf. Mater)
2. Natus ante saecula [53:20]	All	Christmas III	Notker	"Dies sanctificatus"
3. Hanc concordi [53:345]	All	St. Stephen	Notker	"Concordia" (cf. Ephiphaniam)
4. Iohannes Iesu Christo [53:276]	All	St. John Evangelist	Notker	"Romana" (cf. Dic nobis/Clara gaudia)
5. Laus tibi Christe cui sapit [53:256]	**Bu**	Holy Innocents	Notker	"Justus ut palma maior"
6. Haec sunt sacra festa [37:259]	All	St. Sylvester	Italian (Nonantola?)	"Eia turma"
7. Laude mirandum [34:13]	**Rc, Rn**	Octave of Christmas	Italian (north)	"Captiva"
8. Festa Christi [53:50]	All	Epiphany	Notker	"Trinitas"
9. Concentu parili [53:171]	All	Purification	Notker	"Symphonia"
10. Virginis venerandae [53:395]	**Bu, Rc**	St. Fusca	East-Frankish	"Filia matris"
11. Ecce vicit [53:73]	All	Easter Sunday	Romanic	"Epiphaniam" (cf. Concordia)
12. Clara gaudia [53:71]	All	Easter Monday	West-Frankish	"Dic nobis/Clara gaudia" (cf. Romana)
13. Dic nobis [53:69]	All	Easter Tuesday	Romanic	"Dic nobis/Clara gaudia" (cf. Romana)
14. Eia recolamus [53:23]	All	Octave of Easter	East-Frankish	"Eia turma"
15. Sanctae crucis celebremus [37:24]	**Rc, Rn**	Invention holy cross	Italian (north)	"Sanctum diem"
16. Laus tibi Christe patris [53:258]	All	Ss. Senesius and Theopontius	East-Frankish	"Mirabilis Deus"
17. Summi triumphum [53:114]	All	Ascension	Notker	"Captiva"
18. Rex omnipotens [53:111]	**Rc**	Ascension	West-Frankish	"Occidentana" (cf. Rex omnipotens)
19. Sancti spiritus assit [53:119]	All	Pentecost	Notker	"Occidentana" (cf. Rex omnipotens)
20. Alme mundi rex [37:187]	All	St. John the Baptist	Italian	"Hodiernus sacratior"
21. Pretiosa sollemnitas [53:332]	All	St. Peter	Italian (north)	?
22. Petre summe [53:336]	All	St. Peter	Notker	"Concordia" (cf. Ephiphaniam)
23. Sancti merita Benedicti [54:52]	**Rc, Rn**	Translation of St. Benedict	Italian (north)	"Occidentana" (cf. Rex omnipotens)
24. Candida contio melos [7:184]	**Rc**	Translation of St. Benedict	Romanic	"Romana" (cf. Dic nobis/Clara gaudia)
25. Laurenti David [53:283]	All	St. Lawrence	Notker	"Romana" (cf. Dic nobis/Clara gaudia)
26. Congaudent angelorum chori [53:179]	All	Assumption of Blessed Virgin Mary	Notker	"Mater" (cf. Christi hodiernae)
27. Felix valde {fragment} [34:84]	**Rn**	Assumption of Blessed Virgin Mary	Italian (north)	"Metensis minor" (cf. Stans a longe)
28. Summa stirpe [10:20]	All	Birth of the Blessed Virgin Mary	East-Frankish	"Dies sanctificatus"
29. Alma fulgens crux praeclara [37:25]	All	In exaltation of Holy Cross	Italian	——
30. Summi regis [53:312]	All	Michael Archangel	East-Frankish	?
31. Clare sanctorum senatus [53:367]	All	Ss. Simon and Jude	Notker	"Aurea"
32. Omnes sancti seraphin [53:196]	All	All Saints	Notker	"Vox exultationes"
33. Sacerdotem Christi Martinum [53:294]	All	St. Martin	East-Frankish	"Beatus vir"
34. Deus in tua virtute [53:210]	All	St. Andrew	East-Frankish	"Nimis honorati sunt"
35. Ad templi huius limina [53:402]	**Rc, Rn**	Dedication of a Church	Italian (north)	"Eia turma"
36. Benedicta semper sancta [53:139]	All	Trinity Sunday	?	"Benedicta semper"
37. Stans a longe [53:158]	All	Sunday XI after Pentecost	West-Frankish	"Stans a longe" (cf. Metensis minor)
38. Laeta mente [53:103]	All	Sunday XIII after Pentecost	Notker	"Exultate Deo"
39. O quam mira [53:118]	All	Sunday XVII after Pentecost**	Notker	"Confitemini"
40. Almiflua caelorum [34:92]	All	Sunday XXII after Pentecost	Italian	——

*I have shortened manuscript abbreviations for this table, as follows: **Bu** = Bologna, Biblioteca Universitaria, MS 2824; **Rc** = Rome, Biblioteca Casanatense, MS 1741; **Rn** = Rome, Biblioteca Nazionale Centrale, MS 1343. See "Commentary" below for further details.

†East and West Frankish sources had different sets of titles to the sequences melodies in the repertory (often different names for the same or closely related melodies). I have used the title associated with the tradition from which it came. Thus, the tune for *Ecce vicit* was called "Epiphaniam" in West-Frankish sources; the East-Frankish counterpart, which is related but not identical, is called "Concordia." I have cross-referenced the melodies in parentheses for convenience. For Italian pieces using northern melodies, the title most closely associated with the likely model is used. See Bower, "From Alleluia to Sequence," for the most thorough discussion of melodies and the issues involving their titles.

Assigned to Sunday XIX after Pentecost in **Rn.

The melodies of the imported works in the Nonantolan manuscripts are transmitted with the same kind of careful attention as the texts. For example, the parallelism of corresponding phrases of the individual couplets is scrupulously followed, setting these sources apart from most other Italian sequence manuscripts, such as the Mantuan source VEcap 107, where ornamental figures create frequent departures from strict parallelism. Furthermore, in the multiple settings of the same melody in the Nonantolan sources (both within single manuscripts and among all three), there is a close correspondence, suggesting an awareness of, and fidelity to, both melodic details and large-scale structure. A good example is the melody "Romana," which appears with five different texts in the Nonantolan sources, and where the only significant departures are the structural changes between East- and West-Frankish settings that had already been made in the ninth century. The care with which these early melodies were transmitted makes the Nonantolan sequences indispensable to any edition of Notker's sequences.[82]

In turning to sequences of Italian origin, it is helpful to make the distinction between those based on standard-form sequences, often set to well-known international melodies, and the indigenous Italian works that often exhibit archaic and idiomatic traits. The Italian texts set to the popular international melodies are often modeled after an earlier text in syntax and syllable alignment. *Haec sunt sacra festa* (no. 6), for the Feast of St. Silvester, provides a good example. It was clearly modeled on the well-known East-Frankish text *Eia recolamus* (also in the Nonantolan repertory, no. 14). *Haec sunt sacra festa* adopts key words and phrases from *Eia recolamus;* and where the texts go their separate ways, phrase structure and the frequent use of assonance on the letter "a"—internally as well as at verse endings—continue to show the interdependence of the texts. *Haec sunt sacra festa* is actually a crucial link in a complex cluster of texts that tie the Nonantolan sources with VEcap 107. Although this web is too complex to untangle here, it is worth investigating. In a separate study of the variants and liturgical placement, I was able to suggest that *Haec sunt sacra festa* may have been written in Nonantola.[83] *Sancti merita Benedicti* (no. 23) provides another example of an Italian text set to an international melody.

Of the eleven sequences with texts of presumably Italian origin, five have melodies that are also likely Italian creations (nos. 4, 12, 13, 24, 25), inasmuch as they have not been found set to other texts in manuscripts outside of Italy. *Alma fulgens crux praeclara* (no. 29) exhibits some of the archaic characteristics of variation-versus principle. *Almiflua caelorum* (no. 40) and *Preciosa sollemnitas* (no. 21) are closer to the standard-form sequences of the North in that they hold fairly strictly to a syllabic style throughout, except for neumatic-melismatic flourishes at the beginning of each. The melodies, however, do not behave quite like the large-scale northern tunes. Their ambitus is more restricted and the line lengths do not vary to any great extent, thereby not contributing to any sort of perceptible large-scale plan with climactic high points. *Pretiosa sollemnitas* consistently uses an unusual four-note cadential gesture (aFaG), which is made more prominent by its being repeated in the second half of each couplet, creating an echo effect.

Alme mundi rex (no. 20) behaves more like a standard-form melody, except that the sixth phrase has melismatic outbursts on the repetition of the word Alleluia. The text is an odd combination of simple expression and convoluted syntax, but the melismas on the exclamations of Alleluia in phrase 6 create a powerful sense of climax in a way that is very different from the large international melodies and texts. *Sanctae crucis celebremus* comes closer to the archaic style noted in *Lux de luce* and *Alma fulgens crux praeclara*. It is not a variation-versus like *Lux de luce*, but contains some similarities in its relatively restricted range, reliance on cadential patterns, and its ornamental, neumatic character.

The repertory of sequences from the Abbey of San Silvestro at Nonantola during the eleventh century provides a microcosm of the wide spectrum of styles current in the genre ca. 1000, including classic standard-form sequences of Notker and his West-Frankish counterparts, aparallel sequences, and representative Italian pieces. The precise, diastematic musical notation with clefs, which in many cases offers the earliest readable versions of the East-Frankish sequences, the care with which music and text were notated, and the level of Latinity displayed in the manuscripts, make this repertory of song worthy of exploration through scholarly investigation and performance.

Notes on Performance

The notated versions of the sequences sung at Nonantola as we have them, and as transcribed here, are but dried bones—evidence of a healthy, living body of music that was performed there in the eleventh and twelfth centuries. Just how to breathe life back into the silent, skeletal notation of any medieval music creates both the joy and uneasiness of grappling with performance practice, inasmuch as there is little surviving evidence and that today we are many centuries removed from the ancient living tradition. No ordinals (*ordines*) have survived from Nonantola. Lacking adequate performance directions that these manuscripts and other testimony might provide, modern performance decisions concerning music from the Nonantolan repertory must be largely conjectural. This is hardly surprising, considering that no other center in Europe provides completely sufficient documentary evidence on how sequences were performed during the tenth and eleventh centuries. With respect to chant performance in general, both scholars and performers have long struggled to unlock the key to "authentic" historical performance. The debate on proper interpretation has, at times, been highly charged, with advocates of different views strongly attached to their positions. Often the same evidence has been used to justify radically different solutions to fundamental problems, such as the interpretation of rhythm.[84]

The performance of the early medieval sequence—more than any other category of chant—has given rise to an extraordinary range of theories and performance options. This richness of possibilities owes to the unusual ways in which the early sequence was transmitted. The co-existence in the early West-Frankish manuscripts of versions of the same pieces with texts (as *prosae*) and without texts (as *sequentiae*), along with evocative titles ascribed to most melodies, has wide-ranging implications for performance. The central issue is whether the *sequentiae* were meant to be performed on their own as pure melismas, and, if so, in what relationship to the texted versions. Performance options that allow for simultaneous performance of melismatic and texted versions, as well as of instrumental performance, make the situation even more complex. At least five general theories have emerged about the role of the melismatic versions of the melodies in performance:

1. the melismatic versions (*sequentiae*) were performed in their entirety without connection to the syllabic versions (*prosae*);[85]

2. they were not performed at all, but simply served to provide a clearer idea of the melodic profile than the syllabic settings;[86]

3. they were performed a phrase at a time as melismas on the syllable "a" after each phrase sung with text;[87]

4. they were performed simultaneously with the texted, syllabic settings;[88]

5. they were performed on musical instruments.[89]

If one adds considerations of soloistic or choral performance and the possibilities of alternating performance forces between halves of the couplet, these basic theories are expanded into well over a dozen possibilities.

Performance practice differed, too, from time to time and place to place. Sequences were performed in their textless state, that is, as *sequentiae*, in at least some West Frankish centers. Hiley, for example, has shown from his studies of repertories from Cluny and Winchester that textless sequence melodies were both performed and disseminated.[90] Strong evidence has come to light that performance of sequences without texts occurred at Arras and Cambrai, as well.[91] On the other hand, careful study of the format and notational conventions in East-Frankish sources has led Haug to conclude that textless melodies were less important and probably not sung separately from a texting of any given melody.[92] The singing of sequences seems to have been the task at times for the choir and at others the soloists. Indeed, Planchart cites examples of divergence in performance from one occasion to another even in the same church, adding that sequences "seem to have remained in a no man's land between choral and soloistic chant."[93] All of these possibilities provide a range of historically plausible or demonstrable options for modern performers.

However one chooses to deploy performance forces and to deal with the relationship between texted and untexted versions, there are fundamental steps that need to be taken in preparing for any performance of this music. Planchart has articulated these in a wise and practical way in his edition of the southern Italian Proper tropes:

> [T]he singer must be able to declaim easily the text of any trope and chant without the music. This becomes particularly important in some of the syllabic settings and absolutely crucial in sequences and prosulas, where the chant composers set off subtle tensions between the stress accents of the Latin text and the tonic accents implied by the melodic ductus. This is one of the most satisfying aspects of this music to both performer and listener, but it requires absolute ease of pronunciation of the text per se.[94]

As in the other volumes in this series, Latin texts and translations are provided in the commentaries for the individual sequences, which should be studied carefully as part of preparation for performance. Planchart's remarks concerning tempo and sensitivity to the acoustical space of performance to assure intelligibility of text are also very helpful.[95]

Italian manuscripts generally transmit sequences in a straightforward way, with text and melody together in their syllabic form. There are no collections of textless *sequentiae*, as in a number of West-Frankish manuscripts. A few nondiastematic manuscripts, like VEcap 107 and Ra 123 regularly include a melismatic version of each phrase after the syllabic version. The Nonantolan manuscripts retain what seems to be a vestige of this practice in that the first phrase of each sequence is repeated as a melisma with simply the word "Alleluia" underlaid. Since the word "Alleluia" rarely fits into the sequence text itself, it seems most appropriate to consider these phrases as vestigial, and omit them in performance unless they are indeed integral to the text itself.

The Nonantolan sequences are open to the same broad range of performance possibilities as their northern counterparts. Many of these possibilities have been explored by the Schola Hungarica in a recording of fifteen of the Nonantolan sequences, along with other chants from the abbey.[96] When one looks deeply into text and music and pays particular attention to the details, approaches to performance suggest themselves that allow the unique aspects of individual pieces to be highlighted.[97] The Schola Hungarica recording might be used as a model for possible solutions to performance questions. Yet in preparing a performance there is no substitute for becoming intimately acquainted with these pieces, knowing the text with the ease of a long-familiar folk song and having the tune running smoothly through the mind. From this secure base of word and tone something special can happen in performance, whether one sings a piece straight through in its syllabic version or explores other options outlined here. Under such conditions of performance one can readily appreciate why Richard Crocker calls the sequence "one of the most important kinds of music produced in the West," and why, when sung elegantly, others will develop a similar appreciation of its achievement.

Notes

1. See *New Grove,* s.v. "Sequence," 141.
2. Lori A. Kruckenberg-Goldenstein, "The Sequence from 1050–1150: Study of a Genre in Change," (Ph.D. diss., University of Iowa, 1997), 44, lists liturgical placements found outside of the Mass, which include hymn replacements at Vespers and the Night Office; also in some traditions in the Easter and Pentecost Vigils, and in liturgical dramas.
3. For an excellent overview of recent research, including an extensive bibliography, see *MGG*[2], s.v. "Sequenz," by Lori Kruckenberg, and idem, "The Sequence," 7–41, which contains a survey of literary and musical scholarship on the genre.
4. Transitional and "second-epoch" sequences have been the focus of important recent studies by Susan Boynton, "Rewriting the Early Sequence: 'Aureo flore' and 'Aurea virga'," in *Comitatus* 25 (1994): 21–42; Kruckenberg-Goldenstein, "The Sequence"; and Margot Fassler, *Gothic Song: Victorine Sequences and Augustinian Reform in Twelfth-Century Paris* (Cambridge, 1993).
5. For a survey and assessment of the earliest documents, both literary and early musical manuscripts, see Kruckenberg-Goldenstein, "The Sequence," 50–65.
6. See René-Jean Hesbert, *Antiphonale Missarum Sextuplex* (Brussels, 1935).
7. For Amalarius's use of the term, see *Liber officialis,* book 3, chapter 16, in Jean-Michael Hanssens, ed., *Amalarii episcopi opera liturgica omnia* (Rome, 1948–50), 2:304. For *Ordo Romanus* V see Michel Andrieu, *Les Ordines Romani du haut moyen âge,* Spicilegium Sacrum Lovaniense, 23 (Louvain, 1960), 2:215.
8. For a critical analysis see Andreas Haug, "Ein neues Textdokument zur Entstehungsgeschichte der Sequenz," in *Festschrift Ulriche Siegele zum 60. Geburtstag,* ed. Rudolf Faber (Kassel, 1991), 9–19.
9. For a critical edition of the *Liber Hymnorum,* including the preface with German translations, see Wolfram von den Steinen, *Notker der Dichter und seine geistige Welt,* 2 vols. [vol. 1: Introduction and Commentary; vol. 2: Edition] (Bern, 1948). For an English translation of Notker's preface, see Crocker, *The Early Medieval Sequence* (Berkeley and Los Angeles, 1977), 1–2.
10. See Kruckenberg-Goldenstein, "The Sequence," 62–66, for an overview of sources.
11. The late-tenth-century Aquitanian manuscript Paris, Bibliothèque Nationale, lat. 1118 contains 140 sequences with texts and 74 sequence melodies without text, as well as seven later additions; see Richard Crocker, "The Repertoire of Proses at Saint Martial de Limoges (Tenth and Eleventh Centuries)," (Ph.D. diss., Yale University, 1957), 95–126; also Heinrich Husmann, *Tropen- und Sequenzenhandschriften,* RISM, BV1 (Munich-Duisburg, 1964), 124–26. Another tenth-century Aquitanian manuscript (Paris, lat. 1084) contains 130 sequences with text and 108 textless melodies, with eleven later additions; see Crocker, "The Repertoire," 56–94; and Husmann, *Tropen- und Sequenzenhandschriften,* 120–22.
12. For a general picture of manuscripts containing sequences, see Hiley, *Western Plainchant: A Handbook* (Oxford, 1993), 313–17. See also the survey of manuscripts in *New Grove,* s.v. "Sources, MS, II: Western Plainchant," by John Emerson, which includes manuscripts containing sequences in his listing of important chant sources, arranged by century. Husmann's *Tropen- und Sequenzenhandschriften* provides descriptions of the principal trope and sequence manuscripts, but he does not include most graduals that contain sequences, and thus omits many important sources for the sequence from Italy and elsewhere in Europe.
13. See von den Steinen, *Notker der Dichter,* 1:162. The *Liber Hymnorum* was dedicated to Luitward of Vercelli in 884, but presumably finished by 880. Susan Rankin suggests that many of the texts must have been composed by 871, since Marcellus, one of Notker's teachers at St. Gall, died in 871; see Rankin, "The Earliest Sources of Notker's Sequences," *EMH* 10 (1991): 202.

14. For a chronological listing of the most important musical manuscripts from a broad area in south-west France, including St. Martial, see Hiley, *Western Plainchant,* 596–97. For an overview of the significance of the monastery in music history see *New Grove,* s.v. "St. Martial," by Alejandro Planchart and Susan Fuller.

15. See Hiley, *Western Plainchant,* 172. The question of melodic "identity" in sequences is emerging as more complex than hitherto considered. In *The Early Medieval Sequence,* Crocker looks for commonalties between different settings of similar melodies to unearth the ninth-century forms, and hence tends to reduce related melodies to a single one. Yet, there were often significant differences between these melodies in East- and West-Frankish versions, perhaps because they continued to develop and evolve in an aural tradition before they were fixed in notation. For example, Crocker (*Early Medieval Sequence,* 189) considers the West-Frankish *Rex omnipotens* and Notker's *Sancti spiritus assit* to share the same melody ("Occidentana"). However, there are significant enough differences for two West-Frankish manuscripts (Paris, lat. 887 and nouv. acq. lat. 1871) to transmit the melodies as two separate *sequentiae* (using the incipit of each text as melody titles). Such melodies might well be examined more closely for ways in which they are different, as well as similar.

16. Melody titles are referred to in roman type in quotes, whereas incipits for sequence texts appear in italics.

17. N. de Goede, *The Utrecht Prosarium,* Monumenta musica Neerlandica, 6 (Amsterdam, 1965), xxv–xxvi, classifies the melody titles into groups; see also Kruckenberg, "Sequenz," for a similar classification. For editions of melodies see Anselm Hughes, *Anglo-French Sequelae* (London, 1934).

18. Hughes, *Anglo-French Sequelae,* 56, counts 46 texts; but others have been identified. See Richard Crocker, "Some Ninth-Century Sequences," *JAMS* 20 (1967): 385–89; also Calvin Bower, "An Alleluia for Mater," in *Essays on the Music of J. S. Bach and Other Divers Subjects: A Tribute to Gerhard Herz,* ed. Robert L. Weaver (Louisville, Ky., 1982): 98–116.

19. See n. 9 above.

20. The latest possible date of the Jumièges antiphoner Notker saw is the 850s, according to Rankin, "The Earliest Sources," 203.

21. Facsimiles of folios of East- and West-Frankish sequence manuscripts are readily available. See Crocker, *Early Medieval Sequence,* 454–58; Bruno Stäblein, *Schriftbild der einstimmigen Musik* (Leipzig, 1975), 184–87; or Hiley, *Western Plainchant,* 416, plate 6. A new facsimile of two complete St. Gall manuscripts has recently been published in Wulf Arlt and Susan Rankin, eds., *Stiftsbibliothek Sankt Gallen Codices 484 und 381,* 3 vols. (Winterthur, 1996). For an evaluation of the differences between East- and West-Frankish notational approaches, see Karl-Heinz Schlager, "Beobachtungen zur frühen Sequenz in ost- und westfränkischer Überlieferung," *Gordon Athol Anderson In Memoriam,* (Henryville, Pa., 1984), 2:531–43, and Andreas Haug, *Gesungene und schriftlich dargestellte Sequenz: Beobachtungen zum Schriftbild der ältesten ostfränkischen Sequenzenhandschriften* (Neuhausen-Stuttgart, 1987).

22. A few examples of an unusual hybrid form of the sequence are found in the West-Frankish sequentiaries. These are the so-called partially texted sequences, which have text for only a few phrases; the rest of the melody is transmitted in its textless form. Bruno Stäblein, "Zur Frühgeschichte der Sequenz," *Archiv für Musikwissenschaft* 18 (1961): 1–33, identified nine such pieces. For a recent discussion, see Alejandro Planchart, "An Aquitanian Sequentia in Italian Sources," in *Recherches Nouvelles sur les Tropes Liturgiques,* CT, ed. Wulf Arlt and Gunilla Björkvall (Stockholm, 1993), 371–93. Planchart explores the transmission of the melody "Exsultet elegantis" in Italian sources.

23. Among all surviving East-Frankish manuscripts, only St. Gall, Stiftsbibliothek 484, transmits a collection of untexted *sequentiae* as a group. The manuscript is unique in that the melodies were copied from the bottom of the page up, the reasons for which remain puzzling; see Kruckenberg-Goldenstein, "The Sequence," 109.

24. The term *"sequela"* is not found in any medieval manuscripts but was created to refer to the textless melodies; it was apparently first used by Léon Gautier in *Les Tropes* (Paris, 1886), 14, and adopted by Hughes, *Anglo-French Sequelae,* but it has not gained any currency in the scholarly literature.

25. See Crocker, *Early Medieval Sequence,* 6: "Through the study of them [Notker's sequences] we can gain a reliable idea of the sequence in the ninth century, and from that idea, in turn, we could decide about other sequences for whose dating no basis other than stylistic comparison is available. . . . The firm witness of a ninth-century dating is one of the most important aspects of Notker's *Liber hymnorum.*"

26. For Crocker's restored versions of two sequences, see *Early Medieval Sequence,* 68 (*Haec dies quam excelsus*) and 86 (*Ecce vicit*).

27. See Kruckenberg-Goldenstein, "The Sequence," 86–139, especially 125–26. In assessing East- and West-Frankish sources, she asserts, "it is not just the existence of two regional repertories that is of interest, but also the separation and lack of overlap of the Eastern and Western traditions—a separation that holds firmly until at least the end of the eleventh century" (125). That tropes were not subjected to the same strict division strengthens her proposal: "Trope repertories indicate that cross-regional exchange was common, whereas sequence repertories do not" (131).

28. Kruckenberg-Goldenstein has nicely summarized the work of David Hiley (with Western sources) and Karl-Heinz Schlager and Andreas Haug (with Eastern sources). See also Planchart, "An Aquitanian Sequentia," 392–93, who sees Crocker's chronology of development of the sequence from aparallel to more expanded works beginning "to crumble." Recent and ongoing work by Calvin Bower is also challenging some of Crocker's basic assumptions and conclusions; see his "An Alleluia for Mater," "Alleluia, Confitemini Domino, Quoniam Bonus—An *Alleluia, Versus, Sequentia,* and Five *Prosae* Recorded in Aquitanian Sources," in *Music in the Theater, Church, and Villa: Essays in Honor of Robert Lamar Weaver and Norma Wright Weaver,* ed. Susan Parisi (forthcoming); and "From Alleluia to Sequence: Some Definitions of Relations," paper presented at the Symposium "Western Plainchant in the First Millenium" in honor of James McKinnon, University of North Carolina, Chapel Hill, 17 January 1999. Bower's use of vocabulary from Medieval music theory in describing and analyzing sequence melodies is a significant new contribution to the field; see idem, "The Grammatical Model of Musical Understanding in the Middle Ages," in *Hermeneutics and Medieval Culture,* ed. Patrick Gallacher and Helen Damico (Albany, N.Y., 1989), 133–45.

29. *Early Medieval Sequence,* 370.

30. These stylistic aspects are obvious in listening to or examining the notation of a sequence. See, for example,

Congaudent angelorum chori (no. 26 in this edition). Andreas Haug, "Neue Ansätze im 9. Jahrhundert," in *Die Musik des Mittelalters,* ed. Hartmut Möller and Rudolf Stephan (Kassel, 1991), 113, displays this sequence on the page as to clarify the many interrelationships between phrases, as well as the most typical cadential pattern (notated as a *pes stratus* in the neumatic notation). See also Lucas Kunz, "Die Textgestalt der Sequenz *Congaudent angelorum chori,*" *Deutsche Vierteljahrsschrift für Literaturschrift und Geisteswissenschaft* 28 (1954): 273–86; and Bower, "An Alleluia for Mater."

31. See *Early Medieval Sequence,* 382–88, for a brilliant discussion of this large-scale design in the sequences, including graphic displays of three melody profiles (p. 383). Kruckenberg presents schematic synopses of eight sequences melodies in her article, "Sequenz."

32. For the literary references in individual sequences by Notker and those in his orbit, see von den Steinen, *Notker der Dichter,* 1:534–613.

33. See *Early Medieval Sequence,* 43. Crocker refers to Notker's prose on several occasions as Ciceronian, also asserting that "Notker was concerned to sound 'patrician' rather than 'patristic'," (40), but the patristic influence on his Latin and texts seems as strong as the classical models. In comparing sequence texts from the "Gallo-English" area with those of Notker, Guido Maria Dreves pointed to the shallower substance and "strange Latinity" (*merkwürdig Latinität*) of the Western texts; see *Prosarium Lemovicense: Die Prosen der Abtei St. Martial zu Limoges, aus Troparien des 10., 11. und 12. Jahrhunderts,* AH 7 (Leipzig, 1889), 2.

34. In Crocker's words: "In the hands of Notker of St. Gall, an accomplished poet, the texts predominate; but with the exuberant musicality of the West-Frankish cantors the melodies became the most striking feature." See "Medieval Chant," in *Early Middle Ages to 1300,* The New Oxford History of Music, 2, ed. Richard Crocker and David Hiley (Oxford, 1990), 257.

35. For a detailed study of this group, see Klaus Heinrich Kohrs, *Die aparallelen Sequenzen* (Munich and Salzburg, 1978). See also Kruckenberg, "Sequenz." Bower, in "Alleluia, *Confitemini,*" offers a detailed analysis of five *prosae* long considered to be "aparallel" and reveals a more complex structure, involving repetition, which had gone unnoticed in previous discussions of the pieces.

36. There are two aparallel sequences in this edition, nos. 38 and 39.

37. See Kruckenberg-Goldenstein, "The Sequence," 82–83.

38. For an overview of repertories in Italian centers, see Lance W. Brunner, "The Sequences of Verona, Biblioteca Capitolare CVII and the Italian Sequence Tradition," 2 vols. (Ph.D. diss., University of North Carolina, 1977), 1:156–95. For a broader overview of regions throughout Europe, see Hiley, *Western Plainchant,* 563–607. See also Nancy van Deusen, "Style, Nationality and the Sequence in the Middle Ages," *Journal of the Plainsong and Mediaeval Music Society* 5 (1982): 44–55. Alejandro Planchart describes how tropes and sequences imported from the North interacted with the local tradition in *BTC I,* xiv.

39. For example, the early facsimiles published in PM, including the gradual from Einsiedeln, Stiftsbibliothek, 121 (Solesmes, 1894) and Saint Yrieix, Paris, Bibliothèque Nationale, lat. 903 (Solesmes, 1925), did not reproduce those sections that contained sequences and tropes.

40. See the recent essays on both centers in *MGG²,* s.v. "Sankt Gallen," by Andreas Haug, and s.v. "Saint Martial," by Max Haas. Important manuscripts from these centers appeared in PM. Laon and Chartres are represented in the same series in PM 10 (Laon 239) and PM 11 (Chartres 47).

41. In the trope repertory, for example, see Paul Evans, *The Early Trope Repertory of Saint Martial de Limoges* (Princeton, N.J., 1970), and Charles M. Atkinson, "The Earliest Agnus Dei Melody and its Tropes," *JAMS* 30 (1977): 1–19.

42. See Brunner, "The Sequences of Verona 107," 1:178.

43. See *Early Medieval Sequence,* 371, where Crocker exclaims over these pieces, "How bright they sound, how gratefully they sing!"

44. See Planchart's overview of modern chant scholarship with respect to these matters in *BTC I,* xii.

45. The editors of *AH* were particularly perplexed with the southern Italian sequences; thus, of *Candent sidera:* "This previously unknown sequence from Southern Italy is transmitted in the Beneventan sources, unfortunately as usual, in an even more wretched cloak (*noch armseligeren Gewande*) than the little gifted singer originally had given it" (*AH* 53:214). See similar comments in *AH* 53:105, 106, 168, et passim.

46. To get a glimpse of the broadened scope of research in the sequence, compare the bibliography in *MGG¹,* s.v. "Sequenz," by Bruno Stäblein, with the bibliography in *MGG²,* s.v. "Sequenz," by Lori Kruckenberg. In the realm of tropes, the Corpus Troporum project has initiated a comprehensive critical edition of trope texts throughout Europe.

47. See Lance W. Brunner, "Catalogo delle sequenze in manoscritti di origine italiana anteriori al 1200," *Rivista italiana de musicologia* 20 (1985): 191–276, for a listing of manuscripts copied before 1200 that contain sequences. To this should be added a fragment from L'Aquila containing four sequences and discovered by Agostino Ziino; see his "Sequenze in una fonte sconosciuta dell'Italian centrale," in *La Sequenza Medievale. Atti del convengno internazionale Milano 7–8 aprile 1984,* ed. Agostino Ziino (Lucca, 1992), 155–71.

48. For a list of southern Italian manuscripts containing sequences, see Lance W. Brunner, "A Perspective on the Southern Italian Sequence: The Second Tonary of the Manuscript Monte Cassino 318," *EMH* 1 (1981), 126–27, table 2. For descriptions of these manuscripts (with the exception of Udine 26), see *BTC I,* xv–xix; sequences are also included in the Propers of the Mass with Tropes in Southern Italy, see *BTC I,* xxii–xxxiii.

49. Facsimiles include Benevento, VI. 34 (PM 15); Rome, Biblioteca Angelica, 123 (PM 18); Giuseppe Vecchi, ed., *Troparium sequentiarium Nonantulanum, Cod. casanat. 1741* (Modena, 1955); Max Lütolf, ed., *Das Graduale von Santa Cecilia in Trastevere (Cod. Bodmer 74),* 2 vols. (Cologny-Geneva, 1987); Piacenza, Biblioteca Capitolare, MS 65 (New York, 1998), with commentary by Brian Møller Jensen.

50. The number is based on Brunner, "Catalogo."

51. Stäblein, *Schriftbild,* 102, offers some startling speculation on the loss of manuscripts; he mentions that Bernhard Bischoff estimated that only about one medieval manuscript in a thousand has survived.

52. Alejandro Planchart has pointed out on a number of occasions the remnants of older chant recycled as tropes and the occasional absurd juxtaposition of style and content, especially in the Beneventan sources. See, for example, "Old Wine in New Bottles," in *De musica et cantu: Studien zur Geschichte der Kirchenmusik und der Oper: Helmut Hucke zum 60. Geburtstag,* ed. Peter Cahn and Ann-Katrin Heimer (Hildesheim, 1993), 41–65; and "On the Nature of Transmission and Change in Trope Repertories," *JAMS* 41 (1988): 215–49, especially 238–40. He has also pointed to similar

tendencies in northern Italian sources; see his "Notes on the Tropes in Manuscripts of the Rite of Aquileia," in *Essays on Medieval Music*, ed. Graeme M. Boone (Cambridge, Mass., 1995), 333–69. For general aspects of trope transmission in central and northern Italy, see James Borders, "The Northern and Central Italian Trope Repertoire and Its Transmission," in *Atti del XIV Congresso della società internazionale di Musicologia*, 3 vols., ed. Lorenzo Bianconi (Turin, 1990), 3:543–53.

53. The ongoing research of scholars like Calvin Bower, Lori Kruckenberg, and David Hiley, suggests that we may be able to be more specific about melody origin through musical analysis, rather than relying primarily on the texts.

54. The term "Romanic" seems preferable to the more cumbersome "Anglo-Romanic."

55. See Brunner, "The Sequences of Verona 107," 1:161, table 8.

56. The same tendency can be seen with Italian tropes, which according to Planchart "apparently did not travel far within the peninsula itself," *BTC I*, xlviii.

57. See Brunner, "The Sequences of Verona 107," 1:161.

58. Brunner, "A Perspective," 138, table 4. In the trope repertory the number of Proper tropes found only in south Italian manuscripts outnumbers pan-Italian tropes in the same manuscripts by 4:1 (40 to 10); see *BTC 1*, xliv, xlvi (tables 2 and 3).

59. Bruno Stäblein, "Die Sequenzmelodie 'Concordia' und ihr geschichtlicher Hintergrund," in *Festschrift Hans Engel zum siebzigsten Geburtstag* (Kassel, 1964), 378, referred to this tendency toward acclamation as "a type of 'degeneration' of the sequence principle in the direction of litany or psalmody."

60. The text, punctuation, and numbering of the verses is taken from *AH* 53:106. For a transcription of the entire piece, see Lance W. Brunner, "The Italian Sequence and Stylistic Pluralism: Observations about the Music of the Sequences for the Easter Season from Southern Italy," in *La Sequenza Medievale*, 38.

61. See Ritva Jacobsson, "Short Reflexions on Beneventan Easter Sequence Texts," in *La Sequenza Medievale*, 138–39.

62. Brunner, "Catalogo," 264; see also Jacobsson, "Short Reflexions," 139.

63. "Lux de luce: The Origin of an Italian Sequence," *MQ* 57 (1971): 40–61.

64. See "Die Sequenzmelodie 'Concordia'," 377.

65. See Brunner, "The Sequences of Verona 107," 1:185–95.

66. Planchart, "An Aquitanian Sequentia," gives another fascinating example of how the interchange between north and south gave birth to a unique piece out of an instinctual response to something new and unfamiliar. In talking about the introduction of the Aquitanian *sequentia* "Adorabo" into southern Italy, he envisaged a bewildered scribe who probably never saw "anything quite like it, since *sequentiae* normally did not make it to this part of the world. He viewed the piece like a sort of overgrown alleluia with six verses and proceeded to provide it with prosulas" (380).

67. See Brunner, "The Italian Sequence and Stylistic Pluralism," 30–38, where the complex of pieces is discussed in detail.

68. The CT series has adopted the format of editing individual lines of tropes, or "elements," rather than sets of tropes, as they appear in manuscripts, since the sets vary so much. Although in the editions the elements are isolated, it is nevertheless possible, with the help of the commentary, to reconstruct any given manuscript version.

69. See James Borders's overview of the history of the abbey in *Early Medieval Chant from Nonantola, Part I: Ordinary Chants and Tropes*, Recent Researches in the Music of the Middle Ages and Early Renaissance, vol. 30, pp. x–xii.

70. Ibid., x.

71. For a description of manuscripts and complete inventories, see ibid., xii–xxxi.

72. See Borders, "The North and Central Italian Trope Repertory," 545. The trope *Ecce iam Christus* appears in some Italian manuscripts as a sequence, but in the Nonantola sources it is a trope; see Brunner, "Catalogo," and Borders, *Early Medieval Chant from Nonantola, Part II: Proper Chants and Tropes*, Recent Researches in the Music of the Middle Ages and Early Renaissance, vol. 31, p. 3.

73. See Brunner, "The Sequences of Verona 107," for a study of the 61 sequences in this collection.

74. Borders, *Early Medieval Chant from Nonantola, I*, x–xii.

75. Heinrich Pfaff, "Die Tropen und Sequenzen der Handschrift Rom, Bibl. Naz. Vitt. Em. 1343 (Sessor. 62) aus Nonantola," (Ph.D. diss., Munich, 1948), 38–47.

76. Ibid., 42.

77. See *New Grove*, s.v. "Nonantola," by John Emerson.

78. Pfaff, "Die Tropen und Sequenzen," 35.

79. Borders, *Early Medieval Chant from Nonantola, I*, x. See also Borders "The North and Central Italian Trope Repertory," 546.

80. Von den Steinen, *Notker der Dichter*, 2:195.

81. *Laus tibi Christe cui* (no. 5 in the edition), found only in Bu 2824, is the only other Notker text in the Nonantolan repertory and does require several emendations. See critical apparatus for a list of manuscript sigla.

82. Yet Crocker, in *Early Medieval Sequence*, preferred to use the Aquitanian transmission of the melodies, even though that tradition was sharply divided from that of the east. Crocker made his choice consciously, perhaps to limit the number of sources in order to make the study workable. Nevertheless, the Nonantolan versions broaden Crocker's more limited perspective.

83. See Brunner, "The Sequences of Verona 107," 110–15.

84. For an overview of the main controversies, see Lance W. Brunner, "The Performance of Plainchant: Some Preliminary Observations of the New Era," *Early Music* 10 (1982): 316–28.

85. There is mounting evidence that *sequentiae* were sung in their textless state from the ninth century at least into the thirteenth century. The conciliar canon from Meaux attests to such performance as early as 845 (see n. 7, above). See David Hiley, "The Sequence Melodies Sung at Cluny," in *De musica et cantu*, 131–41, and Hiley, "The Repertory of Sequences at Winchester," in *Essays on Medieval Music*, 153–93. Margo Fassler, *Gothic Song*, 62, observed that "the practice of singing the sequence without text is not viewed as superior to using the words, but rather as a special practice of some churches." Calvin Bower's recent work has also argued for the primacy and independence of the *sequentiae* in the early history of the genre (see n. 24, above).

86. Handschin, "Trope, Sequence, and Conductus," in *Early Medieval Music up to 1300*, New Oxford History of Music, vol. 2, ed. Anselm Hughes (Oxford, 1954), 158. In *New Grove*, s.v. "Sequence," Crocker seems to concur with the direct performance: "Given the inconclusive nature of the evidence, and for other reasons as well, it seems advisable to consider the primary form of the work of art to be the singing of the melody with text, straight through, as found in the prosaria."

87. The alternation of syllabic and melismatic forms in a number of manuscripts (VEcap 107, Ra 123, Pn lat. 1119,

etc.) suggests such a performance. See Planchart, *BTC I*, xxxvi. See also Heinrich Husmann "Sequenz und Prosa," *Annales Musicologiques* 2 (1954): 69–76. For a recording that presents soloists singing the text, followed by repetition of the melismatic versions sung by the choir, listen to *Epiphaniam Domino,* on *The Worcester Fragments*, Accademia Monteverdiana, Denis Stevens, director (Nonesuch, H-71308).

88. Joseph Smits van Waesberghe, "Zur ursprünglichen Vortragsweise der Prosulen, Sequenzen und Organa," in *Bericht über den siebenten Internationalen Musikwissenschaftlichen Kongress, Köln 1958* (Kassel, 1959), 251–54.

89. Ewald Jammers, *Musik in Byzanz, im päpstlichen Rom und im Frankenreich* (Heidelberg, 1962), 287–89; Andreas Holschneider, "Instrumental Titles to the Sequentiae of the Winchester Tropers," in *Essays on Opera and English Music in Honour of Sir Jack Westrup*, ed. F. W. Sternfeld, Nigel Fortune, and E. Olleson (Oxford, 1975), 8–18.

90. Hiley, "The Sequence Melodies Sung at Cluny," 138–41; he suggests that melodies may indeed have existed first in their textless state until the subsequent textings "caught the melodies in a syllabic net" (132). See also Hiley, "The Repertory of Sequences at Winchester." Bower, "From Alleluia to Sequence," gives perhaps the most straightforward assertion that sequences were untexted melismas, with texts supplied only later.

91. Kruckenberg-Goldenstein, "The Sequence," 108.

92. See Haug, *Gesungene und schriftlich dargestellte Sequenz.*

93. *The Repertory of Tropes at Winchester*, 2 vols. (Princeton, 1977), 1:51, n. 2.

94. *BTC I*, xxxvi.

95. Ibid., xxxvii.

96. Quint 903084.

97. I have written about this process in a separate essay, "The Tao of Singing: On the Schola Hungarica's Interpretation of the Nonantolan Sequences," *Music in the Theater, Church, and Villa* (forthcoming).

Critical Apparatus

List of Manuscript Sigla

Bc 7	Bologna, Civico Museo, MS Q7
Bu 2748	Bologna, Biblioteca Universitaria, MS 2748
Bu 2824	Bologna, Biblioteca Universitaria, MS 2824
BAs 5	Bamberg, Staatliche Bibliothek, Lit. 5
BV 34	Benevento, Biblioteca Capitolare, MS 34 (*olim* 25)
BV 35	Benevento, Biblioteca Capitolare, MS 35 (*olim* 26)
BV 38	Benevento, Biblioteca Capitolare, MS 38 (*olim* 27)
BV 39	Benevento, Biblioteca Capitolare, MS 39 (*olim* 28)
BV 40	Benevento, Biblioteca Capitolare, MS 40 (*olim* 29)
CHb 2	Chieti, Biblioteca Capitolare, MS 2
Cb 74	Cologny-Geneva, Bibliotheca Bodmeriana, MS C.74 (*olim* Phillipps 16069)
IV 60	Ivrea, Biblioteca Capitolare, MS 60
Kf 29	Killiney County [Dublin], Franciscan Library, Dún Mhuire MS B 29
Lbl 19768	London, British Library, Additional MS 19768
Mbs 14843	Munich, Bayerische Staatsbibliothek MS clm. 14843
MCa 318	Montecassino, Archivio della Badia, MS 318
MCa 546	Montecassino, Archivio della Badia, MS 546
MC comp	Montecassino, Archivio della Badia, MS Compactiones
MOd 7	Modena, Biblioteca Capitolare (Duomo), MS O.I.7
MOd 16	Modena, Biblioteca Capitolare (Duomo), MS O.I.16
Mza 75	Monza, Biblioteca Capitolare (Basilica), MS C.12/75
Mza 76	Monza, Biblioteca Capitolare (Basilica), MS C.13/76
Mza 77	Monza, Biblioteca Capitolare (Basilica), MS C.14/77
NV 1	Novara, Archivio, MS 1
Ob 222	Oxford, Bodleian Library, MS Douce 222
PAc 47	Padua, Biblioteca Capitolare, MS A 47
PAs 697	Padua, Biblioteca del Seminario Vescovile, MS 697
Pn 1669	Paris, Bibliothèque Nationale, MS nouv. acq.lat. 1669
PCsa 65	Piacenza, Biblioteca e Archivio de San Antonio, MS 65
PS 119	Pistoia, Biblioteca Capitolare (Cattedrale), MS C 119
PS 121	Pistoia, Biblioteca Capitolare (Cattedrale), MS C 121
Ra 123	Rome, Biblioteca Angelica, MS 123
Rc 1741	Rome, Biblioteca Casanatense, MS 1741
Rc 3830	Rome, Biblioteca Casanatense, MS 3830
Rn 1343	Rome, Biblioteca Nationale Centrale Vittorio Emanuele III, MS 1343 (olim Sessoriano 62)
Rv 9	Rome, Biblioteca Valliceliana, MS C 9
Rv 52	Rome, Biblioteca Valliceliana, MS C 52
Rvat 602	Rome, Biblioteca Apostolica Vaticana, Urb. lat. 602
Rvat 5319	Rome, Biblioteca Apostolica Vaticana, Vat. lat. 5319
Rvat 10645	Rome, Biblioteca Apostolica Vaticana, Vat. lat. 10645
SEz 2	Sevilla, Library of the de Zayas Family [private], MS 2
SIc 15	Siena, Biblioteca Comunale, MS F.IV.15
Tn 18	Turin, Biblioteca Nazionale Universitaria, MS F.IV.18
Tn 20	Turin, Biblioteca Nazionale Universitaria, MS G.V.20
UDa 26	Udine, Biblioteca Arcivescovile, MS Q.26
VCd 146	Vercelli, Biblioteca Capitolare (Duomo), MS 146
VCd 161	Vercelli, Biblioteca Capitolare (Duomo), MS 161
VCd 162	Vercelli, Biblioteca Capitolare (Duomo), MS 162
VCd 186	Vercelli, Biblioteca Capitolare (Duomo), MS 186
VEcap 90	Verona, Biblioteca Capitolare, MS XC (85)

VEcap 107   Verona, Biblioteca Capitolare, MS CVII (100)
VO 39   Volterra, Biblioteca Guarnacci, MS. L.3.39

List of Works Cited

Arlt, *Ein Festoffizium* = Arlt, Wulf. *Ein Festoffizium des Mittelalters aus Beauvais*. 2 vols. Cologne, 1970.

Brunner, "Catalogo" = Brunner, Lance. "Catalogo delle sequenze in manoscritti di origine italiana anteriori al 1200." *Rivista italiana di musicologia* 20 (1985): 191–276.

Brunner, "The Sequences of Verona 107" = Brunner, Lance W. "The Sequences of Verona, Biblioteca Capitolare CVII and the Italian Sequence Tradition." 2 vols. Ph.D. diss., University of North Carolina, 1977.

Brunner, "Tao of Singing" = Brunner, Lance W. "The Tao of Singing: On the Schola Hungarica's Interpretation of the Nonantolan Sequences." *Music in the Theater, Church, and Villa: Essays in Honor of Robert Lamar Weaver and Norma Wright Weaver*. Edited by Susan Parisi. Forthcoming.

Crocker, *Early Medieval Sequence* = Crocker, Richard. *The Early Medieval Sequence*. Berkeley and Los Angeles, 1977.

Crocker, "Repertoire" = Crocker, Richard. "The Repertoire of Proses at Saint Marital de Limoges." 2 vols. Ph.D. diss., Yale University, 1957.

Crocker, "The Sequence (*Gattung*)" = Crocker, Richard. "The Sequence." *Gattungen der Musik in Einzeldarstellungen: Gedenkschrift Leo Schrade*. Edited by Wulf Arlt, Ernst Lichtenhahn, and Hans Oesch, 269–322. Bern, 1973.

Crocker, "Sequence" = *New Grove*, s.v. "Sequence," by Richard Crocker.

Damilano, "Sequenze" = Damilano, Piero. "Sequenze bobbiensi. *Rivista italiana di musicologia* 2 (1967): 3–35.

de Goede, *Utrecht Prosarium* = de Goede, N., ed. *The Utrecht Prosarium*. Monumenta Musica Neerlandica, 6. Amsterdam, 1965.

Drinkwelder, *Sequentiar* = Drinkwelder, Otto. *Ein deutsches Sequentiar aus dem Ende des 12. Jahrhunderts*. Graz, 1914.

Fassler, *Gothic Song* = Fassler, Margot. *Gothic Song: Victorine Sequences and Augustinian Reform in Twelfth-Century Paris*. Cambridge, 1993.

Handschin, "Trope" = Handschin, Jacques. "Trope, Sequence, Conductus." *Early Medieval Music up to 1300*. New Oxford History of Music, vol. 2. Edited by Anselm Hughes, 128–74. Oxford, 1954.

Haug, "Neue Ansätze" = Haug, Andreas. "Neue Ansätze im 9. Jahrhundert." In *Die Musik des Mittelalters*. Edited by Hartmut Möller and Rudolf Stephan, 94–128. Laber, 1991.

Hiley, *Sequences for St. Benedict* = Hiley, David, ed. *Eight Sequences for St. Benedict and St. Scholastica*. London, 1980.

Hiley, *Western Plainchant* = Hiley, David. *Western Plainchant: A Handbook*. Oxford, 1993.

Hughes, *Sequelae* = Hughes, Anselm. *Anglo-French Sequelae*. London, 1934.

Kunz, "Textgestalt" = Kunz, Lucas. "Die Textgestalt der Sequenz 'Congaudent angelorum chori'." *Deutsche Vierteljahrsschrift für Literaturwissenschaft und Geistesgeschichte* 28 (1954): 273–86.

Moberg, *Schwedischen Sequenzen* = Moberg, Carl Allan. *Über die schwedischen Sequenzen*. 2 vols. Uppsala, 1927.

Negro, "Le sequenze" = Negro, Francesca. "Le sequenze della tradizione liturgica padovana." *Contributi per la storia della musica sacra a Padova*. Edited by Guilio Cattin and Antonio Lovato, 43–92. Padua, 1993.

Reichert, "Structurprobleme" = Reichert, Georg. "Strukturprobleme der älteren Sequenz." *Deutsche Vierteljahrsschrift für Literaturwissenschaft und Geistesgeschichte* 23 (1949): 227–51.

Roederer, *Festive Troped Masses* = Roederer, Charlotte, ed. *Festive Troped Masses from the Eleventh Century: Christmas and Easter in the Aquitaine*. Collegium Musicum: Yale University, 2d ser., vol. 11. Madison, 1989.

Schlager, *Alleluia-Melodien* = Schlager, Karlheinz, ed. *Alleluia-Melodien II ab 1100*. Monumenta Monodica Medii Aevi, vol. 8. Kassel, 1987.

Schubiger, *Sängerschule* = Schubiger, Anselm. *Die Sängerschule St. Gallens von achten bis zum zwölften Jahrhundert*. Einsiedeln, 1858.

Stäblein, *Hymnen* = Stäblein, Bruno, ed. *Hymnen I: Die mittelalterlichen Hymnenmelodien des Abendlandes*. Monumenta Monodica Medii Aevi, vol. 1. Kassel, 1956.

Stäblein, *Schriftbild* = Stäblein, Bruno. *Schriftbild der einstimmigen Musik*. Leipzig, 1975.

Stäblein, "Die Sequenzmelodie" = Stäblein, Bruno. "Die Sequenzmelodie 'Concordia' und ihr geschichtlicher Hintergrund." *Festschrift Hans Engel zum siebzigsten Geburtstag*. Edited by Horst Heussner, 364–92. Kassel, 1964.

Stäblein, *Vat. lat. 5319* = Stäblein, Bruno and Margareta Landwehr-Melnicki. *Die Gesänge des altrömishen Graduale Vat. lat. 5319*. Monumenta Monodica Medii Aevi, vol. 2. Kassel, 1970.

von den Steinen, "Anfänge" = von den Steinen, Wolfram. "Anfänge der Sequenzendichtung." *Zeitschrift für schweizerischen Kirchengeschichte* 40 (1946): 190–212, 241–68; and 41 (1947): 19–48, 122–62.

von den Steinen, *Notker der Dichter* = von den Steinen, Wolfram. *Notker der Dichter und seine geistige Welt*. 2 vols. [vol. 1: Introduction and Commentary; vol. 2: Edition] Bern, 1948.

Vecchi, *Troparium* = Vecchi, Giuseppe, ed. *Troparium sequentiarium Nonantolanum: Cod. Casanat. 1741*. Monumenta Lyrica Medii Aevi Italica, I: Latina. Modena, 1955.

Editorial Methods

Arrangement and Identification of Sequences

The sequences are presented in the liturgical order found in Rc 1741, which contains the most comprehensive collection of sequences of the three principal Nonantolan manuscripts. The four sequences that lie outside this main grouping have been inserted in their proper liturgical place within the present edition. These include *Rex omnipotens* (no. 18), a later addition to Rc 1741, *Christi hodiernae* (no. 1) and *Laus tibi Christe cui sapit* (no. 5), both from Bu 2824, and *Felix valde O Maria* (no. 27), which survives only as a fragment at the end of Rn 1343. The forty sequences in the Nonantolan repertory are numbered according to liturgical order.

Text incipits of the sequences are included in the headings to individual pieces in the commentary and in the music. Because these incipits also serve as uniform titles in the edition, their spelling has been standardized for ease of access and recognition according to normal classical spellings reported in Lewis and Short, *A Latin Dictionary*. Thus *Sancti spiritus assit* is the uniform title for Notker's well known sequence for Pentecost, despite the Nonantolan scribes rendering the third word "adsit." Proper names, including *Deus* but not *dominus*, are also capitalized in the uniform titles but nowhere else unless indicated in the typical manuscript readings. Finally, the manuscript source of the chant selected as the typical reading, along with inclusive folio numbers, is signaled by boldface type in the commentaries; the source is also indicated at the beginning of the first line of the music.

Selection and Presentation of Versions and Variants

In most cases, the versions of sequences in this edition come from Rc 1741. The decision to treat this manuscript as the typical source (rather than Rn 1343, which Borders adopted as the typical source in the first three volumes of *Early Medieval Chant from Nonantola*) is based on two observations. First, Rc 1741 contains a somewhat larger collection of sequences (37 compared to 33 in both Rn 1343 and Bu 2824). Second, the availability of a facsimile of Rc 1741 (Vecchi, *Troparium*) invites comparison with the original notation. Although Rn 1343 is slightly older and more closely related to Bu 2824 than Rc 1741, as Borders observed, all three manuscripts present very similar readings, with no manuscript consistently presenting versions of chants that are more correct textually or musically than those of the other two manuscripts. In any case, all the available Nonantolan readings may be easily reassembled from the variants listed in the commentaries.

Texts and Translations

Texts in the edition are rendered diplomatically. In exceptional cases, however, editorial emendations have been made to clarify meaning. These are always given in square brackets. The Alleluia phrase, which repeats musically the opening phrase of each sequence, has been omitted in the text editions, since the Alleluia is rarely part of the text itself. These phrases have been retained, however, in the musical transcriptions.

Punctuation marks are very rare in the Nonantolan manuscripts, but the scribes did use capital letters to mark the beginnings of new periods. The capitalization of the typical readings has been faithfully retained. The text edition maintains the clear couplet division of the text according to the length of the musical phrases. Where the scribe used a capital letter with a line to indicate sub-phrase structure, the text and translation indicate this and begin a new line. The musical settings of these texts however, are printed as through-composed.

Spellings have also been retained from the manuscript sources in both the commentary and the music. Hence the letters *i* and *j* are treated as the same letters (i), following the practice of the Nonatolan scribes. Only text variants that have a bearing on meaning, syntax, or pronunciation are reported in the commentary. Thus, variants of orthography, such as differences in the use of the letters *c* and *t* in words like *gratias*, are not indicated. Moreover, although the *e-caudata* (in Rc 1741) or *ae* ligature (in Rn 1343 and Bu 2824) are presented in the typical readings as in the manuscript source, the differing practices of the scribes with respect to their use are not reported, nor are variants noted. Errors in a single word or letter of the typical text have been corrected in translation and cued in the commentary.

Standard contractions and suspension found in the texts—such as ꝑ for *per*, ꝓ for *pro*, ꝗ for *qui*, ƀ; for -*bus*, and the *nomina sacra* including *Xpristus* for *Christus*—have been resolved in the texts of the edition and commentary without comment. Truncated or heavily abbreviated phrases, however, have been reproduced as they are found in the typical source, with abbreviations expanded within angle brackets. All other editorial additions are placed within square brackets.

English translations are provided for all the Latin texts. These translations employ modern liturgical

English in the style of the New American Catholic Edition of the Bible (New York, 1961) and *The Saint Andrew Daily Missal* (Bruge, 1962). Translations were made with the help of the editors of Corpus Troporum in Stockholm, with the final versions produced by Gunilla Iversen, whose help has been invaluable. Calvin Bower was also very generous in sharing his elegant English translations of Notker texts, for which he is planning an edition. The style and wording of the translations remain the responsibility of the present editor.

The Notation of Music in the Edition

Following modern scholarly custom, chants in this edition are notated in stemless black noteheads on five-line staves, usually with treble clef transposed down an octave. Two sequences with D-final and low tessitura are transcribed in bass clef (no. 2, *Natus ante saecula*, and no. 28, *Summa stirpe*). In addition to stemless noteheads, two special signs are also employed. The first is an italic *n* for the oriscus, which signals a prolongation of the preceding note or a note repetition. The second is the liquescent, which is transcribed as two slurred notes, the second being smaller and in parentheses as in Roederer, *Festive Troped Masses;* the slurs are placed under the notes with a verticule. Nonantolan scribes used liquescent neumes in connection with most diphthongs and liquid consonants. Although the singing of B-flat is occasionally indicated in Rc 1741 by an additional green line (besides the yellow and red ones), these do not occur in the sequences and no B-flats have been added editorially to the music.

All notes sung to a single syllable are printed under a slur. Slurs within slurs indicate ligated notes; gapped slurs show sub-groupings of notes within aggregate neumes. The manuscript readings generally correspond in the sub-groupings of neumes; the few variants that do occur are not reported in the critical apparatus because they have not been judged to affect performance significantly. Although bar lines were obviously not notated by the Nonantolan scribes, single bars are employed in the edition at the ends of phrases, which constitute the major musico-poetic articulation within each piece. Double bars are used at the ends of pieces.

Single hyphens have been inserted between syllables in the text indicating divisions according to the rules of syllabification in Latin classical verse. Thus *Chris-te* is preferred over *Chri-ste*, and *Be-ne-dic-tus* over *Be-ne-di-ctus*.

Pitch is designated in the commentary according to the medieval gamut, beginning on the lowest line of the bass clef:

Γ A B C D E F G a b c d e f g

Commentaries

Each commentary includes:

- SOURCE of text and music gives the location of each chant in the Nonantolan manuscripts, including the rubric for that specific chant, if one is given in the manuscript. The main source of the text and music in the edition is indicated in **boldface.**

- ITALIAN CONCORDANCES are provided to show how each sequence is disseminated in other Italian sources. This section provides an implicit commentary on the network of relationships between centers within Italy, as well as a guide for further exploration of individual sequences.

- REFERENCES to books, editions, periodical articles and dissertations in which information about the chant may be found (see the lists of abbreviations and works cited). For the most popular, international pieces the listings are selective, but for those undertaking a comprehensive investigation, the references given will lead one to older or less detailed studies, as well as other editions.

- A TEXT COMMENTARY provides brief comments on the meaning and liturgical or historical background of the texts. When text and aspects of transmission have already been studied in detail or are related to the Nonantolan readings, these are pointed out, but not repeated or necessarily summarized here. (Notker's texts, for example, have been carefully studied by von den Steinen in *Notker der Dichter*; he offers detailed commentary on Notker's literary references, as well as meaning and structure in the texts.) Where no page numbers are cited, the pages are the same as given in the references section, immediately preceding the commentary.

- THE TEXT AND TRANSLATION of the main source.

- DISTINCTIVE VARIANTS list the significant textual variants in the Nonantolan sources, with occasional references to other sources, especially those in northern and central Italian sources, including both text and musical variants.

- MELODIC VARIANTS are given for the Nonantolan manuscripts based on the approaches of Stäblein, *Hymnen*, and Schlager, *Alleluia-Melodien*. The manuscript source of the melodic variants is indicated in boldface type. Thereafter follow individual words in italics, with the unaffected syllables in parentheses. The letter of the medieval gamut represents the pitches on the scale (see above). Liquescent notes are indicated in parentheses and the oriscus is represented by a tilde (~) placed next to the letter name designating its pitch. Letters are grouped in two ways, either with a space between groups of letters to indicate groupings of neumes over the same syllable or with an apostrophe to indicate a syllable break. Individual variants are separated by a semicolon; variants in the different manuscript sources are separated by a period.

1. *Christi hodiernae pangimini*

SOURCES

Bu 2824 fols. 18v–20v (no rubric)

ITALIAN CONCORDANCES

Bc 7 (23r–23v); Bu 2748 (pp. 104–8); BV 34 (18v–19r); IV 60 (10v–11r); MCa 318 (p. 283*); MCa 546 (72r–73r); Mod 7 (10r–11v); Mza 75 (86r–86v); Mza 76 (31v–32r); Mza 77 (148r–149r); Ob 222 (83r–84r); PAc 47 (21r–22r); PCsa 65 (228r–228v); PS 121 (18r–19r); Ra 123 (201r–202r); SIc 15 (36v–137v); VCd 146 (96r–96v); VCd 161 (114r–115r); VEcap 90 (59v–60v); VEcap 107 (72r–74r); VO 39 (27r–28r).

REFERENCES

AH 7:42; 53:25; Arlt, *Ein Festoffizium*, 142; Brunner, "The Sequences of Verona 107," 1:93–95, 2:4; Brunner, "Catalogo," 219; Crocker, "The Sequence (*Gattung*)," 296; Crocker, *Early Medieval Sequence*, 183–88; Hughes, *Sequelae*, 55; von den Steinen, "Anfänge," 41:30–33.

TEXT COMMENTARY

This Christmas sequence was widely dispersed in both Italy and West Francia. It is found in the ninth-century collection VEcap 90, as well as the Toul manuscript Mbs 14843 (from ca. 900), and is therefore the earliest surviving notated text set to the very popular melody "Mater." The text is rather artless in its direct account of the Nativity. Von den Steinen ("Anfänge," 41:30) has called attention to the primitive quality of the text as well as the way it is set to music. Crocker (*Early Medieval Sequence*, 186–87) suspects that [5a], with its use of the angelic hymn, is an interpolation.

TEXT AND TRANSLATION

[1]   Christi <h>odierne pagimini omnis una
[2a] Voce simul consona nativitatis magne
[2b] Quod verbum caro factum exibere se voluit
[3a] Mundo quam redemit iam venerat de sede patris dominus
[3b] Nunciat angelus pastoribus ingenti current gaudio
[4a] Presepio puerum maria posuit in stabulum
[4b] Vagiens infantulum a quo regitur omnis mundus
[5a] Vigilantes pastores audiunt chorum
      Angelicum in cælis psallentes gloria laus decus in excelsis deo
[5b] Quem prophete cuncti predicaverunt olim
      Iam apparet forma quam induit dominus quem virgo mater pannis tegit
[6a] Exiguo tegitur diversorio qui arva condidit et polum
[6b] Non ostrum elegit non aurificum non rutilum venit in locum
[7a] Maria genitrix que exultabat incontaminato alvo enixa est auctorem omnium dominum
[7b] Ioseph valde se simul recolabat ammirando retractabat quod rei acta huiuscemodi veniret
[8a] Monitus somno ab angelo ut in egiptum fugeret cum parvulo
[8b] Herodem impium perderet qui queret cristum dominum occidere
[9a] Nos ergo ipsum adoremus ipsumque deprecemur simul omnes
[9b] Nostris ut relaxet delictis æternis donet bonis in æterna secula amen

*

[1]   Let everyone sing of Christ on this day
[2a] With a single consonant voice of the great nativity,
[2b] For the Word made flesh has willed to reveal Himself
[3a] To the world, which He redeemed.
      Now the Lord has come from the throne of the Father.
[3b] The angel announces to the shepherds, who hasten with boundless joy.
[4a] In a manger Mary has placed the babe, in a stable
[4b] The little infant is crying, the one by whom the whole world is ruled.
[5a] The shepherds keeping watch hear the choir on high singing "Glory, praise, honor to God in the highest."
[5b] The one whom all the prophets foretold long ago, now appears in the form that the Lord has put on, that form which His virgin mother in turn wrapped in swaddling cloths.
[6a] He is sheltered in a meager lodging, He who created the heavens and the earth,
[6b] He did not choose purple, nor gold; He did not come into a regal place.
[7a] Mary, the Mother, rejoiced, for from her pure womb she had given birth to the author of all things, to the Lord.
[7b] And Joseph at the same time was deep in meditation, considering with admiration what might come from an event such as this.
[8a] In a dream He was told by an angel, that He should escape into Egypt with the little boy,
[8b] That He should flee the heartless Herod, who slyly sought to kill Christ.
[9a] So let us adore Him and all together pray to Him,

[9b] That He might release us from our offenses, that He might grant us eternal blessings for ages unending. Amen.

DISTINCTIVE VARIANTS

The Italian concordances are fairly unified in the transmission of this sequence. [8] is unstable, producing a number of variants, but mostly in text alignment rather than melodic shape. For more detailed discussion, see Brunner, "The Sequences of Verona 107."

MELODIC VARIANTS

None.

2. *Natus ante saecula*

SOURCES

Rc 1741 fols. 53v–55r Seq\<uentia\>
Rn 1343 fols. 20v–21r Seq\<uentia\>
Bu 2824 fols. 24v–26r Seq\<uentia\>

ITALIAN CONCORDANCES

Bu 2748 (pp. 101–4); IV 60 (9r–9v); MCa 318 (p. 257*); MOd 7 (12v–13r); Ob 222 (84r–84v); PAs 697 (47r–47v); VEcap 107 (71r–72r); VO 39 (26v–27r).

REFERENCES

AH 53:20; Brunner, "The Sequences of Verona 107," 2:1; Brunner, "Catalogo," 247; Crocker, "Repertoire," 2:52; Crocker, *Early Medieval Sequence*, 234–38; Drinkwelder, *Sequentiar*, 18; de Goede, *Utrecht Prosarium*, 6; Schubiger, *Sängerschule*, 6; von den Steinen, *Notker der Dichter*, 1:266–70, 559–60, 2:12.

TEXT COMMENTARY

As Crocker points out (*Early Medieval Sequence*, 236), Notker's Christmas text *Natus ante saecula* is unique in the early repertory in that it has both opening and closing doubles, perhaps suggesting lost singles at the beginning and end. Yet there is no evidence of this and the text seems complete as it has come down to us. Von den Steinen pointed to a number of connections with earlier texts (see *Notker der Dichter*, 1:559). The transmission in Italy was relatively stable, with extant versions coming primarily from northern Italy. For facsimiles of the beginning of this sequence from Bu 2824 and Rn 1343, see plates 1 and 2.

TEXT AND TRANSLATION

[1a] Natus ante secula dei filius invisibilis interminus
[1b] Per quem fit machina cęli ac terrę maris et in his degentium
[2a] Per quem dies et hora labant et se iterum reciprocant
[2b] Quem angeli in arce poli voce consona semper canunt
[3a] Hic corpus adsumpserat fragile Sine labe originalis criminis de carne marię virigins, quo primiparentis culpam evęque lasciviam tergeret
[3b] Hoc pręsens dies ista loquitur Pręlucida adaucta longitudine quo sol verus radio sui luminis vetustas mundi depulerat genitus tenebras
[4a] Nec nox vacat novi sideris luce quod magorum oculos terruit scios
[4b] Nec gregum magistris defuit lumen quos prestrinxit claritas militum dei
[5a] Gaudet dei genitrix quam circumstant obstetricum vice concinentes angeli gloriam deo
[5b] Christe patris unice qui humanam nostri causa formam assumpsisti refove supplices tuos
[6a] Et quorum participem te fore dignatus es hiesu dignanter eorum suscipe preces
[6b] Ut ipsos divinitatis tuę participes deus facere digneris unice dei

*

[1a] Born before the beginning of time, the Son of God, beyond perception, without limit,
[1b] Through whom the workings of heaven and earth was made, of the sea, and all things that dwell therein,
[2a] Through whom the days and hours flicker and then are rekindled,
[2b] Whom the angels in the celestial realm continually proclaim with harmonious voice,
[3a] He had taken on a feeble body—without the stain of original sin, from the flesh of the Virgin Mary—through which the guilt of the first parent and the lust of Eve might be wiped clean.
[3b] Hence the present short day, this day of brilliant light, speaks forth, growing in length, because the true Sun, the newly begotten Son, by the rays of its light, had expelled the long-standing darkness.
[4a] Neither did the night lack the light of the new star, for it struck fear in the knowing eyes of the magi.
[4b] Nor was the light invisible to the shepherds, for they were awestruck by the glory of the heavenly host.
[5a] Rejoice, O Mother of God, whom, in place of a midwife, angels surround singing "Glory of God."
[5b] O Christ, only begotten of the Father, you who have taken human form for our sake, restore your humble servants;
[6a] And, O Jesus, you humbled yourself that you might share in their suffering; deign to receive their prayers,
[6b] So that you might deign to make them companions in your divinity, O only begotten God!

DISTINCTIVE VARIANTS

Rn 1343 [3a] *fragilem* for *fragile*; *lascivia* for *lasciviam*; [3b] *sancta* for *ista*; *vetusta* for *vetustas*. **Bu 2824** [3b] *sancta* for *ista*; *quod* for *quo*; *depulerit* for *depulerat*; [4a] *nos vocat novis* for *nox vacat novi*; *teruit* for *terruit*; *suos* for *scios*; [4b] *magistri* for *magistris*; [5b] *causam* for *causa*; [6b] *Et* for *Ut*.

MELODIC VARIANTS

Rn 1343 [3a] *(car)ne* F; *cul(pam)* DD~; [3b] *loqui(tur)* C'D; [4b] *lu(men)* DD~; [5a] *vi(ce)* ED; [5b] *for(mam)* E(D)~. **Bu 2824** [3a] *cul(pam)* DD~; [3b] *loqui(tur)* C'D; [4b] *lu(men)* DD~; [5a] *vi(ce)* ED.

3. *Hanc concordi*

SOURCES

Rc 1741 fols. 56v–58r Seq<uentia>
Rn 1343 fols. 22r–22v Seq<uentia>
Bu 2824 fols. 28r–29r Seq<uentia>

ITALIAN CONCORDANCES

BV 34 (21v–22r); Bu 2748 (pp. 112–15); Cb 74 (14r–14v); MCa 318 (p. 283*); MCa 546 (73r–73v); MOd 7 (16v–17r); NV 1 (199r–199v); Ob 222 (88r–88v); PAc 47 (27r–27v); PAs 697 (48r–48v); PS 121 (23v–24r); Rvat 5319 (153r–154r); Tn 18 (18v–19r); VEcap 107 (76r–76v); VO 39 (28v–29v).

REFERENCES

AH 53:345; Brunner, "The Sequences of Verona 107," 1:70–77, 2:7; Brunner, "Catalogo," 235; Crocker, *Early Medieval Sequence*, 79–83, 90–93; Drinkwelder, *Sequentiar*, 21; de Goede, *Utrecht Prosarium*, 8; Handschin, "Trope," 154; Hughes, *Sequelae*, 29; Moberg, *Schwedishen Sequenzen*, n. 15a; Schubiger, *Sängerschule*, 26; Stäblein, "Die Sequenzmelodie," 375–76; 387–92; von den Steinen, *Notker der Dichter*, 1:365–69, 582–84, 2:14.

TEXT COMMENTARY

Notker's text for the first martyr, St. Stephen, has a particularly refined sense of diction, where the layout of the text is skillfully matched with the melodic structure (see Crocker's discussion in *Early Medieval Sequence*, 92–93). See von den Steinen, *Notker der Dichter*, 1:582–83, for a number of Notker's sources and textual allusions. The melodic transmission often includes gentle ornamental elaborations, which Stäblein ("Die Sequenzmelodie," 376–79) considered characteristic of the sequence in Italian sources.

TEXT AND TRANSLATION

[1] Hanc concordi famulatu colamus sollemnitatem
[2a] Auctoris illius exemplo docti benigno
[2b] Pro persecutorum precantis fraude suorum
[3a] O stephane signifer regis summi bone nos exaudi
[3b] Proficuę qui es pro tuis exauditus inimicis
[4a] Paulus tuis precibus stephane te quondam persecutus christo credit
[4b] Et tecum tripudiat in regno cui nullus persecutor appropinquat
[5a] Nos proinde nos supplices ad te clamantes et precibus te pulsantes
[5b] Oratio sanctissima nos tua semper conciliet deo nostro
[6a] Te petrus christi ministrum statuit Tu petro normam credendi astruis ad dextram summi patris ostendendo quem plebs furens crucifixit
[6b] Te sibi christus elegit stephane Per quem fideles suos corroborat se tibi inter rotatus saxorum solacio manifestans
[7] Nunc inter inclitas martyrum purpuras coruscas cornonatus

*

[1] Let us in harmonious obedience celebrate this holy day,
[2a] As taught us by the kind example of its founder,
[2b] Who prayed in the face of the treachery of his persecutors.
[3a] Hear us, O Stephen, you consummate standard-bearer of the good King on high,
[3b] As you were once heard to pray beneficially for your enemies.
[4a] Through your prayers, O Stephen, Paul, who once persecuted you, believed in Christ.
[4b] And with you he dances in that kingdom where no persecutor can approach.
[5a] So may we, your supplicants, crying to you and hurling prayers at you,
[5b] May your most holy prayer constantly reconcile us with our God.
[6a] Peter ordained you a minister of Christ, and you offered Peter the model of belief,
by showing at the right hand of the highest Father, Him whom the raging mob had crucified.
[6b] You, O Stephen, Christ chose for Himself, to strengthen his faithful servants,
revealing Himself to you as a solace amid the barrage of stones.
[7] Now you radiate amid the illustrious purple of the martyrs, wearing your crown.

DISTINCTIVE VARIANTS

Rn 1343 [1] *solemptatem* for *sollemnitatem*; [7] *Tunc* for *Nunc*. The melodic settings often include neumatic ornamentation, especially in the Ravenna sources Mod 7 and Pac 47.

MELODIC VARIANTS

Rn 1343 [1] *solemptatem* d′c′aa′G; [3a] *(ste)pha(ne)* EE~; *(ex)au(di)* aa(G); [3b] *tu(is)* aa~; *(ini)mi(cis)* aa~; [4b] *(tripudi)at* EE~; *reg(no)* E; *(appro)pin(quat)* aa(G); [5a] *(cla)man(tes)* GG~; *(pul)san(tes)* aa~; [5b] *sem(per)* GG~; *nos(tro)* aa~; [6a] *(osten)den(do)* GG~; [6b] *in(ter)* abc; *(sax)o(rum)* GG~; *(mani)fes(tans)* aa~; [7] *(pur)pu(ras)* c; *(co)rus(cas)* aa~. **Bu 2824** [3a] *(ste)pha(ne)* EE~; *(ex)au(di)* aa(G); [3b] *tu(is)* aa~; *(ini)mi(cis)* aa~; [4b] *(tripudi)at* EE~; *(appro)pin(quat)* aa(G); [5a] *(cla)man(tes)* GG~; *(pul)san(tes)* aa~; [5b] *sem(per)* GG~; *nos(tro)* aa~; [6a] *(osten)den(do)* GG~; [6b] *in(ter)* abc; *(sax)o(rum)* GG~; *(mani)fes(tans)* aa~; [7] *(co)rus(cas)* aa~.

4. *Iohannes Iesu Christo*

SOURCES

Rc 1741 fols. 59v–60v Sequentia
Rn 1343 fols. 23r Seq\<uen\>n\<tia\>
Bu 2824 fols. 30v–31v Seq\<uentia\>

ITALIAN CONCORDANCES

Bu 2748 (pp. 115–18); BV 34 (24v–25r); Cb 74 (16v–17r); IV 60 (19v–20r); MCa 318 (p. 257*); MCa 546 (73v–74r); Mod7 (20v–21r); Mza 75 (86); Mza 76 (27v–28r); Mza 77 (147r–148r); Ob 222 (88v–89r); PAc 47 (31v–32v); PAs 697 (48v–49r); PCsa 65 (229v–230r); PS 121 (24v–25r); Ra 123 (199v–200r); Rvat 5319 (154r–154v); Tn 18 (22v–23r); Tn 20 (30r–30v); VCd 146 (99v–100r); VCd 161 (118r); VCd 162 (178v–179r); VEcap 107 (77v–78r); VO 39 (29v–30r).

REFERENCES

AH 53:276; Brunner, "The Sequences of Verona 107," 1:77–82, 2:9; Brunner, "Catalogo," 238; Crocker, *Early Medieval Sequence*, 146–59; de Goede, *Utrecht Prosarium*, 11; Moberg, *Schwedishen Sequenzen*, n. 26; Schubiger, *Sängerschule*, 3; Stäblein, *Vat. lat. 5319*, 612; von den Steinen, *Notker der Dichter* 1:361–65, 581–82, 2:16.

TEXT COMMENTARY

As with other texts set to the melody "Romana" (nos. 12, 13, 24, 25), the lines of text are relatively equal to correspond to the musical phrases, which are close in length for [3]–[7]. Such a plan is unusual in the early repertory. Half of the lines of this sequence begin with some form of the second-person singular pronoun *tu*, which as Crocker points out, has resonance in the prototype *Te Deum laudamus*. Von den Steinen has revealed many literary sources for different parts Notker's text (*Notker der Dichter*, 1:581–82). *Iohannes Iesu Christo* has the most complete concordances in Italian manuscripts of any sequence.

TEXT AND TRANSLATION

[1] Iohannes hiesu christo multum dilecte virgo
[2a] Tu eius amore carnalem
[2b] In navi parentem liquisti
[3a] Tu leve coniugis pectus respuisti messiam secutus
[3b] Ut eius pectoris sacra meruisses fluenta potare
[4a] Tuque in terra positus gloriam conspexisti filii dei
[4b] Quę solum sanctis invita creditur contuenda esse perhenni
[5a] Te christus in cruce triumphans matri suę dedit custodem
[5b] Ut virgo virginem servares atque curam suppenditares
[6a] Tute carcere flagrisque fractus testimonio pro christi es gavisus
[6b] Idem mortuos suscitas inque hiesu nomine venenum forte vincis
[7a] Tibi summus tacitum ceteris verbum suum pater revelat
[7b] Tu nos omnes sedulis precibus apud deum semper commenda
[8] Iohannes christi care

*

[1] John, the pure one, deeply beloved by Jesus Christ,
[2a] Because of your love for Him,
[2b] You left your earthly father in the boat.
[3a] You renounced a wife's soft bosom to follow the Messiah,
[3b] So that at his breast you might be worthy to drink the sacred stream.
[4a] In your life on earth you gazed on the glory of God's Son,
[4b] Which, according to our creed, can be seen only by saints in eternal life.
[5a] You were the one to whom Christ in His triumph on the cross, committed the care of His Mother,
[5b] So that you, the one chaste, might attend the Virgin and generously see to her needs.
[6a] You, broken by prison and scourges, rejoiced in your witness for Christ,
[6b] Indeed you raise the dead to new life, and are unaffected by deadly poison, all in the name of Jesus.
[7a] To you God the Father unveils His Word, which is concealed to others.
[7b] So, through your ceaseless prayers, may you always be our advocate in the presence of God,
[8] John, beloved of Christ.

DISTINCTIVE VARIANTS

Rn 1343 [2a] *carnale* for *carnalem*; [2b] *parentum* for *parentem*. For a comparison of eleven Italian versions of phrases [1] and [2], see Brunner, "The Sequences of Verona 107," 1:49.

MELODIC VARIANTS

Rn 1343 [1] *chris(to)* cc~; *(vir)go* C; [3a] *pec(tus)* ee~; [4a] *ter(ra)* ee~; *de(i)* ee~; [4b] *(per)hen(ni)* ee(d); [5b] *(suppedi)to(res)* ee~; [6b] *for(te)* E(D); [7b] *om(nes)* EE~; *(com)men(da)* ee~; [8] *ca(re)* ee~. **Bu 2824** [2b] (li)qui(sti) ee~; [3a] *pec(tus)* ee~; [4a] *ter(ra)* ee~; [4b] *(per)hen(nis)* ee(d); [5b] *(suppedi)to(res)* ee~; [6b] *for(te)* E(D); [7b] *om(nes)* EE~; *(com)men(da)* ee~; [8] *ca(re)* ee~.

5. Laus tibi Christe cui sapit

SOURCES

Bu 2824 fols. 32v–36v Seq<uentia>

ITALIAN CONCORDANCES

CHb 2 (flyleaf verso); IV 60 (21v); Ob 222 (89v–90r); PAs 697 (49r–49v); PCsa 65 (230); Tn 18 (24r–24v); VEcap 107 (78r–78v).

REFERENCES

AH 53:256; Brunner, "The Sequences of Verona 107," 2:10; Brunner, "Catalogo," 243; Crocker, *Early Medieval Sequence*, 296–98; de Goede, *Utrecht Prosarium*, 12; Hughes, *Sequelae*, 48; von den Steinen, *Notker der Dichter* 1:342–47, 574–75, 2:18.

TEXT COMMENTARY

Von den Steinen (*Notker der Dichter*, 1:342–47) explored the theological aspects of Notker's text and his solution to the difficult task of creating a song that praises the children who were martyred, while at the same time justifying why God allowed such a slaughter to take place. Crocker considered this text one of Notker's mature efforts and called attention to a poem by Gottschalk of Orbais, which Notker may have drawn from for his text. For a discussion of the problems associated with the melody, see de Goede, *Utrecht Prosarium*, xcix–c.

TEXT AND TRANSLATION

[1] Laus tibi criste
[2a] Cui sapit quod videtur ceteris esse surdastrum
[2b] Famulatum cuius omnis competit sexus et etas
[3a] Recentes atque teneri milites [h]erodiano ense trucidati te hodie predicaverunt
[3b] Licet necdum potuerunt ligula effusione tamen te criste sui sanguinis preconati sunt
[4a] Lac cum cruore fundentes ad deum clamitaturum
[4b] Ut apud illi quem gena miseret et innocentes
[5a] Quis adletarum fortissimus umquam Exercti-bus tantam christe suis contulit victoria[m]
[5b] Quantum vagiens quoevulis tuis Tu prestitisti mittens eos caelum renaturus perpetim
[6a] O christi precones clari floresque martirum corusci
[6b] Et confessorum insigens gemule sanctorum
[7a] Atque sterilium in mundo virginum
[7b] Clari filioli dulces pusioli os iuvate precibus
[8a] Quas christus innocentem mortem vestram miserans
[8b] Pro sese maturatam placitus exaudiens
[9] Nos regno suo dignetur

*

[1] Praise be to you, O Christ,
[2a] To You who knows that which seems beyond all others' ken,
[2b] Whom every sex and age strives to serve
[3a] Today, the young and tender soldiers, slain by Herod's blade, proclaim You:
[3b] Though not yet able to speak, they glorified You, O Christ, not with their little tongues but with shedding their own blood,
[4a] In offering forth milk together with blood as a cry unto God
[4b] Who has pity on these innocent orphans, their cheeks wet with tears. (read *Uda pupilli*)
[5a] Who, O Christ, mightiest among champions, has ever conferred so great a victory upon his armies
[5b] As You, yourself a little child, granted to your peers, sending them to reign without end in Heaven?
[6a] O bright heralds of Christ, and His gleaming flowers of the Martyrs,
[6b] And glorious gems of the Holy Confessors, (read *insignes*)
[7a] And of the Virgins, barren in the world,
[7b] Dear little sons, sweet little boys, help us through your prayers! (read *nos iuvate*)
[8a] That Christ might have pity on your innocent death,
[8b] Hastened on His behalf and graciously hear your prayers,
[9] And thus hold us worthy of His kingdom.

DISTINCTIVE VARIANTS

None.

6. Haec sunt sacra festa

SOURCES

Rc 1741 fols. 62r–63v Seq<uentia>
Rn 1343 fols. 24r–24v Seq<uentia>
Bu 2824 fols. 35r–36v Seq<uentia>

ITALIAN CONCORDANCES

MCa 318 (p. 277*); Mza 76 (170r–170v); PCsa 65 (246v–247r); PS 121 (74r–75r); VEcap 107 (79r–79v); VO 39 (23v–24r).

REFERENCES

AH 37:259; Brunner, "The Sequences of Verona 107," 1:110–15, 2:12; Brunner, "Catalogo," 235; Hughes, *Sequelae,* 24; Negro, "Le sequenze," 86.

TEXT COMMENTARY

This North-Italian sequence is a setting of the melody "Eia turma." The text is modeled on the more popular text *Eia recolamus* (no. 14) and is generic enough to be used for any saint. Assonance on "a" permeates both texts. A study of the variants suggests the Nonantolan reading may preserve the original text and it is possible that it was created there. For a comparison of the two sequences and a more detailed discussion of the text, see Brunner, "The Sequences of Verona 107," 1:112–15. See also the TEXT COMMENTARY for *Ad templi huius limina* (no. 35), the other Nonantolan sequence set to "Eia turma," which has an unusual version of the melody.

TEXT AND TRANSLATION

[1] Hęc sunt sacra festa laudibus magnis digna
[2a] Nostra hac die carmina penetrent templa precibus siderea
[2b] Sancti silvestri meritis merita nobis imploremus prospera
[3a] Inter ethereos cives tuos post delicta nos sancte silvester revoca
[3b] Tuarum ovium margarita preciosa tu gemma plebis fulgida
[4a] Tu dux gregis lęta iocundę pręvidisti tuis vitę pabula
[4b] Servans custos ovium caulas efferas abegisti insidias
[5a] Nunc alias tenens patrias angelorum delicias
[5b] Terram eden rura pinguia magnis deliciis plena
[6a] Ne nos te quęsumus deseras baiulansque oves tuas
[6b] Dispersas petimus revoca sublevaque prece tua
[7a] Ne sit procul tua cura ne simus hostis pręda mortis tela violent mentis animam
[7b] Frangimur belli pugna dextera sine tua tua sit victoria christi gratia
[8a] Iudicem postula deleat nostra crimina
[8b] Quęsumus impetra remissionis veniam
[9a] Pastor tuam familiam sancte silvester guberna
[9b] Atque deo ut munera hostiam quoque representa
[10] Ut digni fruamur gloria

*

[1] The holy feast is here, worthy of great praise.
[2a] On this day, let our songs penetrate the heavenly sanctuaries with prayers.
[2b] Through Holy Silvester's merits let us beseech that our merits may be propitious for us.
[3a] Summon us back among the heavenly citizens, Holy Silvester, after our transgressions.
[3b] You are the precious pearl of your sheep, the splendid gem of your people.
[4a] As leader of your flock, you have provided your followers with the joyful nourishment of a blessed life.
[4b] As guardian of the sheep you have removed the treacherous snares.
[5a] Now you reach the delightful home of the angels,
[5b] The land of Eden, the fertile land full of great delight.
[6a] We ask that you not to desert us and carry your sheep on your shoulder.
[6b] We pray to you, bring back those who are scattered and lift them up through your prayer.
[7a] Let your care not be far off, so that we do not become the enemies' prey,
that the spears of death shall not violate our soul.
[7b] Without the help of your right hand we are broken by the combat of war;
may the victory be yours through the grace of Christ.
[8a] Implore the Judge that He might absolve our sins.
[8b] We ask that you obtain the favor of forgiveness.
[9a] Shepherd, Holy Silvester, lead your servants
[9b] And display as well the offering to God as gifts,
[10] So that we shall be worthy to delight in glory.

DISTINCTIVE VARIANTS

Rn 1343 [7a] *scit* for *sit*. A couplet was added after phrase [8] in the following Italian manuscripts: Mza 77, MOd 16, PS 121, and VEcap 107; see Brunner, "The Sequences of Verona 107," 2:13.

MELODIC VARIANTS

Rn 1343 [2a] *si(derea)* G; [2b] *(implo)remus* aa~'G; [3a] *tu(os)* a; *(silves)ter* G; [3b] *(marga)ri(ta)* a; *(ple)bis* G; [4a] *(vi)tę* G; [4b] *(ef)fe(ras)* c; *in(sidias)* G; [5a] *de(licias)* d; [5b] *(delici)is* d; [6a] *o(ves)* d; [6b] *pre(ce)* d; [7a] *cura* g'c; *pre(da)* g; [7b] *pug(na)* g; *tu(a)* g; [8b] *(remissio)nis* d; [9a] *tu(am)* ed; [9b] *de(o)* ed. **Bu 2824** [2b] *(implo)remus* aa~'G; [3a] *tu(os)* a; *(silves)ter* G; [3b] *(marga)ri(ta)* a; *(ple)bis* G; [4a] *(vi)tę* G; [4b] *(ef)fe(ras)* c; *in(sidias)* G; [5a] *de(licias)* d; [5b] *(delici)is* d; [6a] *o(ves)* d; [6b] *pre(ce)* d; [7a] *cu(ra)* g; *pre(da)* g; [7b]

pug(na) g; *tu(a)* g; [8b] *(remissio)nis* d; [9a] *tu(am)* ed; [9b] *de(o)* ed.

7. Laude mirandum

SOURCES

Rc 1741 fols. 64v–66r Seq<uentia>
Rn 1343 fols. 25r–25v Seq<uentia> In oct<ava> d<omi>ni

ITALIAN CONCORDANCES

VEcap 107 (81r–82r).

REFERENCES

AH 34:13; Brunner, "The Sequences of Verona 107," 1:77–82; Brunner, "Catalogo," 241.

TEXT COMMENTARY

The piece survives in only five manuscripts, four of Italian provenance (including MOd 16, not listed among the concordances because of its late date) and the Reichenau manuscript BAs 5. Blume (*AH* 37:8) could not decide between North Italian or East Frankish origin, but von den Steinen simply stated it was written in Reichenau in the second half of the tenth century (*Notker der Dichter*, 1:553). *Laude mirandum* was carefully modeled on *Summi triumphum*, also set to "Captiva." For a discussion of their relationship, see Brunner, "The Sequences of Verona 107," 1:123–24.

TEXT AND TRANSLATION

[1] Laude mirandum digna prosequamur regem
[2a] Qui primum frondosa paradisi parentem sede miserans
[2b] Expulsum dolosi virulento serpentis hausto poculo
[3a] Humano nasci pro genere voluit
[3b] Per virginalis aulę auream portam mundo veniens perdito
[4a] Celsa polorum descendens arce summus tulit membra servilia dominus
[4b] Ut nos legis lator archos gravi nexos sarcinarum ligamento legalium solveret
[5a] Masculus hodie circumciditur tipicus
[5b] Innocens penitus atque omnium labe facinorum purissimus
[6a] In circumcisam sic viciis lucido instruens exemplo
[6b] Sanctorum pręclaris animam cętibus esse proturbandam
[7a] Hodie ex eulogio matris angelico hiesus dictatu acceperat vocabulum
[7b] Qui suum diabolicis populum vinculis suae solveret munere gratię salvator ipse salutifero purgans peccamina remedio
[8a] Te virgo virginum te stella maris clara sancta theotocos cernui precamur
[8b] Ut omni scelerum zizania pravorum carnis ac spiritus simul resecata
[9a] Virtutum ac morum nitidos floribus servulos amenis
[9b] Maiores cum parvis senes ac iuvenes sexus utriusque
[10] Unico filio precibus commendes circumcisos

[1] Let us sing worthy praises to the wondrous King,
[2a] Who in compassion for the first parent who was expelled from the leafy seat of paradise,
[2b] When he drank from the poisonous cup of the cunning serpent
[3a] Was willing to be born for the sake of man.
[3b] Coming through the golden door of the virginal chamber to the ruined world
[4a] Descending from the high reaches of heaven the supreme Lord took on the body of a servant
[4b] So that the law-giver Himself, the archon, might liberate us, who had been bound by the burden of the law.
[5a] Today the little boy is circumcised
[5b] Wholly innocent and entirely pure, without the stain of any sins.
[6a] Thus, with His brilliant example, He teaches cutting the soul away from vices
[6b] To be among the shining hosts of saints instead of [among] the rabble.
[7a] Today, after the Mother's praise, Jesus had accepted His designation according to the angel's word.
[7b] He should liberate His people from the snares of the Devil in giving His grace, Himself the savior who purifies from sins with His healing remedy.
[8a] O Virgin of virgins, star of the sea, Holy Mother of God, prostrate we pray to you
[8b] That when every ripple of perverse sins is rinsed out of both flesh and the spirit
[9a] You commend your servants, shining with beautiful flowers of virtues and character,
[9b] High and low together, old and young, men and women,
[10] All encompassed by your prayers to Your one born Son.

DISTINCTIVE VARIANTS

Rn 1343 [8a] *theotocon* for *theotocos*; [8b] *Et omnis* for *Ut omni*.

MELODIC VARIANTS

Rn 1343 [1] *(Alle)lu(ia)* DED . . . ; [3b] *por(tam)* E(D); [5b] *pu(rissimus)* a; [6a] *vi(ciis)* D; *(in)stru(ens)* D;

(ex)em(plo) EE(D); [6b] *(Sancto)rum* a; *(tur)ban(dam)* EE(D); [7a] *vo(cabulum)* a; [7b] *pur(gans)* b(a); [8a] *(pre)ca(mur)* EE~; [8b] *(rese)ca(ta)* EE~; [9a] *(a)me(nis)* EE~; [9b] *(utri)us(que)* EE~.

8. Festa Christi

SOURCES

Rc 1741 fols. 67v–69r Seq<uentia>
Rn 1343 fols. 26r–26v Seq<uentia>
Bu 2824 fols. 38r–39v Seq<uentia>

ITALIAN CONCORDANCES

BV 35 (4v–5r); IV 60 (28v–29r); MCa 318 (p. 283*); MCa 546 (76r–76v); PAs 697 (49v–50v); VCd 161 (120r*); VEcap 107 (83r–84r).

REFERENCES

AH 53:50; Brunner, "The Sequences of Verona 107," 2:16; Brunner, "Catalogo," 231; Crocker, *Early Medieval Sequence*, 308–13; Drinkwelder, *Sequentiar*, 25; de Goede, *Utrecht Prosarium*, 15; Moberg, *Schwedishen Sequenzen*, no. 16b; Schubiger, *Sängerschule*, 9; von den Steinen, *Notker der Dichter* 1:280–84, 563–64, 2:22.

TEXT COMMENTARY

This text is discussed in detail by Crocker, *Early Medieval Sequence*. After a straightforward liturgical exhortation, three themes are explored: the Epiphany [2–4], Herod's wrath in the slaughter of the Innocents [5], and John's baptism of Jesus [6–8]. Phrase [7a] contains the only place in the *Liber Hymnorum* where God speaks directly, which is drawn from the Gospels (Matt. 3:13–17; Luke 3:22). By including all these themes, Notker seems to have intended the piece for the season of Epiphany, rather than the feast specifically, as Crocker points out. Although there are relatively few Italian sources, these are spread from the south to the north of Italy.

TEXT AND TRANSLATION

[1] Festa christi omnis christianitas celebret
[2a] Quę miris sunt modis ornata cunctisque veneranda populis
[2b] Per omnitenentis adventum atque vocationem gentium
[3a] Ut natus est christus est stella magis visa lucida
[3b] At illi non cassam putantes tanti signi gloriam
[4a] Secum munera deferunt parvulo offerunt ut regi cęli quem sidus predicat
[4b] Atque aureo tumidi principis lectulo transito christi presepe quęritant
[5a] Hinc ira sevi herodis fervida Invidi recens rectori genito bethleem parvulos pręcepit ense crudeli perdere
[5b] O christe quantum patri exercitum Iuvenis doctus ad bella maxima populis prędicans colligis sugens cum tantum miseris
[6a] Anno hominis trigesimo Subtus famuli se incliti inclinaverat manus deus consecrans nobis baptisma in absolutione criminum
[6b] Ecce spiritus in specie Ipsum alitis innocuę uncturus sanctis pre omnibus visitans semper ipsius contentus mansione pectoris
[7a] Patris etiam intonuit vox pia veteris oblita sermonis penitet me fecisse hominem
[7b] Vere filius es tu meus michimet placitus in quo sum placitus hodie te mi fili genui
[8] Huic omnes auscultate populi redemptori

*

[1] Let the whole of Christendom celebrate the feasts of Christ,
[2a] Which are distinguished by many wonders and, because of the advent
[2b] Of Him who holds all things and the invitation to all nations, are worthy of honor by all peoples.
[3a] When Christ was born, a brilliant star was seen by the magi.
[3b] But they, reflecting that the glory of such a great sign was not without meaning,
[4a] They brought with them gifts to a little child, that they might offer them to the King of Heaven, whom the star foretold.
[4b] And passing the golden bed of the haughty prince,
they searched for Christ's manger.
[5a] Then cruel Herod, burning with rage, jealous of the new-born ruler,
decrees that the young boys of Bethlehem be destroyed by the merciless sword.
[5b] O Christ, knowing of the great conflict while yet a babe, what a great army you assembled for the Father, and thereby you bore witness to humanity while still a suckling among the most disconsolate.
[6a] In the thirtieth year of His manhood, God submitted Himself to the hands of His glorious servant, consecrating for us baptism for the remission of sins.
[6b] And lo, the Spirit in the form of an innocent bird came to anoint Him before all saints, content for all times to dwell in His heart.
[7a] The devoted voice of the Father sounded forth, forgetting His former words, that He was sorry to have made man.
[7b] "You truly are my Son, pleasing to me, in whom I am reconciled.
Today, my Son, I have begotten You."
[8] O all you peoples, listen to this teacher!

Distinctive Variants

Rn 1343 [5b] *populus* for *populis*. **Bu 2824** [5a] *genitum* for *genito*.

Melodic Variants

Rn 1343 [1] *(christiani)tas* GG~; *(Alle)lu(ia)* ab(a); [2a] *(vene)ran(da)* aa(G); [2b] *(ad)ven(tum)* aa(G); [3a] *chris(tus)* bb~; [3b] *cas(sam)* bb~; [4a] *(si)dus* GG~; [4b] *(prese)pe* GG~ [5a] *(crude)li* GG~; [6b] *sanc(tis)* g(f); *sem(per)* dd~; *(mansio)ne* GG~; [8] *(ausculta)te* GG~. **Bu 2824** [1] *(christiani)tas* GG~; *(Alle)lu(ia)* ab(a); [2a] *(vene)ran(da)* aa(G); [2b] *(ad)ven(tum)* aa(G); [3a] *chris(tus)* bb~; [3b] *cas(sam)* bb~; [4a] *(si)dus* GG~; [4b] *(prese)pe* GG~; [6a] *(absolutio)ne* GG~; [6b] *sanc(tis)* g(f); *sem(per)* dd~; *(mansio)ne* GG~; [8] *(ausculta)te* GG~.

9. Concentu parili

Sources

Rc 1741 fols. 70v–72r Seq\<uentia\>
Rn 1343 fols. 27r–28r Seq\<uentia\>
Bu 2824 fols. 43v–45v Seq\<uentia\>

Italian Concordances

Bu 2748 (pp. 122–26); BV 35 (16v–17v); MCa 318 (p. 284*); MOd 7 (216v–217r); Mza 77 (150v–151v); PAs 697 (50v–51v); Ra 123 (208v–209v); VCd 146 (101v–102r); VCd 161 (120v–121r); VCd 162 (181v–182r); VEcap 107 (85v–86v).

References

AH 53:171; Brunner, "The Sequences of Verona 107," 2:20; Brunner, "Catalogo," 221; Crocker, *Early Medieval Sequence*, 227–35; Drinkwelder, *Sequentiar*, 27; de Goede, *Utrecht Prosarium*, 20; Schubiger, *Sängerschule*, 12; von den Steinen, *Notker der Dichter* 1:315–20, 571–73, 2:24.

Text Commentary

Blume (*AH* 53:173) pointed out that in many manuscripts a phrase is added that uses the same melody as the first two lines, which von den Steinen (*Notker der Dichter*) estimates was added two or three generations after Notker. This additional line, found in many German and a few Italian sources, as well as in Winchester, in effect changes the opening double to a triple, but may have been seen as allowing the opening line to stand as a single, followed by a double, although they use essentially the same melody. The Nonantolan sources interestingly do not have this addition. Crocker provides detailed commentary on this unusual piece, with its long and regular lines of text, where the length of the lines is extended "past what their melodic substance will permit" (*Early Medieval Sequence*, 231). The syntax is simple and straightforward, containing "some of the longest, most sustained lines in his [Notker's] repertory" (232).

Text and Translation

[1a] Concentu parili hic te maria veneratur populus teque piis colit cordibus

[1b] Generosi abraham tu filia veneranda regia de davidis stirpe genita

[2a] Lętare mater et virgo nobilis gabrihelis archangeli quoque oraculo credita genuisti clausa filium

[2b] In cuius sacratissimo sanguine emundatur universitas perditissimi generis ut promisit deus abrahę

[3a] Te virga arida aaron flore speciosa te figurat maria sine viri semine nato florida

[3b] Tu porta iugiter serata quam ezechihelis vox testatur maria soli deo pervia esse crederis

[4a] Sed tu tamen matris virtutum dum nobis exemplum cupisti commendare subisti remedium pollutis statutum matribus

[4b] Ad templum detulisti tecum mundandum qui tibi integritatis decus deus homo genitus adauxit intacta genitrix

[5a] Lętare quam scrutator cordis et renum probat habitatu proprio singulariter dignam sancta maria

[5b] Exulta cui parvus arrisit tum maria qui lętari omnibus et consistere suo nutu tribuit

[6a] Ergo quique colimus festa parvuli christi propter nos facti eiusque pię matris marię

[6b] Si non dei possumus tantam exsequi tardi humilitatem forma sit nobis eius genitrix

[7a] Laus patri glorię qui suum filium gentibus et populo revelans israhel nos sociat

[7b] Laus eius filio qui suo sanguine nos patri concilians supernis sociavit civibus

[8] Laus quoque sancto spiritui sit per ęvum

*

[1a] With one accord this people reveres you, O Mary, and venerates you with devoted hearts.

[1b] You are the daughter of noble Abraham, born of the royal lineage of David.

[2a] Rejoice, O Mother and Virgin renowned! who, trusting the oracle of Gabriel, undefiled, bore a Son

[2b] In whose most sacred blood the whole of the ruined race is cleansed, just as God promised Abraham.

[3a] Aaron's rod, barren but splendid in flowering, prefigures you, O Mary, blossoming with a son without man's seed.

[3b] You are the gate forever closed, to which Ezekiel's voice bears witness, O Mary, you are held to be accessible to God alone.

[4a] But you, wanting to give for us an example of motherly virtue, submitted to the remedy mandated for mothers unclean.
[4b] You brought Him with you to the temple to be cleansed, who, as God-born man, heightened the glory of your virginity, Mother undefiled.
[5a] Rejoice! He who searches our hearts and innermost parts has proven you alone worthy of His own indwelling, O Holy Mary!
[5b] Exult! O Mary, on you the infant then did smile, at whose gift all rejoice, at whose command all exist.
[6a] Therefore so all we who celebrate the feast of Christ, made a child on our behalf, and His Holy Mother Mary,
[6b] If we are not able in our frailty to attain God's profound humility, then let His Mother be our model.
[7a] Praise be to the Father of Glory, who by revealing His Son to the gentiles and His people alike joins us to Israel.
[7b] Praise be to His Son, who by reconciling us to His Father with His blood has joined us to the saints above;
[8] Praise, too, be to the Holy Spirit forever.

DISTINCTIVE VARIANTS

Rn 1343 [5a] the text scribe copied *pro habitatu* twice, but the neume scribe, recognizing the error, did not provide neumes for the repetition.

MELODIC VARIANTS

Rn 1343 [1a] *hic* D; *(Allelu)ia* ... FED E~ ...; [3a] *aa(ron)* bb~; *(speci)o(sa)* aa~; [3b] *(ezechi)he(lis)* aa~; *esse* aa~'GG~; [4a] *(vir)tu(tum)* aa~ *(commen)da(re)* GG~; [4b] *de(cus)* GG~; *(in)tacta* aa~'GG~; [5a] *sanc(ta)* aa~; [7a] *(re)ve(lans)* bb~; [8] *sanc(to)* aa(G); *ę(vum)* aa~. **Bu 2824** [1a] *hic* D; *(Allelu)ia* ... FED E~ ...; [3a] *aa(ron)* bb~; *(speci)o(sa)* aa~; [3b] *(ezechi)he(lis)* aa~; *(es)se* GG~; [4a] *(vir)tu(tum)* aa~ *(commen)da(re)* GG~; [4b] *de(cus)* GG~; *(intac)ta* GG~; [5a] *sanc(ta)* aa~; [7a] *(re)ve(lans)* bb~; [8] *sanc(to)* aa(G); *ę(vum)* aa~.

10. Virginis venerandae

SOURCES

Rc 1741 fols. 73r–73v Seq<uentia> In N<atale> S<anctae> fuscę
Bu 2824 fols. 42r–43r Seq<uentia> de vir<gine>

ITALIAN CONCORDANCES

Bu 2748 (pp. 200–202); BV 39 (152r–152v); IV 60 (33r); MOd 7 (38v–39r); Pac 47 (220v–221r); PAs 697 (50v); PCsa 65 (247); Ra 123 (210r–210v); Rv 52 (159v); VCd 146 (114v–115r); VCd 161 (133v); VCd 162 (200r–200v); VEcap 107 (116r–116v).

REFERENCES

AH 53:395; Brunner, "The Sequences of Verona 107," 64; Brunner, "Catalogo," 267; Crocker, "Repertoire," 2:78; de Goede, *Utrecht Prosarium*, 18; Moberg, *Schwedishen Sequenzen*, n. 67; Schubiger, *Sängerschule*, 34; von den Steinen, *Notker der Dichter* 1:428–31, 600, 2:105.

TEXT COMMENTARY

This straightforward but well written text had been ascribed to Notker, but von den Steinen ruled out his authorship, attributing it rather to one of his students, possibly the same composer of *Deus in tua virtute*, the "Andreasdichter" (*Notker der Dichter*, 1:428–31). The reference to the parable of the wise and foolish virgins in [7] is obvious (Matt. 25). The piece is dedicated to St. Fusca in Rc 1741, and is included with the chants for Epiphany in Bu 2824, where it has a generic rubric, *de virgine*, but the text uses the name of Agnes. Fusca was a girl of fifteen who lived in Ravenna in the mid third century when she was martyred. Her feast, celebrated on 13 February, is usually shared with Maura, her nurse who was speared to death in martyrdom along with her mistress. See S. Baring-Gould, *The Lives of the Saints*, 16 vols. (London, 1897), 2:286–87. The Italian concordances show a stable transmission with very few variants.

TEXT AND TRANSLATION

[1] Virginis venerandę de numero sapientum festa celebremus fuscę
[2a] Filię matris summi regis sacrosanctę marię
[2b] Quam sibi in sororem dei adoptavit filius
[3a] Hęc corpus suum domuit freno ieiunii
[3b] Et luxuriam secuit ense agonię
[4a] Ista hęc contra cunctos mortis dimicavit impetus
[4b] Et hostem cruentum freta christi dextra straverat
[5a] Hęc sponsum ab aula cęli sese invisentem alacris
[5b] Corde iocundo secuta eius est ingressa thalamum
[6a] Tute iam dulcibus plena deliciis
[6b] Christo miserias nostras suggerito
[7] Nobis consolationem precando

*

[1] From the multitude of wise virgins, let us celebrate the feast of Fusca, the venerable virgin,
[2a] A daughter of the most Holy Mary, Mother of the sublime King:
[2b] The Son of God has taken her to Himself as a sister!
[3a] This virgin subdued her body with the discipline of fasting,

[3b] And cut off wantonness with the sword of suffering;
[4a] This virgin herself struggled against all deadly passions
[4b] And, with the support of Christ's right hand, scattered the cruel enemy.
[5a] The Bridegroom approaching her from the heavenly palace
[5b] She gladly followed, with heart rejoicing, and has entered His bed chamber.
[6a] Now safely filled with sweet delights,
[6b] Bring our sorrows before Christ,
[7] And beg for our consolation.

DISTINCTIVE VARIANTS

Bu 2824 [1] *Agnetis* for *fuscae*; [2a] *Agnetis* for *mariae*.

MELODIC VARIANTS

Bu 2824 [1] *(fes)ta* c; *Agnetis* F'G'G; *(Al)le(luia)* ... cd~accb ... ; [2a] *(re)gis* c; [2b] *(de)i* c; [4a] *(mor)tis* c; *(dimica)vit* GG~; [4b] *(fre)ta* c; *(dex)tra* GG~; [5a] *au(la) e(d)*; *(se)se* c; *(invisen)tem* GG~; [5b] *(iocun)do* ed; *(e)ius* c; [7] *(consolati)onem* a'G; *(pre)can(do)* aa~.

11. Ecce vicit

SOURCES

Rc 1741 fols. 76v–78v Seq<uentia>
Rn 1343 fols. 29r–29v Seq<uentia>
Bu 2824 fols. 48v–50v Seq<uentia>

ITALIAN CONCORDANCES

Bu 2748 (pp. 126–30); BV 34 (145r–146r); BV 35 (74v–75r); BV 38 (63v–64v); BV 39 (47r–48r); BV 40 (40r–41r); IV 60 (73r–73v); MCa 318 (p. 284*); MOd 7 (113v–114v); Mza 76 (99r–99v); Mza 77 (151v–153r); NV 1 (201r–201v); Ob 222 (94v–95v); PAc 47 (142r–143v); Pn 1669 (93v–95r); PCsa 65 (236v–237r); PS 121 (38r–39r) and (91r–91v); Ra 123 (217r–218r); SIc 15 (139r–139v); Tn 18 (168v–169r); VCd 146 (102v–103r); VCd 161 (122r–122v); VCd 162 (184r–185r); VEcap 107 (89v–90v); VO 39 (35r–35v).

REFERENCES

AH 7:63; 53:73; Brunner, "The Sequences of Verona 107," 1:70–77, 2:25; Brunner, "Catalogo," 227; Brunner, "The Tao of Singing"; Crocker, "Repertoire," 2:32; Crocker, *Early Medieval Sequence*, 76–87; Hughes, *Sequelae*, 29; Stäblein, "Die Sequenzmelodie," 386–92.

TEXT COMMENTARY

The *dragma* in [3a], rendered here by silver coin, was about a day's wage for a laborer (see Luke 15:8). Crocker saw the Easter sequence *Ecce vicit* as the likely model for Notker's *Hanc concordi*, and later *Petre summe*. He felt that the version of *Ecce vicit* that has come down to us had accrued a number of additions, which weaken the piece by creating discontinuities and jumbling the central narrative of Christ's battle to defeat death. By locating and removing redundancy and inconsistency he posits a restored version, which may have been the one on which Notker modeled his own masterpieces. Whether or not one finds Crocker's restored version convincing, his discussion of text and melody is excellent and instructive (*Early Medieval Sequence*, 75–93). Italian concordances are strong and have a relatively stable transmission.

TEXT AND TRANSLATION

[1a] Ecce vicit radix david leo de tribu iuda
[1b] Mors vicit mortem et mors nostra est vita
[2a] Mirabella et stupenda satis inter omnes victorias
[2b] Ut moriens superaret fortem cum callida versutia
[3a] Domum eius ingressus est rex eternus et averni confregit vasa
[3b] Dragmam secum quę perierat portavit et patefecit regni claustra
[4a] Paradisi portam quę clausa fuerat
[4b] Per lignum vetitum et culpam lętalem in hoc ęvo
[5a] Quam commisit protoplastus reseravit dextra per stipitem etherea
[5b] Susceperat mors indemnem quem tenere numquam potuerat propter culpam
[6a] Dum ambiit inlicita quę tenebat iuste perdidit adquisita
[6b] Ampliare voluerat in successus sed remansit evacuata
[7a] In se refusa defecit extremitas ut quibus ad vitam fuerat largitus ingressus donaret et regressus ad percipiendam veniam
[7b] Hic verus est agnus legalis qui multis se manifestavit figuris tandem se pro mundo hostiam dedit patri ut redimeret plasma suum
[8a] Hic lapis est angularis quem reprobaverunt ędificantes
[8b] Iam factus est in caput anguli super omnes in excelso
[9] Regnum eius magnum et potestas eius prima per secula

*

[1a] Behold, the root of David, the lion of the tribe of Judah has conquered!
[1b] Death has conquered death, and death is our life!
[2a] The miraculous and overwhelming combats are beyond all victories!
[2b] For He, in dying, has conquered the mighty one through a crafty trick.

xli

[3a] The King eternal entered the house of the enemy and shattered the vessels of hell.
[3b] He carried with Him the silver coin that was lost and threw open the bolt of the kingdom:
[4a] The door of paradise—which had been locked
[4b] By the forbidden tree and the fatal sin
[5a] Committed by the first man of our age—has been opened by the Eternal Right Hand through another tree.
[5b] Death grabbed hold of the sinless one, of Him whom death could never hold through guilt,
[6a] And when death encircled that to which it had no claim, it also lost that which it had justly acquired.
[6b] Death had desired to increase its holdings, but was left empty handed. (read *successu*)
[7a] The final ending failed by consuming itself, so that to those given an entrance to life were given as well an access for knowing grace.
[7b] This is the true and lawful lamb, the one made known in many signs and symbols, the one who finally offered himself to the Father as sacrifice, that He might redeem those who are His very own.
[8a] This is the corner stone that the builders rejected.
[8b] Now He is made the head of the corner, exalted above all others.
[9] Great is His Kingdom, and His power foremost through all ages.

DISTINCTIVE VARIANTS

Rn 1343 [6a] *ambigit* for *ambiit*; [7b] *sua* for *suum*.
Bu 2824 [7b] *sui* for *suum*.

MELODIC VARIANTS

Rn 1343 [1a] *iu(da)* aa~; *(Allelu)ia* ... dcaa~G; [1b] *mor(tem)* a(G); *vi(ta)* aa~; [2a] *(Mi)ra(bella)* FF~E; *om(nes)* aa~; *(victo)ri(as)* aG; [2b] *(mo)ri(ens)* ED; *(versu)ti(a)* aG; [3a] *va(sa)* aa~; [3b] *(por)ta(vit)* GG~; *claus(tra)* a(G); [4a] *por(tam)* G(F); [4b] *ę(vo)* aa~; [5a] *(in)dem(nem)* EE(D); *cul(pam)* aa(G); *(adqui)si(ta)* aa~; [7a] *(ve)ni(am)* aG; [8a] *(ędifi)can(tes)* aa~; [8b] *om(nes)* a(G); *(ex)cel(so)* aa(G); [9] *magnum* cc(b)'a; *prima* cc~'a; *(se)cu(la)* aG. **Bu 2824** [1a] *iu(da)* aa~; *(Allelu)ia* ... dcaa~G; [1b] *mor(tem)* a(G); *vi(ta)* aa~; [2a] *(Mi)ra(bella)* FF~E; *om(nes)* aa~; *(victo)ri(as)* aG; [2b] *(mo)ri(ens)* ED; *(versu)ti(a)* aG; [3a] *(ę)ter(nus)* a(G); *va(sa)* aa~; [3b] *(por)ta(vit)* GG~; *claus(tra)* a(G); [4a] *por(tam)* G(F); [4b] *ę(vo)* aa~; [5a] *(proto)plas(tus)* EE~; [5b] *(in)demp(nem)* EE(D); *cul(pam)* aa(G); [6a] *(adqui)si(ta)* aa~; [7a] *(ve)ni(am)* aG; [8a] *(ędifi)can(tes)* aa~; [8b] *om(nes)* a(G); *(ex)cel(so)* aa(G); [9] *magnum* cc(b)'a; *prima* cc~'a; *(se)cu(la)* aG.

12. *Clara gaudia*

SOURCES

Rc 1741 fols. 80r–81r Fer<ia> ii Seq<uentia>
Rn 1343 fols. 30r–30v Seq<uentia>
Bu 2824 fols. 51v–53r Seq<uentia>

ITALIAN CONCORDANCES

Bu 2748 (pp. 137–40); BV 34 (135v–136v); BV 35 (75v–76r); BV 38 (57r–57v); BV 39 (39v–40v); BV 40 (32v–33r); Cb 74 (81v–82r); IV 60 (79v–80r); MCa 318 (p. 257*); MOd 7 (111r–111v); Mza 76 (107r–107v); Mza 77 (154v–155r); Ob 222 (95v–96v); PAc 47 (140r–141r); Pn 1669 (84v–85v); PCsa 65 (233r–233v); PS 121 (39v–40r) and (91v, incomplete); Ra 123 (218v–219r); Rvat 5319 (156r–156v); Tn 18 (88v–89v); VCd 146 (103v–104r); VCd 161 (123r–123v); VCd 162 (185v–186r); VEcap 107 (88v–89v); VO 39 (36v–37r).

REFERENCES

AH 7:66; 53:71; Brunner, "The Sequences of Verona 107," 1:77–82, 2:24; Brunner, "Catalogo," 220; Crocker, "Repertoire," 2:26; Crocker, *Early Medieval Sequence*, 153–59; Hughes, *Sequelae*, 70.

TEXT COMMENTARY

Clara gaudia recounts the familiar Easter theme of Christ's battle and victory over death. Phrases [7] and [8] are of equal length and, because this is so rare, it is likely that lines were added. Blume (*AH* 53:73) suggested that [7] may have been an addition, but Crocker argued that [7a] and [8b] were added, since without them the narrative moves more naturally (*Early Medieval Sequence*, 154–55). The piece was popular in Italy, where the transmission was fairly stable; see Brunner, "The Sequences of Verona 107," 2:88.

TEXT AND TRANSLATION

[1] Clara gaudia festa paschalia
[2a] Congaudet cetus per omnia
[2b] Dulce decantans alleluia
[3a] In qua christus per crucem redemit animas inferno deditas
[3b] A protoplasto quotquot in hoc seculo progenitę fuerant
[4a] Patriarcharum omniumque simul prophetarum regum pontificum
[4b] Detinebantur claustro tartareo mortis cruore retrusę
[5a] Donec victor mortis dominus omnium atque sanctus sanctorum
[5b] Cum crucis tropheo infernum penetrans abegit claustra seva

xlii

[6a] Quis es demones ululant lucifer qui nostra ut deus solvis vincula cuncta
[6b] Fugatis tenebris fulget at theatralis orror rutilo lumine perlustratus
[7a] Clamabant sancti advenisti o iam domine regum rex ave
[7b] Quem olim vates cecinere iam nos habes redemptos rex ave
[8a] Tunc hiesus cum lęta sanctorum gloria processit morte victa
[8b] Cui psallere laudes sub omni carmine non cesset omnis ętas
[9] Decantans alleluia

*

[1] Bright joys, paschal feast,
[2a] The crowd rejoices everywhere,
[2b] Sweetly singing "Alleluia."
[3a] In this feast when Christ, through the cross, redeemed the souls condemned to Hell,
[3b] All those who had been in this world begotten of the first man (Adam),
[4a] And of all the patriarchs and prophets, of all the kings and priests together.
[4b] They were fettered in the hellish dungeons, bound by the blood of death,
[5a] Until the conqueror of death, the Lord of all and the Saint of saints,
[5b] With the victorious sign of the cross, penetrated Hell and banished the horrid prison.
[6a] "Who are you, enlightening one," the demons wail, "You who like a God frees us from all our shackles?"
[6b] With the darkness put to flight, the spectacular horror moreover begins to be illuminated with dazzling rays of light.
[7a] The saints cried: "Now you have come, O Lord, hail, King of kings!"
[7b] You whom the prophets once foretold, now you have us redeemed; hail O King!"
[8a] Then, after death was defeated, Jesus went forth amidst the joyous glory of the saints.
[8b] May all ages never cease to sing praises to Him, in every song
[9] Singing "Alleluia!"

MELODIC VARIANTS

Rn 1343 [3b] *quot(quot)* ee~; [4a] *(Patriar)cha(rum)* ee~; *(ponti)fi(cum)* ed; [4b] *(Detine)ban(tur)* ee(d); [5a] *(sanc)to(rum)* ee~; [5b] *se(va)* ee~; [6a] *cunc(ta)* ee(d); [6b] *(perlu)stra(tus)* ee~; [7a] *sanc(ti)* ee(d); [7b] *va(tes)* ee~; *(re)demp(tos)* ed(c); [8a] *(proces)sit* ed; *vic(ta)* ee~; [8b] *om(ni)* g(f); *ę(tas)* ee~ [9] *(allel)lu(ia)* ee(d). **Bu 2824** [3b] *quot(quot)* ee~; [4a] *(Patriar)cha(rum)* ee~; *(ponti)fi(cum)* ed; [4b] *(Detine)ban(tur)* ee(d); [5a] *(sanc)to(rum)* ee~; [5b] *se(va)* ee~; [6a] *cunc(ta)* ee(d); [6b] *lu(mine)* d; *(perlu)stra(tus)* ee~; [7a] *sanc(ti)* ee(d); [7b] *va(tes)* ee~; *(re)demp(tos)* ed(c); [8a] *vic(ta)* ee~; [8b] *om(ni)* g(f); *ę(tas)* ee~ [9] *(allel)lu(ia)* ee(d).

13. Dic nobis

SOURCES

Rc 1741 fols. 81v–83r Fer<ia> iii Seq<uentia>
Rn 1343 fols. 31r F<e>r<ia> iii Seq<uentia>
Bu 2824 fols. 53v–55r Seq<uentia>

ITALIAN CONCORDANCES

Bc 7 (25v–26r); BV 34 (131r–132r); BV 35 (73r–73v); BV 38 (54r–54v); BV 39 (36r–36v); BV 40 (29r–29v); Cb 74 (83r–83v); IV 60 (76r–76v); MCa 318 (p. 258*); MOd 7 (107v–108v); PAc 47 (134v–135r); Pn 1669 (87r–88r); PCsa 65 (234r–234v); PS 121 (37v–38r) and (90v–91r); Ra 123 (216r–216v); VEcap 107 (90v–91v); VO 39 (35v–36r).

REFERENCES

AH 7:73; 53:69; Brunner, "The Sequences of Verona 107," 1:77–82, 2:27; Brunner, "Catalogo," 224; Brunner, "The Tao of Singing"; Crocker, "Repertoire," 2:30; Crocker, *Early Medieval Sequence,* 155–59; Crocker, "The Sequence (*Gattung*)," 288; Fassler, *Gothic Song,* 46–47; Hughes, *Sequelae,* 70; von den Steinen, *Notker der Dichter* 1:132.

TEXT COMMENTARY

The text is extraordinary in that it involves a dialogue with the personified Alleluia, which is absent from the liturgy during Lent. It returns to the liturgy again on Holy Saturday at the Easter Vigil Mass. Fassler (*Gothic Song,* 47) likens the Alleluia to one of the Marys coming back from the tomb on Easter morning and the servants in [5], that is, the singers, are like the Apostles who hear the news. The encounter is described in all four Gospels (Matt. 28, Mark 16, Luke 24, and John 20). The Alleluia describes the "new grace" of Christ's triumph over death.

TEXT AND TRANSLATION

[1] Dic nobis quibus e terris nova Alleluia
[2a] Cuncto mundo nuncians gaudia
[2b] Nostram rursus visitans patriam
[3a] Respondens placido vultu dulci voce dixit alleluia
[3b] Angelus michi de christo nunciavit pia miracula
[4a] Resurrexisse dominum sydera cecinerunt voce laudanda
[4b] Mox ego pennas volucris vacuas dirigens lęta per auras

[5a] Redii famulis ut dicam vacuatam legem veterem ac novam regnare graciam

[5b] Itaque plaudite famuli voce clara christus hodie redemit nos a morte dira

[6a] Pater filium tradidit servi interemerunt pro salute nostra

[6b] Sponte subiit filius mortem ut nos redimeret morte ab ęterna

[7a] Nunc requiem rapere licet omnibus et frui vita perpetua

[7b] Nunc colite pariter mecum famuli celebri laude sanctum pascha

[8a] Christus est pax nostra

*

[1] Tell us, Alleluia, from which lands

[2a] You come announcing to the whole world the joyful news,

[2b] Visiting again our homeland.

[3a] With peaceful expression the Alleluia answered in a sweet voice:

[3b] "An angel announced to me holy miracles about Christ:

[4a] With praising voice the heavens sang that the Lord has risen.

[4b] Therefore, at once I rejoice, directing swift wings through the clear air.

[5a] I returned so that I might say to the faithful servants that the old law is abandoned and a new grace reigns.

[5b] Therefore, sing, O faithful servants, with a bright voice; today Christ has redeemed us from a terrible death."

[6a] The Father gave His Son over; the slaves slayed Him for the sake of our salvation;

[6b] Willingly the Son submitted to death so that He might redeem us from eternal death.

[7a] Now, we may all take rest and enjoy eternal life.

[7b] Now, O faithful servants, sing with me in most solemn praise:

[8] The holy paschal lamb, Christ, is our peace.

DISTINCTIVE VARIANTS

None in Nonantolan sources. The Italian concordances are close to each other except where extra syllables require adjustments. The melody for phrase [7] in PCsa 65 differs from the other concordances.

MELODIC VARIANTS

Rn 1343 [1] *no(va)* ee~; *(Allelu)ia* ... cdee~cee~d; [3a] *vul(tu)* e(d); *(alle)lu(ia)* e(d); [3b] *chris(to)* ee~; [4a] *(Resurre)xis(se)* ee~; *(lau)dan(da)* ee~; [4b] *pen(nas)* ee(d); *au(ras)* ee(d); [5a] *di(ra)* ee~; [6a] *ser(vi)* g(f); *nos(tra)* ee~; [6b] *mor(tem)* gg~; *(redime)ret* e; *mor(te)* e(d); *(ę)ter(na)* ee(d); [7a] *perpetu(a)* e'e'ed; [7b] *laud(de)* e(d); *pas(cha)* ee~; [8] *nos(tra)* ee~. **Bu 2824** [1] *no(va)* ee~; *(Allelu)ia* ... cdee~cee~d; [2a] *(gau)di(a)* ed; [3a] *vul(tu)* e(d); *alle)lu(ia)* e(d); [3b] *chris(to)* ee~; [4a] *(Resurre)xis(se)* ee~; *(lau)dan(da)* ee~; [4b] *pen(nas)* ee(d); *au(ras)* ee(d); [5a] *di(ra)* ee~; [6a] *ser(vi)* g(f); *nos(tra)* ee~; [6b] *mor(tem)* gg~; *mor(te)* e(d); *(ę)ter(na)* ee(d); [7a] *perpetu(a)* e'e'ed; [7b] *laud(de)* e(d); *pas(cha)* ee~; [8] *nos(tra)* ee~.

14. Eia recolamus

SOURCES

Rc 1741 fols. 83r–84v Seq<uentia> In oct<ava> pasc<hae>
Rn 1343 fols. 31v–32r (no rubric)
Bu 2824 fols. 40r–42r Seq<uentia>

ITALIAN CONCORDANCES

Bu 2748 (pp. 108–12); BV 34 (146v–147v); BV 38 (65v–66r); BV 40 (42r–42v); IV 60 (24r–24v); MCa 318 (p. 284*); MCa 546 (70v–71v); MOd 7 (11v–12v); NV 1 (200r–200v); Ob 222 (90r–91r); PAc 47 (22r–23r); PAs 697 (46r–46v); PCsa 65 (230v); PS 121 (26v–27v); Ra 123 (192v–193v); Tn 18 (26r–26v); VCd 146 (100r–100v); VCd 161 (118v–119r); VCd 162 (180r–180v); VEcap 107 (80r–81r); VO 39 (30v–31r).

REFERENCES

AH 53:23; Brunner, "The Sequences of Verona 107," 1:109–10, 2:13; Brunner, "Catalogo," 229; Hiley, *Western Planchant,* 173; Drinkwelder, *Sequentiar,* 19; de Goede, *Utrecht Prosarium,* 4; Hughes, *Sequelae,* 24; Moberg, *Schwedishen Sequenzen,* n. 43; Negro, "Le sequenze," 86; Schubiger, *Sängerschule,* 35; von den Steinen, *Notker der Dichter,* 1:270–76, 560–62, 2:94.

TEXT COMMENTARY

This popular text for Christmas is firmly established in the St. Gall manuscripts, but it was also adopted internationally, including England. Von den Steinen considered it the work of a gifted poet a generation or two younger than Notker (*Notker der Dichter,* 1:562). Although primarily sung during one of the three Christmas Masses, the central image in [6a] is derived from the *Exultet iam angelica,* the prayer sung by one of the celebrants on Holy Saturday during the Easter Vigil. Von den Steinen discusses the relationship in some detail (1:271–72). For the reference to *dragma* in [5b], see TEXT COMMENTARY for *Ecce vicit* (no. 11). See also TEXT COMMENTARY for *Haec sunt sacra festa* (no. 6). Rc 1741 and Rn 1343 atypically place the sequence for the Octave of Easter, while Bu 2824 assigns it to Epiphany, a more typical liturgical position.

Text and Translation

[1] Eia recolamus laudibus piis digna
[2a] Huius diei carmina in qua nobis lux oritur gratissima
[2b] Noctis interit nebula pereunt nostri criminis umbracula
[3a] Hodie seculo stella maris est enixa novę salutis gaudia
[3b] Quem tremunt baratra mors cruenta pavet ipsa a quo peribit mortua
[4a] Gemit capta pestis antiqua coluber lividus perdit spolia
[4b] Homo lapsus ovis abducta revocatur ad ęterna gaudia
[5a] Gaudent in hac die agmina angelorum cęlestia
[5b] Quia erat dragma decima perdita et est inventa
[6a] O culpa nimium beata ac redempta natura
[6b] Deus qui creavit omnia nascitur ex femina
[7a] Mirabilis natura mirifice induta assumens quod non erat manens quod erat
[7b] Induitur natura divinitas humana quis audivit talia dic rogo facta
[8a] Quęrere venerat pastor pius quod perierat
[8b] Induitur galea certat ut miles armis arma
[9a] Prostratus in sua propia ruit hostis spicula auferuntur tela
[9b] In quibus fiderat divisa sunt illius spolia capta pręda sua
[10a] Christi pugna fortissima salus nostra est vera
[10b] Qui nos suam ad patriam duxit post victoriam
[11] In qua sibi laus ęterna

*

[1] Come then, let us with reverent praises call to mind
[2a] Songs worthy of this day, in which a most welcomed light is born to us,
[2b] In which the mist of night disperses, and the shadows of our sins disappear.
[3a] Today, for our age, the Star of the sea brings forth the joys of a new salvation,
[3b] Before whom the inhabitants of hell tremble, and cruel death shakes, for before this one, death itself will vanish in death.
[4a] The ancient curse, now the captive, moans, the malicious serpent loses its spoils;
[4b] Fallen man, the sheep led astray, is recalled to eternal joys.
[5a] The celestial hosts of angels rejoice in this day,
[5b] For the tenth coin that had been lost has been found.
[6a] O exceedingly blessed fault for which nature has been redeemed! (read *qua redempta*)
[6b] God, who created all things, is of woman born.
[7a] An indescribable nature, miraculously clothed, becomes that which it was not while remaining that which it was;
[7b] Divinity has been clothed in human nature. Tell me, I ask, who has heard of such a thing being done?
[8a] The loving shepherd has come to seek that which was lost,
[8b] He put on a helmet and battles like a soldier, weapon against weapons.
[9a] The enemy, thrown onto his own arrows, is brought to ruin; snatched away are the weapons
[9b] In which he had trusted; his spoils divided, his prey taken.
[10a] Christ's mighty combat is our true salvation,
[10b] He it is who leads us to the fatherland after the victory,
[11] Where praise is His eternally.

Distinctive Variants

Rn 1343 [1] *festa* added (after *recolamus*, squeezed in after main text already copied); [7a] *quod* for *qui*. **Bu 2824** [7a] *quod* for *qui*.

Melodic Variants

Rn 1343 [1] *festa* c′c; *(pi)is* GG~; [3a] *ma(ris)* aa~; *(salu)tis* G; [3b] *(cru)en(ta)* aa(G); *(per)i(bit)* aa~; [4b] *(ab)duc(ta)* d; [5a] *(ag)mi(na)* cd; *cę(lestia)* d; [5b] *(de)ci(ma)* cd; *est* d; [6a] *(be)ata ac re(dempta)* cd′d′d′c; [6b] *(fe)mi(na)* d; [8a] *per(ierat)* d; [9a] *te(la)* d; [9b] *(di)vi(sa)* ff~e; *su(a)* d; [10a] *pug(na)* ee(d); [11] *(ę)ter(na)* ee(d). **Bu 2824** [1] *(pi)is* GG~; [3a] *ma(ris)* aa~; [3b] *(cru)en(ta)* aa(G); [6a] *(be)ata ac re(dempta)* cd′d′d′c; *(na)tu(ra)* d; [7b] *(hy)ma(na)* gg~; [9a] *te(la)* d; [9b] *(di)vi(sa)* ff~d; *su(a)* d; [10a] *pug(na)* ee(d); [11] *(ę)ter(na)* ee(d).

15. *Sanctae crucis celebremus*

Sources

Rc 1741 fols. 85v–86v (no rubric)
Rn 1343 fols. 81v [fragment] SEQ<UENTIA> IN INVENTIONE SC<ANCT>ÆE CRUCIS

Italian Concordances

BV 35 (99v–100v); BV 38 (77v–78r); BV 39 (72r–72v); BV 40 (54r–54v); IV 60 (87v–87v); MOd 7 (129); PAc 47 (164v–165r); VEcap 107 (105v–106r); VO 39 (38r–38v).

References

AH 37:24; Brunner, "The Sequences of Verona 107," 1:135–43, 2:77; Brunner, "Catalogo," 260; Brunner, "The Tao of Singing"; Hiley, *Western Planchant*, 183.

TEXT COMMENTARY

The text presents a very modest and direct series of invocations and petitions to the Holy Cross. The syntax in the first half is somewhat awkward and not particularly coordinated with the musical structure. Text and melody are both of Italian origin. For discussion of the text and a synoptic transcription of four Italian sources including Rc 1741, see Brunner, "The Sequences of Verona 107," 1:109–10, 2:77–78.

TEXT AND TRANSLATION

[1a] Sancte crucis celebremus devotione veneranda
[1b] Signaculum triumphale per quod salutis sacramentum
[2a] Sumpsimus culpa qui protoparentis heu eramus exules facti patrię
[2b] Redempti ergo gracias agamus qui nos suo sancto redemit sanguine
[3a] In domini crucifixi laude consona voce mellifula concinamus cantica
[3b] O crux spendidissima salus perhennitas vitę virtutibus totis es repleta
[4a] O crux gloriosa o crux adoranda quę precium mundi ferre tu meruisti
[4b] Salva pręsentem humilem plebem in laude tua hodie congregatam
[5]   Quę sola fuisti portare digna talentum

*

[1a] Let us celebrate with reverent devotion the holy cross's
[1b] Victorious symbol, through which we received the sacrament of salvation,
[2a] We who through the fault of the first born were made exiles from our fatherland.
[2b] Redeemed, therefore, let us give thanks to Him who redeemed us through His holy blood.
[3a] To the glory of the crucified Lord, let us sing together mellifluous songs with a consonant voice.
[3b] O cross most splendid, salvation, eternity, you are filled with all of life's virtues.
[4a] O glorious cross, O adorable cross, you who deserved to bear the world's prize,
[4b] Save the humble people present, gathered together today in your praise,
[5]   You who were alone worthy to bear the talent of the world.

DISTINCTIVE VARIANTS

None.

MELODIC VARIANTS

Rn 1343 [fragment] [2b] *(a)ga(mus)* GF; [3a] breaks off at *cru(cifixi)*.

16. *Laus tibi Christe patris*

SOURCES

Rc 1741 fols. 87v–88v Seq<uentia>
Rn 1343 fols. 33r–33v Seq<uentia>
Bu 2824 fols. 56r–57r Seq<uentia>

ITALIAN CONCORDANCES

Bu 2748 (pp. 194–96); Ra 123 (265r–265v); VEcap 107 (114v–115r).

REFERENCES

AH 53:258; Brunner, "Catalogo," 243; Drinkwelder, *Sequentiar,* 23; Hughes, *Sequelae,* 57; von den Steinen, *Notker der Dichter* 2:99.

TEXT COMMENTARY

This text was written by an early tenth-century poet, probably at St. Gall, whom von den Steinen calls the "Innocents poet" (*Notker der Dichter,* 1:349–50). The text, for the Holy Innocents, is generic enough that it was dedicated to Sts. Senesius and Theopontius in all three Nonantolan manuscripts, as well as Ra 123. However, in order to accommodate these martyrs, the last two lines of the text ([6b] and [7]) had to be dropped, because Herod—the only explicit reference to the slaughter of the Innocents—is mentioned in [6b]. Blume saw this as clear proof of Italy's dependence on southern Germany for its sequences (*AH* 53:60). The three Italian concordances not from Nonantola are from the same area in Northern Italy.

TEXT AND TRANSLATION

[1a] Laus tibi christe patris optimi nate deus omnipotentię
[1b] Cui cęlitus iubilat super astra manentis plebis decus armonię
[2a] Quem agmina martyrum sonoris hymnis collaudant etheris in arce
[2b] Quos impii ob nominis odium tui misero stravere vulnere
[3a] Quos pie nunc remuneras in cęlis chirste pro pęnis nitide
[3b] Solita usus gracia qui tuos ornas coronis splendide
[4a] Quorum precibus sacris dele precamus nostrę pie crimina vitę
[4b] Ut quos laudibus tuis reseras nobis istic dones clemens favere
[5a] Illis ęternę dans lumen glorię
[5b] Nobis terrena concede vincere
[6]   Ut liceat serenis actibus pleniter adipisci dona tuę gracię

*

xlvi

TEXT AND TRANSLATION

[1] Eia recolamus laudibus piis digna
[2a] Huius diei carmina in qua nobis lux oritur gratissima
[2b] Noctis interit nebula pereunt nostri criminis umbracula
[3a] Hodie seculo stella maris est enixa novę salutis gaudia
[3b] Quem tremunt baratra mors cruenta pavet ipsa a quo peribit mortua
[4a] Gemit capta pestis antiqua coluber lividus perdit spolia
[4b] Homo lapsus ovis abducta revocatur ad ęterna gaudia
[5a] Gaudent in hac die agmina angelorum cęlestia
[5b] Quia erat dragma decima perdita et est inventa
[6a] O culpa nimium beata ac redempta natura
[6b] Deus qui creavit omnia nascitur ex femina
[7a] Mirabilis natura mirifice induta assumens quod non erat manens quod erat
[7b] Induitur natura divinitas humana quis audivit talia dic rogo facta
[8a] Quęrere venerat pastor pius quod perierat
[8b] Induitur galea certat ut miles armis arma
[9a] Prostratus in sua propia ruit hostis spicula auferuntur tela
[9b] In quibus fiderat divisa sunt illius spolia capta pręda sua
[10a] Christi pugna fortissima salus nostra est vera
[10b] Qui nos suam ad patriam duxit post victoriam
[11] In qua sibi laus ęterna

*

[1] Come then, let us with reverent praises call to mind
[2a] Songs worthy of this day, in which a most welcomed light is born to us,
[2b] In which the mist of night disperses, and the shadows of our sins disappear.
[3a] Today, for our age, the Star of the sea brings forth the joys of a new salvation,
[3b] Before whom the inhabitants of hell tremble, and cruel death shakes, for before this one, death itself will vanish in death.
[4a] The ancient curse, now the captive, moans, the malicious serpent loses its spoils;
[4b] Fallen man, the sheep led astray, is recalled to eternal joys.
[5a] The celestial hosts of angels rejoice in this day,
[5b] For the tenth coin that had been lost has been found.
[6a] O exceedingly blessed fault for which nature has been redeemed! (read *qua redempta*)
[6b] God, who created all things, is of woman born.
[7a] An indescribable nature, miraculously clothed, becomes that which it was not while remaining that which it was;
[7b] Divinity has been clothed in human nature. Tell me, I ask, who has heard of such a thing being done?
[8a] The loving shepherd has come to seek that which was lost,
[8b] He put on a helmet and battles like a soldier, weapon against weapons.
[9a] The enemy, thrown onto his own arrows, is brought to ruin; snatched away are the weapons
[9b] In which he had trusted; his spoils divided, his prey taken.
[10a] Christ's mighty combat is our true salvation,
[10b] He it is who leads us to the fatherland after the victory,
[11] Where praise is His eternally.

DISTINCTIVE VARIANTS

Rn 1343 [1] *festa* added (after *recolamus*, squeezed in after main text already copied); [7a] *quod* for *qui*. **Bu 2824** [7a] *quod* for *qui*.

MELODIC VARIANTS

Rn 1343 [1] *festa* c'c; *(pi)is* GG~; [3a] *ma(ris)* aa~; *(salu)tis* G; [3b] *(cru)en(ta)* aa(G); *(per)i(bit)* aa~; [4b] *(ab)duc(ta)* d; [5a] *(ag)mi(na)* cd; *cę(lestia)* d; [5b] *(de)ci(ma)* cd; *est* d; [6a] *(be)ata ac re(dempta)* cd'd'd'c; [6b] *(fe)mi(na)* d; [8a] *per(ierat)* d; [9a] *te(la)* d; [9b] *(di)vi(sa)* ff~e; *su(a)* d; [10a] *pug(na)* ee(d); [11] *(ę)ter(na)* ee(d). **Bu 2824** [1] *(pi)is* GG~; [3a] *ma(ris)* aa~; [3b] *(cru)en(ta)* aa(G); [6a] *(be)ata ac re(dempta)* cd'd'd'c; *(na)tu(ra)* d; [7b] *(hy)ma(na)* gg~; [9a] *te(la)* d; [9b] *(di)vi(sa)* ff~d; *su(a)* d; [10a] *pug(na)* ee(d); [11] *(ę)ter(na)* ee(d).

15. *Sanctae crucis celebremus*

SOURCES

Rc 1741 fols. 85v–86v (no rubric)
Rn 1343 fols. 81v [fragment] SEQ\<UENTIA\> IN INVENTIONE SC\<ANCT\>Æ CRUCIS

ITALIAN CONCORDANCES

BV 35 (99v–100v); BV 38 (77v–78r); BV 39 (72r–72v); BV 40 (54r–54v); IV 60 (87v–87v); MOd 7 (129); PAc 47 (164v–165r); VEcap 107 (105v–106r); VO 39 (38r–38v).

REFERENCES

AH 37:24; Brunner, "The Sequences of Verona 107," 1:135–43, 2:77; Brunner, "Catalogo," 260; Brunner, "The Tao of Singing"; Hiley, *Western Planchant*, 183.

TEXT COMMENTARY

The text presents a very modest and direct series of invocations and petitions to the Holy Cross. The syntax in the first half is somewhat awkward and not particularly coordinated with the musical structure. Text and melody are both of Italian origin. For discussion of the text and a synoptic transcription of four Italian sources including Rc 1741, see Brunner, "The Sequences of Verona 107," 1:109–10, 2:77–78.

TEXT AND TRANSLATION

[1a] Sancte crucis celebremus devotione veneranda
[1b] Signaculum triumphale per quod salutis sacramentum
[2a] Sumpsimus culpa qui protoparentis heu eramus exules facti patrię
[2b] Redempti ergo gracias agamus qui nos suo sancto redemit sanguine
[3a] In domini crucifixi laude consona voce mellifula concinamus cantica
[3b] O crux spendidissima salus perhennitas vitę virtutibus totis es repleta
[4a] O crux gloriosa o crux adoranda quę precium mundi ferre tu meruisti
[4b] Salva presentem humilem plebem in laude tua hodie congregatam
[5]   Quę sola fuisti portare digna talentum

*

[1a] Let us celebrate with reverent devotion the holy cross's
[1b] Victorious symbol, through which we received the sacrament of salvation,
[2a] We who through the fault of the first born were made exiles from our fatherland.
[2b] Redeemed, therefore, let us give thanks to Him who redeemed us through His holy blood.
[3a] To the glory of the crucified Lord, let us sing together mellifluous songs with a consonant voice.
[3b] O cross most splendid, salvation, eternity, you are filled with all of life's virtues.
[4a] O glorious cross, O adorable cross, you who deserved to bear the world's prize,
[4b] Save the humble people present, gathered together today in your praise,
[5]   You who were alone worthy to bear the talent of the world.

DISTINCTIVE VARIANTS

None.

MELODIC VARIANTS

Rn 1343 [fragment] [2b] *(a)ga(mus)* GF; [3a] breaks off at *cru(cifixi)*.

16. *Laus tibi Christe patris*

SOURCES

Rc 1741 fols. 87v–88v Seq<uentia>
Rn 1343 fols. 33r–33v Seq<uentia>
Bu 2824 fols. 56r–57r Seq<uentia>

ITALIAN CONCORDANCES

Bu 2748 (pp. 194–96); Ra 123 (265r–265v); VEcap 107 (114v–115r).

REFERENCES

AH 53:258; Brunner, "Catalogo," 243; Drinkwelder, *Sequentiar*, 23; Hughes, *Sequelae*, 57; von den Steinen, *Notker der Dichter* 2:99.

TEXT COMMENTARY

This text was written by an early tenth-century poet, probably at St. Gall, whom von den Steinen calls the "Innocents poet" (*Notker der Dichter*, 1:349–50). The text, for the Holy Innocents, is generic enough that it was dedicated to Sts. Senesius and Theopontius in all three Nonantolan manuscripts, as well as Ra 123. However, in order to accommodate these martyrs, the last two lines of the text ([6b] and [7]) had to be dropped, because Herod—the only explicit reference to the slaughter of the Innocents—is mentioned in [6b]. Blume saw this as clear proof of Italy's dependence on southern Germany for its sequences (*AH* 53:60). The three Italian concordances not from Nonantola are from the same area in Northern Italy.

TEXT AND TRANSLATION

[1a] Laus tibi christe patris optimi nate deus omnipotentię
[1b] Cui cęlitus iubilat super astra manentis plebis decus armonię
[2a] Quem agmina martyrum sonoris hymnis collaudant etheris in arce
[2b] Quos impii ob nominis odium tui misero stravere vulnere
[3a] Quos pie nunc remuneras in cęlis chirste pro pęnis nitide
[3b] Solita usus gracia qui tuos ornas coronis splendide
[4a] Quorum precibus sacris dele precamus nostrę pie crimina vitę
[4b] Ut quos laudibus tuis reseras nobis istic dones clemens favere
[5a] Illis ęternę dans lumen glorię
[5b] Nobis terrena concede vincere
[6]   Ut liceat serenis actibus pleniter adipisci dona tuę gracię

*

[1a] Praise to you, O Christ, most noble Son of the Father, omnipotent God,
[1b] To whom the honorable people dwelling above the stars in heaven celebrate in harmony.
[2a] Whom the crowds of martyrs in heaven's palace praise together with resounding hymns.
[2b] Those who the unfaithful in hatred for your name have crushed with painful wound
[3a] Those who you now abundantly reward in Heaven for their pains, O graceful Christ.
[3b] Showing your usual grace you splendidly adorn your followers with the crown.
[4a] Through their blessed prayers we pray, mercifully blot out the transgressions of our life,
[4b] So that, as You reveal those in Your praises, You might lovingly grant to us to find favor there.
[5a] And as You give them the light of the eternal glory,
[5b] Let us to overcome the worldly
[6] So that, through worthy deeds, we might fully achieve the gifts of Your grace.

DISTINCTIVE VARIANTS

Rn 1343 [1b] *Quem* for *Cui*. **Bu 2824** [1b] *Quem* for *Cui*; [6a] *gloriae* for *gracię*.

MELODIC VARIANTS

Rn 1343 [1a] *(omnipo)ten(tię)* a(G); [1b] *Quem* a(G); [4a] *no(strę)* dd~; [4b] *is(tic)* dd~; [5a] *(ę)ter(ne)* dd(c); [5b] *(ter)re(na)* dd~; [6] *(adi)pi(sci)* dd~. **Bu 2824** [1a] *(omnipo)ten(tię)* a(G); [1b] *Quem* a(G); [4a] *no(strę)* dd~; [4b] *is(tic)* dd~; [5a] *(ę)ter(ne)* dd(c); [5b] *(ter)re(na)* dd~; [6] *(adi)pi(sci)* dd~.

17. *Summi triumphum*

SOURCES

Rc 1741 fols. 90v–92v Seq<uentia>
Rn 1343 fols. 34r–34v Seq<uentia>
Bu 2824 fols. 58r–60r Seq<uentia>

ITALIAN CONCORDANCES

BV 38 (92r–92v); BV 39 (89r–90r); BV 40 (69v–70v); IV 60 (91v–92r); MCa 318 (p. 284*); Mza 76 (116r–117r); Mza 77 (155v–156r); NV 1 (201v, fragment); PAs 697 (54v–55r); Ra 123 (228v–229r); VEcap 107 (94r–95r).

REFERENCES

AH 53:114; Brunner, "The Sequences of Verona 107," 1:119–23, 2:47; Brunner, "Catalogo," 264; Brunner, "The Tao of Singing"; Crocker, *Early Medieval Sequence,* 213–18; de Goede, *Utrecht Prosarium,* 87, Schubiger, *Sängerschule,* 20; von den Steinen, *Notker der Dichter,* 1:239–52, 552–54, 2:50.

TEXT COMMENTARY

Notker's text *Summi triumphum*, for the Ascension, is set to the melody "Captiva" and may well be the original text to this melody. Von den Steinen (*Notker der Dichter,* 1:553) made a case that the melody, as well as the text, was written by Notker. The tune and text are unusual in that in couplets 3, 4, 5, and 7 the second line of each is extended by the skillful addition of motives. Crocker offers a helpful schematic diagram and discussion of how music and text work together (*Early Medieval Sequence,* 215). The name "Idithum," used three times in the text, appears in Psalms 39, 62, and 77 in the English Bible under the name "Jeduthun" (38, 61, and 76 in the Vulgate numbering). Idithum was apparently a chief musician of the Temple and a prophet. Von den Steinen (*Notker der Dichter,* 1:240) describes Notker's creative use of this name, which was understood to mean "he who leaps over," to refer to God's leap into the Virgin's womb and sea of time, and then back to Heaven in "His greatest leap."

TEXT AND TRANSLATION

[1] Summi triumphum regis prosequamur laude
[2a] Qui cęli qui terrę regis sceptra inferni iure domito
[2b] Qui sese pro nobis redimendis permagnum dedit precium
[3a] Huic nomen extat conveniens idithum
[3b] Nam transilivit omnes strenuę montes colliculosque bethel
[4a] Saltum de cęlo dedit in virginalem ventrem inde in pellagus seculi
[4b] Postquam illud suo mitigavit potentatu tetras flegetontis assiliit tenebras
[5a] Principis illius disturbato imperio
[5b] Maniplis plurimis inde erutis mundum illustrat suo iubare
[6a] Captivitatemque detentam in ibi victor duxit secum
[6b] Et redivivum iam suis se prebuit servis et amicis
[7a] Denique saltum dederat hodie maximum nubes polosque cursu prepeti transiens
[7b] Celebret ergo populus hunc diem credulus cuius morbida idithun corpora insemet ipso altis sedibus cęli invexit dei filius
[8a] Et tremens iudicem expectat adfuturum ut duo angeli fratres docuerunt
[8b] Qui hiesus a vobis assumptus est in cęlum iterum veniet ut vidistis eum

[9a] Iam idithum nostrum vocibus sedulis omnes imploremus
[9b] Ut ad dextram patris qui sedet spiritum mittat nobis sanctum
[10] In finem seculi ipse quoque semper sit nobiscum

*

[1] The triumph of the highest King let us recount with praise:
[2a] He who rules the scepters of heaven, of earth, having conquered the authority of hell,
[2b] He who gave Himself at great price to redeem us.
[3a] For Him the name "Idithum" is fitting:
[3b] For He vigorously leapt over all the mountains and hills of Bethel.
[4a] He made the leap from Heaven into the virginal womb, hence into the sea of time.
[4b] After He had pacified that sea through His dominion, He leapt to the horrifying darkness of Phlegethon.
[5a] There He threw the reign of the Prince of Darkness into utter confusion,
[5b] Then, with many companies torn away, He illuminated the world with His radiance.
[6a] And captivity, there laid in bonds, He, the Victor, led forth with Himself;
[6b] And then, born anew, He showed Himself to His servants and friends.
[7a] Finally today He made His greatest leap, flying over clouds and the heavens in winged path.
[7b] Thus, the faithful people celebrate this day, those whose sickly bodies Idithum, the Son of God, carried in His very own into the highest seats of heaven,
[8a] And dreading the Judge the people should await what is to come, as the two angels taught the disciples:
[8b] "The same Jesus, taken up from you into Heaven will come again as you now see Him."
[9a] So let us all implore our Idithum with diligent voices,
[9b] That He who sits at the right hand of the Father might send the Holy Spirit to us,
[10] And that this very spirit will always, even unto the end of time, abide with us.

DISTINCTIVE VARIANTS

Rn 1343 [4a] *pelagus* for *pellagus*; [4b] *illum* for *illud*; [7a] *(polos)que cursu* copied twice, second *que* has number (D), but second *cursu* left blank; [7b] *alti* for *altis*; [9a] *impleremus* for *imploremus*.

MELODIC VARIANTS

Rn 1343 [2b] *(redi)men(dis)* E(D); *(de)dit* DD~; [3a] *ex(tat)* EE~; [3b] *(transi)li(vit)* EE~; *mon(tes)* E(D); *(collicu)los(que)* D~; [4a] *(virgin)na(lem)* EE~; [4b] *te(tras)* EE~; [5a] *(il)li(us)* ba; [5b] *mun(dum)* b(a); [6a] *de(tentam)* D; *se(cum)* EE~; [6b] *(a)mi(cis)* EE~; [7a] *(po)los(que)* bb~; [7b] *ip(so)* bb~; *ce̜(li)* bb~; [8a] *(docu)e(runt)* EE~; [8b] *ce̜(lum)* DD~; *e(um)* EE~; [9a] *(implo)re(mus)* EE~; [9b] *sanc(tum)* EE(D); [10] *sem(per)* EE(D); *(no)bis(cum)* EE~. **Bu 2824** [2a] (iu)re DD~; [2b] *(redi)men(dis)* E(D); *(de)dit* DD~; [3a] *ex(tat)* EE~; [3b] *(transi)li(vit)* EE~; *mon(tes)* E(D); *(collicu)los(que)* D~; [4a] *(virgin)na(lem)* EE~; [4b] *te(tras)* EE~; [5a] *(il)li(us)* ba; [5b] *mun(dum)* b(a); [6a] *(Captivitatem)que* EE~; *se(cum)* EE~; [6b] *iam* EE~; *(a)mi(cis)* EE~; [7a] *(po)los(que)* bb~; [7b] *ce̜(li)* bb~; [8a] *(adfu)tu(rum)* DD~; *(docu)e(runt)* EE~; [8b] *ce̜(lum)* DD~; *e(um)* EE~; [9a] *(implo)re(mus)* EE~; [9b] *sanc(tum)* EE(D); [10] *sem(per)* EE(D); *(no)bis(cum)* EE~.

18. Rex omnipotens

SOURCES

Rc 1741 fols. 159r–160v Seq<uentia>

ITALIAN CONCORDANCES

Bc 7 (26v–27r); Bu 2748 (pp. 152–56); BV 34 (179v–180v); BV 35 (109r–110r); BV 38 (94r–95r); BV 39 (91v–92v); BV 40 (72r–73r); Cb 74 (101r–102r); MOd 7 (139v–140r); Ob 222 (101r–101v, incomplete); PAc 47 (175v–177r); Pn 1669 (105v–107r); PCsa 65 (236v–237r); PS 121 (42r–43v); Rvat 5319 (157r–158v): SIc 15 (140r–141r); Tn 18 (105r–106r); VCd 146 (104v–105r); VCd 161 (124r–125r); VCd 162 (186r–187r); VEcap 107 (92v–93v); VO 39 (38v–39v).

REFERENCES

AH 7:83; 53:111; Brunner, "The Sequences of Verona 107," 1:56–70, 2:30; Brunner, "Catalogo," 258; Crocker, "Repertoire," 2:70; Crocker, *Early Medieval Sequence*, 189–98; Crocker, "Sequence," 146; Drinkwelder, *Sequentiar*, 33; Hughes, *Sequelae*, 32; Moberg, *Schwedishen Sequenzen*, n. 14a; Stäblein, *Vat. lat. 5319*, 623; von den Steinen, "Anfänge," 41:150–52.

TEXT COMMENTARY

This text offers a long narrative of the Ascension, based closely on accounts in the New Testament. After an acclamatory introduction [1–2] the text draws on John (20:22–23) and Matt. (28:19), then from [6] to the petition in [11] from Acts 1:4–11. For a detailed discussion of text and music, see Crocker, *Early Medieval Sequence*, 189–98. For a comparison of *Rex omnipotens* with the two sequences based on the related melody "Occidentana" (i.e., *Sancti spiritus assit*, no. 19, and *Sancti merita Benedicti*, no. 23), see Brunner, "The Sequences of Verona 107," 1:61–70.

TEXT AND TRANSLATION

[1] Rex omnipotens die hodierna
[2a] Mundo triumphali redempto potentia
[2b] Victor ascendit cęlos unde descenderat
[3a] Nam quadraginta postquam surrexerat
[3b] Diebus sacris confirmans pectora
[4a] Apostolorum pacis clara relinquens oscula
[4b] Quibus et dedit potestatem laxandi crimina
[5a] Et misit eos in mundum baptizare cunctas animas
[5b] In patris et filii et sancti spiritus clementia
[6a] Et convescens pręcepit eis ab hierosolimis
[6b] Ne abirent sed expectarent promissa munera
[7a] Non post multos enim dies mittam vobis spiritum paraclitum in terris
[7b] Et eritis michi testes in hierusalem iudea sive samaria
[8a] Et cum hoc dixisset videntibus illis elevatus est et nubes clara
[8b] Suscepit eum ab eorum oculis intuentibus illis aera
[9a] Ecce steterunt amicti duo viri in veste alba
[9b] Iuxta dicentes quid ammiranmini cęlorum alta
[10a] Hiesus enim hic qui assumptus est a vobis ad patris dexteram
[10b] Ut ascendit ita veniet querens talenti commissi lucra
[11a] O deus maris poli arvę hominem quem creasti quam fraude subdola
[11b] Hostis expulit paradiso et captivatum secum traxit ad tartara
[12a] Sanguine proprio quem redemisti deus Illuc et rediit unde primum corruit ad paradisi gaudia
[12b] Iudex cum veneris iudicare sęculum Da nobis petimus sempiternam requiem in sanctorum patria
[13] In qua tibi cantemus alleluia

*

[1] Today, the Almighty King,
[2a] Having redeemed the world with triumphal power,
[2b] Ascends as victor into Heaven, from whence He descended.
[3a] For forty days after He had risen from the dead,
[3b] Divine days when He strengthened the hearts of the apostles,
[4a] Leaving them precious kisses of peace
[4b] Through which He granted them the power of forgiving sins
[5a] And sent them into the world to baptize all souls
[5b] In the mercy of the Father and the Son and the Holy Spirit;
[6a] And having supper with them, He commanded them
[6b] That they should not leave Jerusalem, but that they should await the promised gifts.
[7a] "For not many days hence I shall send the Spirit, the Paraclete, into the world for you,
[7b] And you shall be witnesses unto me in Jerusalem, in Judea, and in Samaria."
[8a] And when He had said this, while they watched, He was lifted up, and a bright cloud
[8b] Received Him out of their sight; as they looked toward heaven,
[9a] Behold, two men wrapped in white clothing stood in front of them,
[9b] Saying "Why are you astonished at in the heavens above?"
[10a] For this Jesus, who has been taken up from you to the right hand of the Father,
[10b] Will come again, just as He has ascended, seeking for the profits from the talents entrusted.
[11a] O God of the sea, and of heaven and earth: man, whom You created, whom he expelled
[11b] From Paradise because of the crafty deception of the enemy and carried with him captive into Hell;
[12a] Whom You, God, redeemed with Your own blood; and You transported him hence, from where he had first shattered the joys of paradise:
[12b] O Judge, when You come to judge the ages, Grant us, we beseech You, eternal rest in the homeland of the saints,
[13] Where all sing to You: Alleluia.

DISTINCTIVE VARIANTS

None.

19. *Sancti spiritus assit*

SOURCES

Rc 1741 fols. 93v–95v Seq<uentia>
Rn 1343 fols. 35r–36r (no rubric)
Bu 2824 fols. 61v–63v Seq<uentia>

ITALIAN CONCORDANCES

Bc 7 (27v–28r); Bu 2748 (pp. 157–61); BV 34 (187v–188v); BV 35 (114r–114v); BV 38 (97v–98v): BV 39 (96r–97r); BV 40 (77v–78r); Cb 74 (105r–106r); IV 60 (94v–95r); MCa 318 (p. 284*); MOd 7 (144v–145r); Mza 76 (119r–119v); Mza 77 (156v–157v); PAc 47 (181r–182r); PAs 697 (55r–56r); Pn 1669 (109v–111r); PCsa 65 (237v); PS 121 (48r–49r); Ra 123 (232r–233r); Rvat 5319 (158r, incomplete); SIc 15 (141r–141v); Tn 18 (108v–109v); Tn 20 (9v–10r); VCd 146 (105v–106v); VCd 161 (126r–126v); VCd 162 (187v–188r); VEcap 107 (95r–96r); VO 39 (40v–41v).

References

AH 53:119; Brunner, "The Sequences of Verona 107," 1:198–203, 2:33; Brunner, "Catalogo," 261; Crocker, "Repertoire," 2:73; Crocker, *Early Medieval Sequence*, 198–203; Damilano, "Sequenze," 11; Drinkwelder, *Sequentiar*, 35; de Goede, *Utrecht Prosarium*, 40; Hughes, *Sequelae*, 32; Reichert, "Structurprobleme," 238–41; Schubiger, *Sängerschule*, 22; Stäblein, *Vat. lat. 5319*, 623; von den Steinen, *Notker der Dichter* 1:181–97, 538–41, 2:54.

Text Commentary

Notker's *Sancti spiritus assit*, for Pentecost, celebrates the gifts of the Spirit, rather than retelling the scriptural account of the Spirit coming to the Apostles, as described in Acts 2:1–13. The text is primarily a series of acclamations. Crocker (*Early Medieval Sequence*) shows convincingly how *Rex omnipotens* served as a model for this text, whereas von den Steinen had seen *Rex omnipotens* as written later (*Notker der Dichter*, 1:154). Crocker points to the remarkable achievement of this piece in its balance of rhetoric and music, with a sophistication and economy that is masterful, and wonders if it is this that accounts for the popularity of the piece in France and England. It was obviously very popular in Italy as well, with a broad range of concordances.

Text and Translation

[1] Sancti spiritus adsit nobis gratia
[2a] Quę corda nostra sibi faciat habitaculum
[2b] Expulsis inde cunctis viciis spiritalibus
[3a] Spiritus alme illustrator hominum
[3b] Horridas nostrę mentis purga tenebras
[4a] Amator sancte sensatorum semper cogitatuum
[4b] Infunde unctionem tuam clemens nostris sensibus
[5a] Tu purificator omnium flagitiorum spiritus
[5b] Purifica nostri oculos interioris hominis
[6a] Ut videri suppremus genitor possit a nobis
[6b] Mundi cordis quem soli cernere possunt oculi
[7a] Prophetas tu inspirasti ut pręconia christi pręcinuissent inclita
[7b] Apostolos confortasti uti tropheum christi per totum mundum veherent
[8a] Quando machinam per verbum suum fecit deus cęli terrę marium
[8b] Tu super aquas foturus eas numen tuum expandisti spiritus
[9a] Tu animabus vivificandis aquas fecundas
[9b] Tu aspirando das spiritales esse homines
[10a] Tu divisum per linguas mundum et ritus adunasti domine
[10b] Idolatras ad cultum dei revocans magistrorum optime
[11a] Ergo nos supplicantes tibi exaudi propicius sancte spiritus
[11b] Sine quo preces omnes casse creduntur et indignę dei auribus
[12a] Tu qui omnium seculorum sanctos Tui nominis docuisti instinctu amplectende spiritus
[12b] Ipse hodie apostolis christi Donans munera insolita et cunctis inaudita seculis
[13] Hunc diem gloriosum fecisti

*

[1] Let the grace of the Holy Spirit be with us,
[2a] The grace that makes our hearts its indwelling place,
[2b] After having expelled from it all spiritual vices.
[3a] O life-giving Spirit, source of light for humankind:
[3b] Dispel the terrible darkness of our soul.
[4a] O Holy One, ever lover of perceptive knowing:
[4b] Mercifully anoint our senses with Your balm.
[5a] You, Spirit, purifier of all wickedness,
[5b] Purify the eyes of our soul,
[6a] So that the supreme source of being might be seen by us,
[6b] The being whom only the eyes of a pure heart can discern.
[7a] You inspired the prophets, to sing the heralding song of Christ!
[7b] You strengthened the apostles, so that they carry Christ's banner through the whole world.
[8a] When God, through His word, created the edifice of heaven and earth and the seas,
[8b] You, O Spirit, expanded your divine breath over it to give it warmth.
[9a] You seeded the waters to bring souls to life:
[9b] You, by breathing out, make mankind spiritual.
[10a] You, O Lord, brought together the world, divided through tongues and customs,
[10b] Recalling idolaters to venerate God, O greatest of teachers.
[11a] Therefore, O Holy Spirit, in your mercy, listen to those of us beseeching you,
[11b] Without whom all prayers are in vain and unworthy for God's ears.
[12a] You who taught the saints throughout all times Through the all encompassing impulse of your divine breath, O Spirit,
[12b] Today You Yourself, endowing the apostles of Christ with a gift extraordinary and incredible to all ages,
[13] Have made this day glorious.

Distinctive Variants

Rn 1343 [8b] *futurus* for *foturus*; *santos* for *sanctus*.
Bu 2824 [8b] *futurus* for *foturus*.

MELODIC VARIANTS

Rn 1343 [1] *nobis* B′A; [2a] *cor(da)* c(b); *(nos)tra* cd; *si(bi)* cc~; *(ha)bi(taculum)* GG~; [2b] *cunc(tis)* c(b); *(spi)ri(talibus)* GG~; [3a] *al(me)* F(E); [3b] *nos(trę)* FF~; [4a] *sanc(te)* E; [4b] *(Infun)de* GG~; [5a] *(flagito)rum* GG~; [5b] *(interior)ris* GG~; [6b] *cor(dis)* GG~; [7a] *(precinuis)sent* GG~; [7b] *(mun)dum* GG~; [8a] *(su)um* cc~; [8b] *(e)as* cc~; *(expandi)sti* GG~; [9a] *(vivifi)can(dis)* F(G); *(a)quas* GG~; [9b] *(aspi)ran(do)* F(E); *(es)se* GG~; [10a] *per* G; [10b] *(magisto)rum* GG~; [11a] *Er(go)* c(b); *(suppli)can(tes)* cc~; *ti(bi)* aa~; *spiri(tus)* G′F; [11b] *om(nes)* cc~; *cas(se)* aa~; *(in)dig(ne)* aa(G); [12a] *sanc(tos)* c(d); *Tu(i)* Gd; [12b] *Do-(nans)* G; *(inaudi)ta* GG~; [13] *(fe)ci(sti)* cc~. **Bu 2824** [1] *(no)bis* GG~; [2a] *cor(da)* c(b); *si(bi)* c; [2b] *(Ex)pul(sis)* c(b); *cunc(tis)* c(b); [3a] *al(me)* F(E); [3b] *nos(trę)* FF~; [4a] *(Ama)tor* GG~; [4b] *(Infun)de* GG~; [5a] *(flagito)rum* GG~; [5b] *(interior)ris* GG~; [6b] *cor(dis)* GG~; [7a] *(precinu)is(sent)* aa~; [7b] *mun(dum)* aa~; [8a] *(su)um* cc~; *ter(re)* aa~; [8b] *(e)as* cc~; *(expandi)sti* GG~; [9a] *(ani)ma(bus)* FF~; *(vivifi)can(dis)* F(G); *(a)quas* GG~; [9b] *(aspi)ran(do)* F(E); *(es)se* GG~; [10a] *(aduna)sti* GG~; [11a] *Er(go)* c(b); *(suppli)can(tes)* cc~; *ti(bi)* aa~; *spiri(tus)* G′F; [11b] *om(nes)* cc~; *cas(se)* aa~; *(in)dig(ne)* aa(G); [12a] *sanc(tos)* c(d); *Tu(i)* Gd; [12b] *Do(nans)* Gd; *(inaudi)ta* GG~; [13] *(fe)ci(sti)* cc~.

20. Alme mundi rex

SOURCES

Rc 1741 fols. 97r–98r Seq<uentia>
Rn 1343 fols. 36v–37r Seq<uentia>
Bu 2824 fols. 66r–67v Seq<uentia>

ITALIAN CONCORDANCES

Bc 7 (29r–29v); BV 34 (230v–231r); BV 35 (125r–125v); BV 38 (129r–129v); BV 39 (154v–155r); BV 40 (119v–120r); Cb 74 (111v–112r); IV 60 (112v–113r); MCa 318 (p. 253*); MOd 7 (154v–155v); PAc 47 (192r–192v); PAs 697 (58v–59r); Pn 1669 (38r–39r); PCsa 65 (242); PS 121 (55v–56v); Ra 123 (236v–237r); VEcap 107 (98r–99r); VO 39 (44r–44v).

REFERENCES

AH 37:187; Brunner, "The Sequences of Verona 107," 1:127–31, 2:36; Brunner, "Catalogo," 212.

TEXT COMMENTARY

Both melody and text of *Alme mundi rex* are almost certainly of Italian origin, with strong concordances throughout the peninsula. The text is an interesting juxtaposition of simple, direct expression and complicated syntax. The piece opens with invocations to Christ the King, but the single petition to Christ beginning in the middle of [3b] and running through [5a] is more complex and effective with its relative clauses in [4]. These refer to John the Baptist, to whom the text is dedicated, but he appears only as the agent of the petition to Christ. The melody is unusual, in that it is largely disciplined and refined, yet the long single phrase [6] has a melismatic passage on the word Alleluia, which gives rise to a number of variants among the concordances. See Brunner, "The Sequences of Verona 107," 1:131, example 19, which compares four versions of the Alleluia in [6].

TEXT AND TRANSLATION

[1] Alme mundi
[2a] Rex christe qui regis secla et arva sataque cuncta
[2b] Tu gubernas astra supra marisque habitacula
[3a] Ipse es qui vocaris alpha et ω inicium et finis lapis quadrus angularis et concordia
[3b] Qui facis prisca nobis presentia quęsumus ut concedas cui superni chori canunt te laudantia
[4a] Per suffragia pręcuroris tui atque baptistę
[4b] Qui inter vates solus maior manet plusquam propheta
[5a] Una cum illo angelico agmine Tuum mirabile conlaudare nomen Valeat falanx nostra
[5b] Iam nunc omnis turba fidei subiecta Levet in excelso canoraque sancta domino dicentia
[6] Dignus es accipere laudes cui canunt cherubin Alleluia Alleluia Agie rex ęterne
[7a] Qui solus regnas cum patre et paraclito
[7b] Per immortalia seculorum secula
[8] Amen dicant omnia

*

[1a] Propitious King of the world,
[2a] Christ, who reigns over the ages, the whole earth and all that grows,
[2b] You govern the stars above and the dwellings of the sea,
[3a] You are the one who is called Alpha and Omega, the beginning and the end, the cornerstone, and the ring.
[3b] You who make the old present to us, we beseech you, to whom the heavenly choirs sing praises, that you grant us,
[4a] Through the aid of your precursor and baptist,
[4b] Who alone among the prophets remains more than a prophet,
[5a] That our host may sing together with that angelic host praising your wondrous name.
[5b] Now let all the faithful crowd raise up on high in singing holy songs to the Lord.
[6] You are worthy of receiving the praises that the cherubim sing to you, "Alleluia, Alleluia, Holy Eternal King."

[7a] You alone reign together with the Father and the Paraclete
[7b] For the ages everlasting.
[8] Let all creation sing Amen.

DISTINCTIVE VARIANTS

Rn 1343 [8b] *falax* for *falanx*.

MELODIC VARIANTS

Rn 1343 [2a] *ar(va)* E(D); *cunc(ta)* EE(D); [3a] *(angu)la(ris)* EE~; *(concor)di(a)* ED; [3b] *ca(nunt)* EE~; [4a] *tu(i)* ED; *(bap)ti(ste)* EE~; [4b] *(ma)net* EE~; *(pro)phe(ta)* EE~; [5a] *il(lo)* b(a); *nos(tra)* EE~; [5b] *tur(ba)* aa(G); [6] *(cheru)bin* a~(G); *(Alle)lu(ia)* acbcd; *(ẹ)ter(ne)* bb(a). **Bu 2824** [2a] *ar(va)* E(D); *cunc(ta)* EE(D); [3a] *(angu)la(ris)* EE~; *(concor)di(a)* ED; [3b] *ca(nunt)* EE~; [4a] *tu(i)* ED; *(bap)ti(ste)* EE~; [4b] *(ma)net* EE~; *(pro)phe(ta)* EE~; [5a] *il(lo)* b(a); *nos(tra)* EE~; [5b] *tur(ba)* aa(G); [6] *(cheru)bin* aa~(G); *(Alle)lu(ia)* acbcd; *(ẹ)ter(ne)* bb(a).

21. Pretiosa sollemnitas

SOURCES

Rc 1741 fols. 99v–100v Seq<uentia>
Rn 1343 fols. 37v–38r Seq<uentia>
Bu 2824 fols. 69r–70v Seq<uentia>

ITALIAN CONCORDANCES

BV 39 (124v–125v); Ra 123 (241r–241v); VEcap 107 (100r–100v).

REFERENCES

AH 7:203; 53:332; Brunner, "The Sequences of Verona 107," 1: 131–34, 2:39; Brunner, "Catalogo," 254; Crocker, "Repertoire," 2:64.

TEXT COMMENTARY

This piece for St. Peter is found in sources from both Italy and West Francia. Because the Italian transmission of the text is much better than the West Frankish, Blume confidently pointed to Italy, even specifying Nonantola as a likely place of origin. (*AH* 53:333). Yet closer scrutiny makes such an assertion suspect. For a discussion of origins and other aspects of the text and tune, see Brunner, "The Sequences of Verona 107," 1:131–34. The text itself paints a picture of the splendor of Heaven, but does so with some very awkward syntax. The poet seemed compulsively concerned with aligning words and accents between corresponding halves of each couplet, rather than with lucid syntax. An unusual aspect of this sequence is the extra four syllables that occur at the end of the second verse of each couplet, save the last, repeating the four-note cadential figure.

TEXT AND TRANSLATION

[1a] Preciosa sollemnitas adest annuata
[1b] Christi secutoris cui tanta vox audita tibi regna
[2a] Mi angelorum consors clara apud agmina dabo ẹtherea nutu porta
[2b] Falanx prophetarum tuo petre egredietur patens amicta veste alba cum corona
[3a] Ubi adstant coram domino mille milia clamantia
[3b] Quẹ non cessant voce congrua nomen eius laudantia in secula
[4a] Ubi cherubin seraphin ardentes amoris igne nulla fuscati nequicia
[4b] Murus refulget ornatus aspersaque gemmis redolent nectar oleum lac et vina roriflua
[5a] Cum quibus fortitur collata clave regni cẹlorum petrus christi athleta regens cuncta
[5b] Ipseque pro nobis intercedere patrem polorum devotione sua atque fide non desistat
[6] Uti digna carmina patri ac filio posita
[7] Proferamus per coẹterna seculorum secula

*

[1a] Today is the precious annual feast
[1b] Of Christ's follower to whom so grand a voice was heard:
[2a] To you, my brother, I shall give the Kingdom among the bright throng of angels on high;
[2b] At your sign, Peter, the gate is opened and the host of prophets shall go forth wrapped in white robes and with crowns,
[3a] Where, in the presence of the Lord, countless thousands stand crying out,
[3b] Never ceasing to praise His name with concordant voice.
[4a] Where cherubim, seraphim burning with the fire of love remain untouched by iniquity.
[4b] The adorned wall shines forth and is sprinkled over with gems, while the nectar, oil, milk, together dripping of dew, send forth their scents,
[5a] Strengthened by these, Peter, Christ's athlete, reigns over all, having collected the key of the kingdom of Heaven.
[5b] Let him not cease to intercede on our behalf to the Father of the heavens with his devotion and faith,
[6–7] So that we might bring forth worthy songs given to the Father and the Son throughout the ages.

DISTINCTIVE VARIANTS

Rn 1343 [5a] *leve* for *clave*. **Bu 2824** [4b] *muros* for *murus*.

MELODIC VARIANTS

Rn 1343 [1a] *(annu)a(ta)* aa~; [1b] *reg(na)* aa(G); [2a] *(ange)lo(rum)* aa~; *cla(ra)* GG~; *(ẹ)the(rea)* F; *(nu)tu* aa(G); *por(ta)* aaG; [2b] *(prophe)ta(rum)* aa~; *e(gredi)e(tur)* G'DD~; *al(ba)* a(G); *(cor)o(na)* a~; [3a] *ad(stant)* GG~; *clamati(a)* F'Ga'G; [3b] *insecu(la)* F'Ga'G; [4a] *nequici(a)* F'Ga'G; [4b] *(re)ful(get)* b(a); *(rori)flu(a)* aa~; [5a] *(ath)le(ta)* aa~; *cunc(ta)* a(G); [5b] *fi(de)* aa~; *(de)sis(tat)* aa~; [6] *dig(na)* F(E); [7] *(Profe)ra(mus)* cc~b; *(coę)ter(na)* a(G). **Bu 2824** [1a] *(annu)a(ta)* aa~; [1b] *reg(na)* aa(G); [2a] *(ange)lo(rum)* aa~; *cla(ra)* GG~; *(ę)the(rea)* F; *por(ta)* aaG; [2b] *(prophe)ta(rum)* aa~; *(egredi)e(tur)* DD~; *al(ba)* a(G); *(co)ro(na)* aa~; [3a] *clamati(a)* F'Ga'G; [3b] *insecu(la)* F'Ga'G; [4a] *nequici(a)* F'Ga'G; [4b] *(re)ful(get)* b(a); *(rori)flu(a)* a~; [5a] *(ath)le(ta)* aa~; *cunc(ta)* a(G); [5b] *fi(de)* aa~; *(de)sis(tat)* aa~; [6] *dig(na)* F(E); [7] *(Profe)ra(mus)* cc~b; *(coę)ter(na)* a(G).

22. *Petre summe*

Sources

Rc 1741 fols. 101r–102r Seq<uentia>
Rn 1343 fols. 38r–38v (no rubric)
Bu 2824 fols. 71r–72v Seq<uentia> al<ia>

Italian Concordances

Bc 7 (29v–30r); Bu 2748 (pp. 164–67); BV 39 (125v–126r); IV 60 (103v–104r); MOd 7 (159r–159v); Mza 76 (129v–130r); Mza 77 (159r–159v); NV 1 (202); PAc 47 (197r–197v); PAs 697 (56v–57r); Pn 1669 (43r–44v); PCsa 65 (239r–239v); PS 121 (58r–59r); Ra 123 (240v–241r); Tn 18 (119r–119v); Tn 20 (11r–11v); VCd 146 (1007r–107v); VCd 161 (128r); VCd 162 (189r–189v); VEcap 107 (99r–99v); VO 39 (45r–45v).

References

AH 53:336; Brunner, "The Sequences of Verona 107," 1:70–77, 2:38; Brunner, "Catalogo," 252; Crocker, *Early Medieval Sequence*, 91–93; Damilano, "Sequenze," 11; Drinkwelder, *Sequentiar*, 41; de Goede, *Utrecht Prosarium*, 51; Hughes, *Sequelae*, 29; Schubiger, *Sängerschule*, 26; Stäblein, "Die Sequenzmelodie," 372–75, 387–92; von den Steinen, *Notker der Dichter*, 1:359–61, 579–81, 2:62.

Text Commentary

Stäblein ("Die Sequenzmelodie," 375) exclaimed that this text had "greatness" (*Grossartigkeit*). The text celebrates both Peter and Paul, who are invoked together in the first two phrases, then given separate lines or phrases to be joined together at the end. Crocker (*Early Medieval Sequence*, 93) considers this a mature text where the melody "seems not only to determine the text's layout but also to suggest, through rhetorical shape, some of the key ideas and images."

Text and Translation

[1] Petre summe christi pastor et paule gentium doctor
[2a] Aecclesiam vestris doctrinis illuminatam
[2b] Per circulum terrę precatus adiuvet vester
[3a] Nam dominus petre cęlorum tibi claves dono dedit
[3b] Armigerum beniamin christus texit suum vasque lectum
[4a] Mare planta te petre christus conculcare tuę dedit karitati
[4b] Umbra tui corporis infirmis debilibusque fecit medicinam
[5a] Spermologon philosophos te paule christus dat vincere sua voce
[5b] Multiplices victorias tu paule christo per populos adquisisti
[6a] Postremo victis omnibus barbaris Ad arcem summi pergitis culminis germanos discordes sub iugo christi pacatos iam coacturi
[6b] Ibi neronis feritas principes Apostolorum pręliis plurimis victores diversę te petre et paule addixerat penę mortis
[7] Te crux associat te vero gladius cruentus mittit christo

*

[1] Peter, Christ's highest pastor, and Paul, teacher of the gentiles,
[2a] The Church, enlightened through your teachings,
[2b] Your prayer has supported throughout the whole earth.
[3a] For the Lord gave you, Peter, the keys to Heaven as a gift.
[3b] Christ protects you, Benjamin, as His shield-bearer, as His chosen vessel.
[4a] To you, Peter, to the one who loves, Christ granted that you tread the sea under your foot.
[4b] He made the shadow of your body into a remedy for the sick and helpless.
[5a] And you, Paul, the babbler, Christ granted that you conquer the philosophers with your voice;
[5b] You, Paul, have won many victories for Christ throughout the nations.
[6a] Finally, when all the barbarians are vanquished, you proceed to the most famous citadel, two unlike brothers, to be brought together in harmony under Christ's yoke.
[6b] There Nero's savageness condemned the princes of the apostles, Peter and Paul, victors in so many struggles, to different death sentences,
[7] The cross joins you <Peter>, and yes, the blood-stained sword sends you <Paul>, to Christ.

DISTINCTIVE VARIANTS

Bu 2824 *Ibi neronis feritas principes* added in margin. [7] *christus* for *christo*. As with *Hanc concordi*, the Italian manuscripts are fairly consistent in their transmission of the text, but syllabic settings often give way to neumatic elaboration, as in MOd 7 (see Brunner, "The Sequences of Verona 107," 1:74).

MELODIC VARIANTS

Rn 1343 [1] *Pa(stor)* GG~; *Alle(luia)* Ga'a; [2a] *ves(tris)* aa~; *(illumi)na(tam)* a~; [2b] *ves(ter)* aa~; [3a] *(cę)lo(rum)* aa~; *cla(ves)* aa~; [3b] *lec(tum)* aa~; [4a] *(concul)ca(re)* aa~; *de(dit)* aa~; [4b] *fe(cit)* aa~; *(medi)ci(nam)* aa~; [5a] *chris(tus)* GG~; *vo(ce)* aa~; [5b] *chris(to)* GG~; *(adqui)si(sti)* aa~; [6a] *sum(mi)* dd~; *(ger)ma(nos)* cc~; *chris(ti)* GG~; [6b] *(ne)ro(nis)* dd~; *(vic)to(res)* cc~; *pau(le)* G(F); *mor(tis)* aa(G); [7] *(cru)en(tus)* aa(G); *chris(to)* aa~. **Bu 2824** [2a] *ves(tris)* aa~; *(illumi)na(tam)* aa~; [2b] *ter(rae)* aa~; [3a] *(cę)lo(rum)* aa~; *cla(ves)* aa~; [3b] *lec(tum)* aa~; [4a] *(concul)ca(re)* aa~; *de(dit)* aa~; [4b] *fe(cit)* aa~; [5a] *chris(tus)* GG~; *vo(ce)* aa~; [5b] *chris(to)* GG~; *(adqui)si(sti)* aa~; [6a] *Pos(tremo)* c; *sum(mi)* dd~; *(ger)ma(nos)* cc~; *chris(ti)* GG~; [6b] *(ne)ro(nis)* dd~; *(vic)to(res)* cc~; *pau(le)* G(F); *mor(tis)* aa(G); [7] *(cru)en(tus)* aa(G); *chris(to)* aa~.

23. *Sancti merita Benedicti*

SOURCES

Rc 1741 fols. 103r–105r Seq<uentia>
Rn 1343 fols. 39r–39v (no rubric)

ITALIAN CONCORDANCES

Bu 2748 (pp. 167–71); MCa 546 (78v–79v); VEcap 107 (51v–52v).

REFERENCES

AH 54:52; Brunner, "The Sequences of Verona 107," 1:56–70, 2:70; Brunner, "Catalogo," 261; Hiley, *Sequences for St. Benedict*, 7–9; Hughes, *Sequelae*, 32.

TEXT COMMENTARY

According to Hiley (*Sequences for St. Benedict*, 3) this text was written ca. 1000, possibly in Monte Cassino, but more likely at Fleury. Blume (*AH* 54:54) on the other hand, thought an origin in a Benedictine abbey in northern Italy more likely, whence the piece spread to many monasteries in southern Germany. The text recounts the miracles attributed to St. Benedict in the Second Dialogue of St. Gregory. For the Latin text of the Dialogue, see J.-P. Migne, *Patrologia Latina* 66:125–204 and U. Moricca, *Gregorii Magni Dialogi* (Rome, 1924), 71–134. There are a number of English translations, e.g., see A. Hoffmann, *The Life and Miracles of St. Benedict* (Collegeville, Minn., 1925). The translation below is based, in part, on that of Hiley's in *Sequences for St. Benedict*, 9.

TEXT AND TRANSLATION

[1] Sancti merita benedicti inclita
[2a] Venerande sanctitatis ac monachorum pręsulis
[2b] Ad laudem hiesu christi organa nostra concrepent
[3a] Nursia felix tulit natum genitrix
[3b] Domina mundi roma fovit alitrix
[4a] Hic ergo pręventus optimo sancti spiritus dono
[4b] Sophiam despexit humanam nactus et angelicam
[5a] Hic fide subnixus integra redintegravit confracta
[5b] Incendia carnis edomat cruce venenum effugat
[6a] Vage mentis monachum reparat fontem rutilat
[6b] Eius iussu de laci abdito ferrum enatat
[7a] Discipulus super aquas siccis pedibus currit corvus mandatum peragit
[7b] Ingentem levigat petram fratrum revocat oculos iam delusos ignibus
[8a] Lapsum monacum per membra tritum sua prece redonavit animę
[8b] Culpam prodidit pręsumpti cibi et hospitem notat culpa simili
[9a] Perfidi regis machinam mente saga denudat
[9b] Prescia mente debita talione pessundat
[10a] Qui clericum hoste pervasum liberat et ventura nunciat
[10b] Qui secretam superbi mentem increpat atque famen mitigat
[11a] Verbo carne solutas ligat iam animas sed absolvit pane mistico
[11b] Cautes absque periculo servant vas vitreum oppressum plangit emulum
[12a] Solo numine enodavit rusticum sed oramine iam extinctum rustici suscitavit filium
[12b] Ipse animam capuani pręsulis vidit lumine in solito supernis importari sedibus
[13] Quibus ipse gloriosus triumphat

*

[1] (In) the glorious merits of Holy Benedict,
[2a] Eminent in sanctity and patron of monks,
[2b] Let our instruments sound together to the glory of Jesus Christ.
[3a] The land of Nursia is happy to bear such a son
[3b] And Rome, ruler of the world, to be his nurse!
[4a] Nevertheless forewarned by the splendid gift of the Holy Spirit,
[4b] He despised earthly knowledge and gained angelic wisdom.
[5a] Relying on a vigorous faith, he made whole the broken vessel.

[5b] He tames the fiery desires of the flesh; he dispels poison by the sign of the cross.

[6a] He restores the monk whose mind had gone astray; he causes a spring to flow red.

[6b] At his bidding, the iron tool floats up from the hidden depths of the lake.

[7a] His disciple runs with dry feet above the water; the raven fulfills his bidding.

[7b] He raises the enormous rock; he brings back the sight of his brothers deceived by fires.

[8a] The fallen monk, by his bruised limbs (by whipping him), he restored by his prayers to peace of soul.

[8b] He notes the sin of eating food before the time, and the guest committing a similar sin.

[9a] By his insight he exposes the tricks of the deceitful king.

[9b] By foresight, he revealed to him the end of his life, the fitting penalty.

[10a] He sets free the cleric who is in the enemy's grip and he foretells the future.

[10b] He rebukes the secret thoughts of the proud and allays famine.

[11a] He binds the souls ensnared by the flesh, but brings them forgiveness with the mystical bread.

[11b] Protecting the glass vessel from the danger of the rock he laments the oppressed enemy.

[12a] Through his divine sway alone he sets the slave free;
and through his prayer he brought back to life a peasant's son who was already dead.

[12b] He saw the soul of the bishop of Capua carried by a marvelous light to the heavenly mansions.

[13] Where he in glory triumphs.

Distinctive Variants

Rn 1343 *angelica* for *angelicam*; [5b] *crucem* for *cruce*; [7b] *fratrem* for *fratrum*; [9a] *machina* for *machinam*; *sagat* for *saga*; [9b] *tallione* for *talione*; [10a] *hostem* for *hoste*; [10b] *mente* for *mentem*; [11a] *solutos* for *sollutas*.

Melodic Variants

Rn 1343 [4b] (hu)ma(nam) FF~; *an(gelica)* GG~; [5a] *(redintegra)vit* GG~; [6a] *men(tis)* G(F); *(fon)tem* GG~; [6b] *ius(su)* GG~; *(fer)rum* GG~; [7a] *(Discipu)lus* GG~; *(manda)tum* GG~; [7b] *(In)gen(tem)* aa(G); *(fra)trem* F; *(delu)sos* GG~; [8a] *(redona)vit* GG~; [8b] *(ci)bi* cc~; *(cul)pa* GG~; [9b] *men(te)* F(E); [10a] *(per)va(sum)* GG~; [10b] *men(te)* GG(F); *(fa)men* GG~; [11a] *(so)lu(tos)* cc~; *li(gat)* aG; *(ab)sol(vit)* aa(G); [11b] *ser(vant)* aa(G); *(plan)git* GG~; [12a] *Sed* Gd; [12b] *Vi(dit)* Gd; [13] *(glori)o(sus)* GG~; *(trium)phat* abcc~.

24. *Candida contio melos*

Sources

Rc 1741 fols. 105r–106v Seq\<uentia\>

Italian Concordances

BV 43 (243r–243v); BV 35 (153r); BV 38 (137r–137v); BV 39 (174r–174v); BV 40 (163v); MCa 318 (p. 252*); VEcap 107 (110r–111r).

References

AH 7:184; 53:392; Brunner, "The Sequences of Verona 107," 1:77–82, 2:41; Brunner, "Catalogo," 217; Crocker, "Repertoire," 2:22.

Text Commentary

This text follows directly after *Sancti merita Benedicti* in Rc 1741 and mentions Benedict in the text. Yet the details of the text do not correspond to Benedict's life. Blume (*AH* 53:392) suggests that the content of couplet [5] implies that piece was originally written for St. Germanus. The sequence is found primarily in Beneventan and French sources; the only other Italian concordances are from Nonantola and VEcap 107.

Text and Translation

[1a] Candida contio melos concrepa

[1b] Tinnula cantibus iungas organa

[2a] Benedictum caste resultet liquido sonore simphonia

[2b] Artifici plectro perita sillabatim stringere neumata

[3a] Fluxerat quondam sopor immania confessoris fessa per membra

[3b] Cui prębens sacra christus viatica intulit grata famina

[4a] Care quid hesitas non est quod metuas dulcem mox petiturus patriam

[4b] Deposcunt sydera civem ad supera quo manet sine fine gaudia

[5a] Quia monita comes excipit egrimonia membra carpens languida

[5b] Die septima supera sequens cęli convexa felix scandit anima

[6a] Plaudens gallia funus excipit ac inclita servat in aula

[6b] Eius per sacra christe suffragia nostra guberna tempora

[7] Amen dicant omnia

*

[1a] O splendid assembly, break forth in song,

[1b] Unite ringing instrumental parts with the melodies,

[2a] And let it sing praise to Benedict with flowing sound in devout harmony,
[2b] And with a skillful plectrum parse practiced melodies syllable by syllable.
[3a] Once a deep sleep had filled the Confessor's weary limbs,
[3b] And while offering him final communion, Christ spoke these joyful words to him:
[4a] "Dear one, why do you hesitate? There is nothing to fear for you who will soon reach the gentle fatherland.
[4b] The stars call their citizen to the heavens, where there is joy without end."
[5a] As our companion received these divine monitions, suffering seized his weary limbs.
[5b] And on the seventh day, his happy soul following, he climbed to the lofty arch of heaven.
[6a] Exulting Gaul receives his body, and preserves it in the illustrious sanctuary.
[6b] Through his blessed intercession, O Christ, guide our lives.
[7] Let all creation sing: Amen.

DISTINCTIVE VARIANTS
None.

MELODIC VARIANTS
None.

25. *Laurenti David*

SOURCES
Rc 1741 fols. 107v–108v Seq<uentia>
Rn 1343 fols. 40v–41r (no rubric)
Bu 2824 fols. 74v–76r Seq<uentia>

ITALIAN CONCORDANCES
Bu 2748 (pp. 172–74); BV 34 (218v–219r); BV 35 (139v–140r); BV 38 (123v–124r): BV 39 (144v–145r); BV 40 (111v–112r); IV 60 (108v–109r); Kf 29 (1v, incomplete); MOd 7 (166r–166v); Mza 76 (134v–135r); Mza 77 (159v–160v); PAc 47 (206r–206v); PAs 697 (57r–57v); PCsa 65 (241r); PS 121 (62r–62v); Ra 123 (245r–245v); Tn 18 (124v–125r); Tn 20 (132rv–132v); VCd 146 (108v); VCd 161 (128v–129r); VCd 162 (191r–191v); VEcap 107 (101v–102v); VO 39 (45v–46r).

REFERENCES
AH 53:283; Brunner, "The Sequences of Verona 107," 1:77–82, 2:42; Brunner, "Catalogo," 242; Crocker, *Early Medieval Sequence*, 149–53; Drinkwelder, *Sequentiar*, 46; de Goede, *Utrecht Prosarium*, 61; Hughes, *Sequelae*, 70; von den Steinen, *Notker der Dichter*, 1:374–79, 584–86, 2:64.

TEXT COMMENTARY
Laurenti David is the fifth and final text in this edition set to "Romana" (or its close relative "Dic nobis/ Clara gaudia"). Crocker considers it a mature piece (later than *Iohannes Iesu*, set to the same melody), based on the mastery of rhetoric and syntax, combined with the melodic shape (*Early Medieval Sequence*, 151). The text recounts significant acts and the passion of the martyred saint. For the sources of Notker's text, see von den Steinen, *Notker der Dichter*, 1:584–85. The piece has strong concordances in Italian manuscripts with relatively consistent transmission.

TEXT AND TRANSLATION
[1] Laurenti david magni martyr milesque fortis
[2a] Tu imperatoris tribunal
[2b] Tu manus tortorum cruentas
[3a] Sprevisti secutus desiderabilem atque manu fortem
[3b] Qui solus potuit regna superare tyranni crudelis
[4a] Cuiusque sanctus sanguinis prodigos facit amor milites eius
[4b] Dummodo illum liceat cernere dispendio vitę presentis
[5a] Cesaris tu fasces contemnis et iudicis minas derides
[5b] Carnifex ungulas et ustor craticulam vane consumunt
[6a] Dolet impius urbis prefectus victus a pisce assato christi cibo
[6b] Gaudet domini conviva favo conresurgendi cum ipso saturatus
[7a] O laurenti miles david invictissime regis ęterni
[7b] Apud illum servulis ipsius deprecare veniam semper
[8] Martir milesque fortis
*
[1] Lawrence, noble David's martyr and mighty warrior:
[2a] The emperor's tribunal,
[2b] The bloodstained hands of the torturers,
[3a] You held them in contempt and followed the desired one and the one mighty in combat,
[3b] The one who alone could overcome the powers of the cruel tyrant,
[4a] And whose sublime love makes his warriors prodigious in blood
[4b] At that moment they are granted to perceive Him as they give up this present life.
[5a] You belittle Caesar's symbols of powers, and you jeer at the threats of the judge.
[5b] In vain the executioner and torturer exhaust their talons and gridiron.

[6a] It is the ungodly magistrate of the city who suffers, vanquished by a roasted fish, by the food of Christ,
[6b] It is the companion of the Lord at table who rejoices, the one rising again with Him feasting on honeycomb.
[7a] O Lawrence, of David's—of the eternal King's—warriors, you are the most invincible:
[7b] In His presence continuously beseech good will toward His servants
[8] Oh martyr and mighty warrior.

DISTINCTIVE VARIANTS

Rn 1343 [7a] *militum* for *miles*. Bu 2824 [7a] *militum* for *miles*.

MELODIC VARIANTS

Rn 1343 [1] *mag(ni)* c(b); [2a] *(tri)bu(nal)* ee~; [2b] *(cru)en(tas)* ee(d); [3a] *for(tem)* ee(d); [3b] *reg(na)* ee(d); [4a] *sanc(tus)* ee(d); *e(ius)* ee(d); [4b] *(pre)sen(tis)* ee(d); [5a] *(con)tem(nis)* g(f); [5b] *(con)su(munt)* ee~; [6a] *urbis presectus* f'g'a' aa~'g; *ci(bo)* ee~; [6b] *(satu)ra(tus)* ee(d); [7a] *militum* e'f'g; [7b] *il(lum)* ee~; *sem(per)* ee(d); [8] *for(tis)* ee(d). Bu 2824 [1] *mag(ni)* c(b); *miles(que)* cd'd; [2a] *(tri)bu(nal)* ee~; [2b] *(cru)en(tas)* ee(d); [3a] *for(tem)* ee(d); [3b] *reg(na)* ee(d); *(ty)ran(ni)* dd~; [4a] *sanc(tus)* ee(d); *e(ius)* ee(d); [4b] *(pre)sen(tis)* ee(d); [5a] *(con)tem(nis)* g(f); [5b] *(con)su(munt)* ee~; [6a] *(pre)sec(tus)* gg~; *ci(bo)* ee~; [6b] *(conresur)gen(di)* ee~; *(satu)ra(tus)* ee(d); [7a] *militum* e'f'g; *(ę)ter(ni)* ee(d); [7b] *il(lum)* ee~; *sem(per)* ee(d); [8] *for(tis)* ee(d).

26. *Congaudent angelorum chori*

SOURCES

Rc 1741 fols. 110r–112r Seq<uentia>
Rn 1343 fols. 41v–42r Seq<uentia>
Bu 2824 fols. 76v–78v Seq<uentia>

ITALIAN CONCORDANCES

Bu 2748 (pp. 174–78); BV 38 (127r–128r); BV 39 (148r–148v); IV 60 (110v–111r); MOd 7 (169r–169v); Mza 77 (160v–161v); PAs 697 (58r–58v); PCsa 65 (241r–241v); PS 121 (63r–64v); Ra 123 (248v–249v); Tn 18 (126v–127r); VCd 146 (108v–109r); VCd 161 (129r–129v); VCd 162 (191v–192r); VEcap 107 (103v–104v); VO 39 (46r–47r).

REFERENCES

AH 53:179; Brunner, "The Sequences of Verona 107," 1:99–100, 2:45; Brunner, "Catalogo," 222; Crocker, *Early Medieval Sequence*, 160–88; Drinkwelder, *Sequentiar*, 47; de Goede, *Utrecht Prosarium*, 3; Haug, "Neue Ansätze," 112–14; Hughes, *Sequelae*, 55; Kunz, "Textgestalt"; Moberg, *Schwedishen Sequenzen*, n. 12; Negro, "Le sequenze," 75; Schubiger, *Sängerschule*, 21; Stäblein, *Schriftbild*, 184–185; von den Steinen, *Notker der Dichter*, 1:299–305, 566–68, 2:66.

TEXT COMMENTARY

The structure of the text has been analyzed in detail by Kunz, "Textgestalt." The transcription of the piece in Haug, "Neue Ansätze," displays the music and text in a form that highlights motivic relationships between phrases. Crocker has written in detail about text and melody and their relationship to possible West-Frankish models, especially *Christi hodiernae* (no. 1 in the present edition). The sequence is unusual because of the irregularity in line length at the end [8–9]. The melody, too, is unusual in that from phrase [5] to the end the co-final d is adopted. The Nonantolan sources present an interesting departure from the other sources, since after the shift to d in [5], the melody is transposed down a fourth to a, in effect, the co-final of the co-final! With the downward transposition the intervals remain the same (since the sixth scale degree does not occur), but the tension of the high tessitura is lost.

TEXT AND TRANSLATION

[1] Congaudent angelorum chori gloriosę virgini
[2a] Quę sine virili commixtione genuit
[2b] Filium qui suo mundum cruore medicat
[3a] Nam ipsa lętatur quod cęli iam conspicatur principem
[3b] In terris cui quondam sugendas virgo mamillas prębuit
[4a] Quam celebris angelis maria hiesu mater creditur
[4b] Qui filii illius debito se cognoscunt famulos
[5a] Qua gloria in cęlis ista virgo colitur Quę domino cęli prębuit hospitum sui sanctissimi corporis
[5b] Quam splendida polo stella maris rutilat Quę omnium lumen astrorum et hominum atque spirituum genuit
[6a] Te cęli regina hęc plebicula piis concelebrat mentibus
[6b] Te cantu melodos super ethera una cum angelis elevat
[7a] Te libri virgo concinunt prophetarum chorus iubilat sacerdotum apostoli christique martyres prędicant
[7b] Te plebes sexus sequitur utriusque vitam diligens virginalem cęlicolas in castimonia emulans.
[8a] Aecclesia ergo cuncta te cordibus teque carminibus celebrat

[8b] Tibi suam manifestat devotionem
[9a] Precatu te supplici implorans maria
[9b] Ut sibi auxilio circa christum dominum esse digneris per aevum

*

[1] The choirs of angels rejoice together with the glorious Virgin,
[2a] Who, without knowing man, begot
[2b] The Son who heals the world with His blood.
[3a] Now, she herself rejoices to behold the Prince of Heaven,
[3b] Him whom on earth she once, as a virgin, gave her breast to suckle.
[4a] O how Mary, the Mother of Jesus, is honored, attended by angels,
[4b] Who know themselves to be the indebted servants of her Son.
[5a] In what glory this Virgin is worshipped in Heaven, who offered to the Lord of Heaven the chamber of her most sacred body.
[5b] How radiantly in the celestial vault shines the star of the sea, who brought forth the light of all stars and of all men, and of all spirits.
[6a] You, O Queen of Heaven, whom this humble congregation extols with devout minds.
[6b] Together with the angels it raises you up with melodious song above the ethereal heights.
[7a] You, O Virgin, the books of the prophets celebrate in song, the chorus of priests praise, and the apostles and martyrs of Christ proclaim.
[7b] You, people of both sexes follow, esteeming virginal life, emulating the heavenly beings in purity.
[8a] The whole church, therefore, praises you with hearts and voices,
[8b] Manifesting its devotion to you,
[9a] Imploring you with suppliant prayer, O Mary,
[9b] That you might deign to be succor for it in the presence of Christ the Lord, throughout the ages.

DISTINCTIVE VARIANTS

Rn 1343 [3a] *Iam* for *Nam;* [4b] *debitos* for *debito.* **Bu 2824** [3a] *Iam* for *Nam.*

MELODIC VARIANTS

Rn 1343 [1] *(angel)lo(rum)* GG~; *(glori)o(sę)* aa~; [2a] *(commixtio)ne* GG~; [2b] *su(o)* cc~; *(cruo)re* GG~; [3a] *(lę)ta(tur)* aa~; *cę(li)* cc~; [3b] *quon(dam)* aa(G); *(su)gen(das)* cc~; [4a] *(ange)lis* aa~; *hiesu* b'c; [5a] *cę(lis)* dd~; *(vir)go* dd~; *(sanctissi)mi* dd~; [5b] *(ma)ris* dd~; *(ho)minum* ee~'d; *(spiritu)um* dd~; [6a] *Te* G; *(plebicu)la* G; *pi(is)* a; *(concele)brat* aa~; [6b] *(e)the(ra)* bb~; [7a] *(prophe)ta(rum)* dd~; *(sacer)do(tum)* dd~; *(marty)res* aa~; [7b] *(utri)us(que)* dd~; *(virgi)na(lem)* dd~; *(casti-moni)a* aa~; [8a] *cunc(ta)* dd~; *(carmini)bus* aa~; [8b] *(mani)fe(stat)* dd~; *(implo)rans* aa~; [9] *(es)se* bb~. **Bu 2824** [1] *(angel)lo(rum)* GG~; *(glori)o(sę)* aa~; [2b] *su(o)* cc~; *(cruo)re* GG~; [3a] *(lę)ta(tur)* aa~; *cę(li)* cc~; *(conspica)tur* GG~; [3b] *quon(dam)* aa(G); *(su)gen(das)* cc~; *(mamil)las* GG~; [4a] *(ange)lis* aa~; *ma(ter)* aa~; [5a] *cę(lis)* dd~; *(vir)go* dd~; [5b] *(ho)mi(num)* ee~; *(spiritu)um* dd~; [6a] *(plebicu)la* G; *pi(is)* a; *(concele)brat* aa~; [6b] *(e)the(ra)* bb~; [7a] *(prophe)ta(rum)* dd~; [7b] *(utri)us(que)* dd~; *(virgi)na(lem)* dd~; [8a] *cunc(ta)* dd~; [8b] *(mani)fe(stat)* dd~; [9] *(es)se* bb~.

27. *Felix valde*

SOURCES

Rn 1343 fol. 81v [fragment]

ITALIAN CONCORDANCES

Bu 2748 (pp. 178–79); MOd 7 (172r–172v); Tn 18 (129v–130r); Tn 20 (179); VEcap 107 (102v–103r); VO 39 (57v–58r).

REFERENCES

AH 34:84; Brunner, "The Sequences of Verona 107," 1:145–47, 2:43; Damilano, "Sequenze," 19; Hughes, *Sequelae,* 70.

TEXT COMMENTARY

Felix valde, for the Assumption of the Virgin Mary, is a splendid text. It is set to "Metensis minor," the same melody as *Stans a longe* (no. 37), and the skill with which it is set is reminiscent of that piece. The central section [3a–5b] moves from the Annunciation to the Nativity to the Assumption directly and elegantly. The text has consistent a-assonance at the ends of lines, and in [4] and [5] rhyme as well. The concordances are grouped in northern Italy, but the piece is also found in a Spanish troper from Huesca. For further discussion of text and melody, see Brunner, "The Sequences of Verona 107," 1:145–47. Since only a few lines of the piece are preserved in Rn 1343, and even these are partially damaged and text and music partially obliterated, the present edition is based on concordances, as well as on the Nonantolan readings of *Stans a longe,* which uses the same melody.

TEXT AND TRANSLATION

[1a] Felix valde
[2a] O Maria incorrupta puerpera
[2b] Tu merito vocaris mundi domina
[3a] Angeli dictis obedisti virgo pudica
[3b] Vernanti flore mox fuisti virgo praegnata
[4a] Illo progenito caeli clamaris regina
[4b] Ipso germinante revivescunt morticina
[5a] Hodie puella morte non es impedita

[5b] Licet temporali nece fores inretita
[6a] Te transeunte laetatur polorum fors beata
[6b] Te adiuvante possimus foveri saecla per cuncta
[7] Felix valde O Maria

*

[1] O Mary most blessed,
[2a] Young mother undefiled,
[2b] You are justly named Our Lady of the Universe.
[3a] As Virgin Pure, you obeyed the words of the angel,
[3b] And you at once became Virgin pregnant with the verdant flower!
[4a] At His birth you are called the Queen of Heaven,
[4b] For as He sprouts forth the dead are given life anew.
[5a] Today, O Maiden, you are not deterred by death,
[5b] Even though you should be ensnared by death in the world of time.
[6a] For the blessed host of the heavens rejoices as you cross over,
[6b] That, with your aid, we might be comforted in that world of eternity.
[7] O Mary most blessed!

DISTINCTIVE VARIANTS

See TEXT COMMENTARY, above.

MELODIC VARIANTS

None.

28. *Summa stirpe*

SOURCES

Rc 1741 fols. 112v–114r Seq<uentia>
Rn 1343 fols. 42v–43r Seq<uentia>
Bu 2824 fols. 79r–80v Seq<uentia>

ITALIAN CONCORDANCES

None.

REFERENCES

AH 10:20; 53:22; Brunner, "Catalogo," 264.

TEXT COMMENTARY

This text to the Virgin Mary, outside the three Nonantolan sources, is found in a few East-Frankish sources, including the mid-tenth-century trope and sequence collection from St. Alban in Mainz (Lbl 19768). Von den Steinen noted the borrowings from Notker's Marian pieces, particularly *Stirpe Maria*, but also from the Song of Songs, the liturgy, and Sedulius (*Notker der Dichter*, 1:560). The Old Testament references to Eve, Cain, and Aaron are obvious in their contrast or prefiguring of Mary's giving birth to a new age. Although likely an East-Frankish text, the a-assonance at the ends of lines is a West-Frankish trait.

TEXT AND TRANSLATION

[1a] Summa stirpe genita virgo maria regum sanctorum filiola
[1b] Hodie rosa de spinis acutis evę orta est mollissima
[2a] Quę stipitem vetustę noxę flore gratię obumbrabat
[2b] Hanc venturam signaverant secli recentis exordia
[3a] Nam virgo extiterat arida Ante cain quam polluisset eandem humore fraterni sanguinis libera livoris flamma nec calens libidinis macula
[3b] Te viri et feminę pręducant Castitatem sequentes cęli reginam seu chorus sub lege principum vel novorum stegma patrum inter quos tu rutilas maxima
[4a] Te sicca virgula aaron monstrat sitibundo cortice trudens gemmulas
[4b] Sic casto corpore filium gigens protulisti cęlis ac terris germina
[5a] Hierusalem filia tu genitrix dei simplicibus columbarum oculis splendes nitida
[5b] Sola exemplo sine nec prius similem visa es nec habere sequentem alma maria
[6a] Quam frequentes celebrant angeli in tuo natali hunc diem sollemnem stella lucida
[6b] Nos gregatos fragiles homines sub tua viscera iugiter tuere pia maria

*

[1a] Virgin Mary, daughter of holy kings, born of the most noble lineage,
[1b] Today the rose most tender is born from the sharp thorns of Eve,
[2a] For Eve cast the lineage of the flower of grace into shadow,
[2b] But now the advent of the new age had heralded her coming.
[3a] For the Virgin had stood there barren—since Cain had polluted that same lineage with his shedding of his brother's blood—freed from the flame of envy, not burning with the grave flaw of desire.
[3b] You men and women proclaim—following the chaste Queen of Heaven—and the chorus of those foremost under the law, or the garland of new fathers, among whom you shine forth most brightly. (read *stemma*)
[4a] You the barren rod of Aaron prefigures, by sprouting little buds from its thirsting bark.
[4b] And thus from your chaste body giving birth to a Son you brought forth shoots before the heavens and earth.

[5a] O Daughter of Jerusalem, You, Mother of God, shine in brilliance before the innocent eyes of doves.

[5b] Alone without exemplar and without precedent, you are here, and there is none to follow you, nurturing Mary.

[6a] How ceaselessly the angels celebrate this solemn day of your birth, O brilliant Star,

[6b] So protect us, frail people gathered together under your heart, O loving Mary.

DISTINCTIVE VARIANTS

Rn 1343 [4a] *gemmula* for *gemmulas*. **Bu 2824** [3b] *tegma* for *stegma*; [4a] *gemula* for *gemmulas*.

MELODIC VARIANTS

Rn 1343 [2a] *(gra)ti(ę)* ED; [2b] *(re)cen(tis)* E(D); [3a] *(pol)lu(isset)* F; (li)vo(ris) GG~; *flam(ma)* DD(C); [3b] *(sequen)tes* F; *seu* F'F; *steg(ma)* GG~; [4a] *mon(strat)* DD~; [4b] *gi(gens)* DD~; [5a] *fi)lia* E'D; [5b] *si(ne)* FF~; [6a] *(sol)lem(nem)* FF(E). **Bu 2824** [2a] *(gra)ti(ę)* ED; [2b] *(re)cen(tis)* E(D); [3a] *(pol)lu(isset)* F; (li)vo(ris) GG~; *flam(ma)* DD(C); *(libidi)nis* DD~; [3b] *(femi)nę* DD~; *(sequen)tes* F; *seu* F'F; *le(ge)* a(G); [5a] *dei* G'F.

29. Alma fulgens crux praeclara

SOURCES

Rc 1741 fols. 114r–115r Seq\<uentia\> In exal\<tatione\> S\<anctae\> ✣ \<crucis\>

Rn 1343 fols. 48r–48v Seq\<uentia\> de S\<ancta\> cruce

Bu 2824 fols. 97v–98v Seq\<uentia\> In exal\<tatione\> s\<anctae\> ✣ \<crucis\>

ITALIAN CONCORDANCES

Bu 2748 (pp. 146–48); BV 34 (165v); BV 35 (99v); BV 38 (77r–77v): BV 39 (71v–72r); BV 40 (53v–54r); Cb 74 (98v); MCa 318 (p. 273*); PAc 47 (214r–214v); PCsa 65 (236r); PS 121 (69r); Ra 123 (225r–225v); VCd 161 (142r); VCd 162 (199r); VO 39 (47v–48r).

REFERENCES

AH 37:25; Brunner, "The Sequences of Verona 107," 1:185–88; Brunner, "Catalogo," 212.

TEXT COMMENTARY

This piece discussed in the introduction.

TEXT AND TRANSLATION

[1a] Alma fulgens crux pręclara splendidior cunctis gloriosa

[1b] Desiderabilis atque dilecta membrorum Christi es adornata

[2a] Tu sola fuisti digna nobilis triumphare

[2b] Ecce enim es exaltata super omnia ligna cedrorum conlaudanda

[3a] Catenę infernorum per te sunt destructę animę sanctorum sunt absolutę

[3b] Tartarea legio est alligata per tuum sanctum signum manus armata

[4] Libera nos semper crux gloriosa

*

[1a] Nurturing, illustrious, magnificent cross, glorious and more splendid than all things,

[1b] Longed for and beloved, with Christ's limbs you were adorned.

[2a] You alone, noble one, were worthy to triumph.

[2b] Behold, for you were elevated above all the cedars, worthy of praising.

[3a] The chains of Hell through you were destroyed, the souls of the holy were redeemed.

[3b] The infernal troop, the armed host, was fettered through your blessed sign.

[4] Free us always, glorious cross!

DISTINCTIVE VARIANTS

Bu 2824 later addition, twelfth century, in northern Italian notation.

MELODIC VARIANTS

Rn 1343 [1a] *(splendi)di(or)* cba; *glo(riosa)* aG; [1b] *dilecta* bb~aG'abaG'G; *a(dornata)* aG; [2a] *(fui)sti* bb~aG; *(nobi)lis* dd~cb …; *(trium)pha(re)* Gaa~G; [2b] *(ex)al(tata)* bb~aG; *con(lau)dan(do)* aG'Gaa~G; [3a] *(in)fer(norum)* bb~aG; *(de)struc(tę)* dd~cb; *(a)nimę sancto(rum)* G'a'c(b)'baG; [3b] *(le)gi(o)* bb~aG; *(alli)ga(ta)* dcb; *sanctum* c(b)'bb~aG; *ma(nus)* aG; [4] *(glori)o(sa)* Gaa~G. **Bu 2824** [1a] *glo(riosa)* aG; [1b] *dilecta* b~aG'abaG'G; *a(dornata)* aG; [2a] *(nobi)lis* dd~cb abaa~G; *(trium)pha(re)* Gaa~G; [2b] *(ex)al(tata)* bb~aG; *con(lau)dan(do)* aG'Gaa~G; [3a] *(in)fer(norum)* bb~aG; *(des)truc(tę)* dd~cb; *(a)nimę sancto(rum)* G'a'c(b)'babaG; [3b] *(le)gi(o)* bb~aG; *(alli)ga(ta)* dd~cb; *tuum* G'a; *ma(nus)* aG; [4] *(glori)o(sa)* Gaa~G.

30. Summi regis

SOURCES

Rc 1741 fols. 116r–117v Seq\<uentia\>
Rn 1343 fols. 43v–44v Seq\<uentia\>
Bu 2824 fols. 82r–83v Seq\<uentia\>

ITALIAN CONCORDANCES

Bu 2748 (pp. 180–83); BV 34 (169v–170v); BV 35 (102r–102v); BV 38 (132v–133r); BV 39 (164r–164v); BV 40 (126r–127r); IV 60 (116v–117r); MCa 318 (p. 284*); MOd 7 (174v–175r); PAc 47 (215r–216v); PAs 697 (59v–60r); Pn 1669 (25r–26r); PCsa 65 (243v); PS 121

(69v–70v); Ra 123 (252v–253r); Tn 18 (133r–133v); VCd 146 (111r–111v); VCd 161 (129v–130r); VCd 162 (192v–193v); VEcap 107 (106v–107r); VO 39 (49r–49v).

References

AH 53:312; Brunner, "The Sequences of Verona 107," 2:47; Brunner, "Catalogo," 264; Drinkwelder, *Sequentiar*, 87; von den Steinen, *Notker der Dichter*, 1:338–42.

Text Commentary

This text for St. Michael was attributed to Alcuin in an eleventh-century addition to a manuscript from Trier. Von den Steinen discussed the text in some detail and dispels any notion that it could have been written in Charlemagne's time when Alcuin was at his court, i.e., 801–4 (*Notker der Dichter*, 1:338–42). Rather it seems to be the work of a tenth-century German poet outside the St. Gall orbit. The language is simple and unadorned, yet the diction elevated. Italian concordances are strong and fairly stable in their transmission of text and melody.

Text and Translation

[1a] Summi regis archangele michahel
[1b] Intende quęsumus nostris vocibus
[2a] Te namque profitemur esse supernorum principem civium
[2b] Tu deum obsecra pro nobis ut mittat auxilium miseris
[3a] Principalis est potestas a domino tibi data peccantes salvificare animas
[3b] Idem tenes perpetuo principatum paradisi omnes civis te honorant superi
[4a] Tu in templo dei turibulum aureum visus es habuisse manibus
[4b] Inde scandens vapor aromatum plurimus pervenit ante conspectum dei
[5a] Quando cum dracone magnum perfecisti pręlium faucibus illius animas abstraxisti plurimas
[5b] Hinc maximum agebatur in cęlo silentium milia milium dicebant salus regi domino
[6a] Audi nos michahęl angele summe huc parum descende de poli sede nobis ferendo opem domini atque levamen indulgentię
[6b] Tu nostros gabrihel hostes prosterne tu raphahel egris affer medelam morbos absterge noxas minue nosque fac interesse gaudiis
[7] Beatorum

*

[1a] O archangel of the highest King! Michael!
[1b] We beg you, turn your ears to our voices;
[2a] We declare you to be the prince of heavenly citizens.
[2b] Entreat God on our behalf, that He might send aid to the wretched.
[3a] The foremost power to rescue souls in sin has been granted to you by the Lord.
[3b] You hold forever that same dominion of Paradise; all heavenly citizens give honor to you.
[4a] In God's temple you are seen to hold the golden censer in your hands;
[4b] Hence the rising incense rich in fragrance ascends before the face of God
[5a] When you waged the mighty battle with the dragon, you snatched away many souls from his jaws.
[5b] Then a profound silence took place in Heaven; thousands upon thousands began to cry: "Salvation to the King, our Lord!"
[6a] O Michael, highest of angels, hear us! Descend a moment from your celestial dwelling to bring us the succor of the Lord and the solace of His love,
[6b] O Gabriel, disperse our enemies; O Raphael, bring healing to the sick, atone for diseases, limit harm, and lead us to participate in the joys
[7] Of the blessed.

Distinctive Variants

None.

Melodic Variants

Rn 1343 [1a] *(archange)le* GG~; [1b] *(nos)tris* GG~; [2a] *es(se)* aa~; *(princi)pem* GG~; [2b] *no(bis)* aa~; *(auxili)um* GG~; [3] *(pec)can(tes)* GG(F); [5a] *mag(num)* aa~; [6a] *(fe)ren(do)* bc(b); *(le)va(men)* a; [6b] *(pro)ster(ne)* cc~b; *(me)de(lam)* cc~b; *(ab)ster(ge)* bc(b); *(mi)nu(e)* G; *(bea)to(rum)* a. **Bu 2824** [1b] *(nos)tris* GG~; [3b] *(pec)can(tes)* GG~; [4a] *tem(plo)* a; [4b] *scan(dens)* a; *(con)spec(tum)* GG~; [6b] *(pro)ster(ne)* cc~b; *(me)de(lam)* cc~b; *(bea)to(rum)* aa~G.

31. *Clare sanctorum senatus*

Sources

Rc 1741 fols. 118r–119r Seq\<uentia\>
Rn 1343 fols. 44v–45r Seq\<uentia\>
Bu 2824 fols. 84r–85r Seq\<uentia\>

Italian Concordances

Bu 2748 (pp. 191–93); BV 34 (235v–236r); BV 35 (149v); BV 38 (133v–134r): BV 39 (166v–167r); BV 40 (127v–128r); MCa 318 (p. 284*); MOd 7 (162r–163r); Mza 76 (145r–145v); Mza 77 (162v–163r); PAc 47 (199r–199v); PAs 697 (61r); PCsa 65 (246r); PS 121 (66v–67r and 75*); Ra 123 (240r–240v and 253v*); Tn 18 (142r–142v); VCd 146 (114r); VCd 161 (132r); VCd 162 (197r); VEcap 107 (113r–113v); VO 39 (37r–38v).

References

AH 53:367; Brunner, "The Sequences of Verona 107," 2:58; Brunner, "Catalogo," 221; Crocker, *Early*

Medieval Sequence, 314–30; Drinkwelder, Sequentiar, 59; de Goede, Utrecht Prosarium, 120; Hiley, Western Plainchant, 416–17, 440–41; Hughes, Sequelae, 60; Schubiger, Sängerschule, 33; von den Steinen, Notker der Dichter, 1:355–59, 578–79, 2:80.

Text Commentary

Notker's text to the Holy Apostles invokes the apostles by name as if in a roll call in the Roman Senate. Peter and Paul are each given a phrase, while Matthew is given a full couplet, but the rest are recited in rapid succession. Despite the straightforward presentation, Notker shows great skill in his rhetorical presentation and in joining it with a melodic ductus that seems closer to the Alleluia than most of the other melodies that Notker set. Crocker offers an extended and brilliant analysis of both text and music (*Early Medieval Sequence*, 314–21). His division of the text into couplets differs slightly from the division indicated in the Nonantolan manuscripts, which continues [7b] through *iudices* (Crocker begins an irregular concluding couplet with *se patres*).

Text and Translation

[1] Clare sanctorum senatus apostolorum princeps orbis terrarum rectorque regnorum
[2a] Aecclesiarum mores et vitam moderare
[2b] Quę per doctrinam tuam fideles sunt ubique
[3a] Antiochus et romus concedunt tibi petre regni solium
[3b] Tirannidis tu paule alexandria invasisti greciam
[4a] Ethiopes orridos mathee agnelli vellere
[4b] Qui maculas nesciant aliquas vestisti candido
[5] Thomas bartholomee
[6a] Iohannes philippe simon iacobique pariles
[6b] Andreas taddee dei bellatores incliti
[7a] En vos occidens et oriens
[7b] Immo teres mundi circulus se patres habere gaudet et expectat iudices
[8] Et idcirco mundus omnis laudes vobis et honores satis debitas supplex impendit

*

[1] Resplendent senate of holy apostles, you foremost of earthly spheres and guide of all realms,
[2a] Govern the customs and life of the churches,
[2b] Which, through your teaching, stand faithful at every hand.
[3a] To you, O Peter, Antioch and Rome cede the throne of the kingdom.
[3b] You, O Paul, have invaded the Alexandrian regime of Greece,
[4a] The rugged Ethiopians, O Matthew, you have clothed
[4b] With the white fleece of the lamb that knows no stains,
[5] Thomas, Bartholomew,
[6a] John, Philip, Simon, and the two Jameses,
[6b] Andrew and Thaddeus, God's glorious warriors,
[7a] Behold you, West and East,
[7b] Indeed, even the circular orbit of the world rejoices to hold you as fathers and expects you to be judges.
[8] And therefore the whole world in supplication offers you praise and honors due to the saints.

Distinctive Variants

Rn 1343 [4a] *agni* for *angelli*. **Bu 2824** [4a] *agni* for *angelli*.

Melodic Variants

Rn 1343 [1] *(ter)ra(rum)* cc~; *(Allelu)ia* cc~acdcbaa~G; [2a] *(Aecclesi)a(rum)* bb~; *vi(tam)* aa~; *(mode)ra(re)* aa~; [2b] *(doc)tri(nam)* bb~; *(u)bi(que)* aa~; [3a] *ro(mus)* bb~; *ti(bi)* dd~; *reg(ni)* c(b); [3b] *pau(le)* b(a); *(alexan)dri(a)* dd~; [4a] *agni* G'b; [6a] *(or)i(ens)* dd~; [6b] *gau(det)* d(c); [7] *om(nis)* d(c); *(ho)no(res)* ee~; *(im)pen(dit)* aa(G). **Bu 2824** [1] *sanc(torum)* a; *(Allelu)ia* cc~acdcbaa~G; [2a] *vi(tam)* aa~; [4a] *agni* G'b; [6b] *gau(det)* d(c); [7] *(im)pen(dit)* aa(G).

32. *Omnes sancti seraphin*

Sources

Rc 1741 fols. 119v–120v In N\<atale\> om\<n\>iu\<m\> s\<an\>c\<t\>or\<m\> Seq\<uentia\>
Rn 1343 fols. 45r–45v Seq\<uentia\>
Bu 2824 fols. 85r–86v Seq\<uentia\>

Italian Concordances

IV 60 (118r–118v); MCa 318 (p. 284*); MOd 7 (177); Mza 76 (141v–142r); Mza 77 (161v, conclusion 164); PAc 47 (218v–219v); PAs 697 (60); PCsa 65 (244r); PS 121 (72v–73r); Ra 123 (254v–255r); Rvat 10645 (78r–78v); Tn 18 (136r–136v); VCd 146 (112v); VCd 161 (130r–130v); VCd 162 (194v–195r); VCd 186 (186v–187r); VEcap 107 (108v–109v); VO 39 (50r).

References

AH 53:196; Brunner, "The Sequences of Verona 107," 2:82; Brunner, "Catalogo," 249; Crocker, *Early Medieval Sequence*, 366–69; Drinkwelder, *Sequentiar*, 53; de Goede, *Utrecht Prosarium*, 20; Moberg, *Schwedishen Sequenzen*, n. 28; Schubiger, *Sängerschule*, 31; von den Steinen, *Notker der Dichter*, 1:328–32, 573–74, 2:78.

Text Commentary

In his piece for All Saints, Notker invokes important members of the Church in a kind of roll call. Crocker called it Notker's "one-time exercise . . . in

West-Frankish Latinity" (*Early Medieval Sequence*, 366). Although such straightforward diction is uncharacteristic of Notker, as Crocker points out, the overall design is indicative of Notker's skill, essentially dividing the text into two large sections [1–4b] and [5a–9], each invoking a portion of the celestial host.

TEXT AND TRANSLATION

[1] Omnes sancti seraphin cherubin throni quoque
[2] Dominationesque principatus potestates virtutes
[3a] Archangeli angeli vos decet laus et honores
[3b] Ordines noveni spirituum beatorum
[4a] Quos in dei laudibus firmavit caritas
[4b] Nos fragiles homines firmate precibus
[5a] Ut spiritales pravitates vestro iuvamine vincentes fortiter
[5b] Nunc et in ęvum vestris simus digni sollemniis interesse sacris
[6a] O quos dei gracia vincere terrea
[6b] Et angeli socios fecit esse polo
[7a] Vos patriarche prophete apostoli confessores martires monachi virgines
[7b] Ed viduarum sanctarum omniumque placentium populus supremo domino
[8a] Nos adiutorium
[8b] Nunc et perhenniter
[9] Foveat protegat ut vestrum in die poscimus gaudiorum vestrorum

*

[1] All you holy seraphim, cherubim, thrones, too,
[2] As well as dominations, principalities, powers, virtues,
[3a] Archangels, angels! Praise and honor befit you,
[3b] You nine-fold order of blessed spirits.
[4a] You whom charity has made strong in the praise of God,
[4b] Strengthen us frail humans through your prayers,
[5a] So that valiantly conquering our spiritual depravities,
[5b] Now and forever, we may be worthy to partake in your sacred rites of worship.
[6a] You whom God's grace made able to conquer worldly things
[6b] And to become companions to the angels in Heaven, (read *angelis*)
[7a] You patriarchs, prophets, apostles, confessors, martyrs, monks, virgins,
[7b] And the company of holy widows, and of all those pleasing to God on high:
[8a] May your assistance
[8b] Now and always
[9] Sustain and protect us as your own, this we pray in this day of your joyful celebration.

DISTINCTIVE VARIANTS

Rn 1343 *terreat* for *terrea*. There are a number of substantial variants among the Italian sources, particularly with respect to the pitch level of the notation, and in [2], with its extra syllable in the first half. See Brunner, "The Sequences of Verona 107," 2:105–6.

MELODIC VARIANTS

Rn 1343 [1] *(se)ra(phin)* a; *(Alle)lu(ia)* . . . cac(b); [2] *(virtu)tes* a; [3a] *(an)ge(li)* cc~; *(ho)no(res)* cc~; [3b] *(no)ve(ni)* cc~; *(spiritu)um* a; *(bea)to(rum)* cc~; [4a] *(laudi)bus* GG~; [4b] *Nos* a; [5a] *(iuvami)ne* GG~; [6b] *Et* Fa; [7a] *(confesso)res* GG~; *(marti)res* GG~; [7b] *(omni)um(que)* GG~; *(popu)lus* GG~; [9] *ves(trum)* FF~; *(ves)tro(rum)* FF~. **Bu 2824** [1] *(Alle)lu(ia)* . . . cac(b); [4a] *(an)ge(li)* cc~; *laus* a; [4b] *(spiritu)um* a; *(bea)to(rum)* cc~; [4a] *(laudi)bus* GG~; [4b] *nos* a; [5a] *(iuvami)ne* GG~; [6b] *Et* Fa; [6a] *(marti)res* GG~; [7b] *(omni)um(que)* GG~; *(popu)lus* GG~; [9] *ves(trum)* FF~; *(ves)tro(rum)* FF~.

33. *Sacerdotem Christi Martinum*

SOURCES

Rc 1741 fols. 121r–122v Seq<uentia>
Rn 1343 fols. 46r–47r Seq<uentia>
Bu 2824 fols. 87r–89r Seq<uentia>

ITALIAN CONCORDANCES

Bu 2748 (pp. 187–91); MOd 7 (179r–180r); Mza 76 (142v–143v); Mza 77 (164–64v; concludes 167r); PAs 697 (60v); PCsa 65 (244v); Ra 123 (257r–257v); Rc 3830 (57v–58v); Rvat 10645 (78v–79v); SEz 2 (9v–11r); VCd 146 (112v–113r); VCd 161 (130v–131r); VCd 162 (195r–196r); VEcap 107 (110r–111r).

REFERENCES

AH 53:294; Brunner, "The Sequences of Verona 107," 2:52; Brunner, "Catalogo," 259; Drinkwelder, *Sequentiar*, 55; de Goede, *Utrecht Prosarium*, 100; Hughes, *Sequelae*, 27; Moberg, *Schwedishen Sequenzen*, n. 28; Schubiger, *Sängerschule*, 32; von den Steinen, *Notker der Dichter*, 1:435–38, 602–3, 2:125.

TEXT COMMENTARY

The text for St. Martin of Tours was part of the St. Gall canon from the time of the earliest surviving manuscripts, suggesting the text might be Notker's (see *AH* 53:294). Von den Steinen's careful textual analysis ruled this out, attributing it rather to a poet active at St. Gall in the second quarter of the tenth century (*Notker der Dichter*, 1:438). The text touches upon aspects of Martin's life; first, mentioning places where he lived or influenced [2–5], then, listing healings and miracles attributed to him [6–8]. The main sources of this information is Sulpicius Severus's *Vita sancti Martini* and *Dialogi,* edited by Karl Felix von Halm, *Corpus scriptorum ecclesiasticorum latinorum* 1 (Vindobonae, 1866). For specific references see *Notker der Dichter,* 1:602–3.

TEXT AND TRANSLATION

[1a] Sacerdotem christi martinum cuncta per orbem canat ęcclesia pacis catholicę
[1b] Atque illius nomen omnis hereticus fugiat pallidus
[2a] Pannonia lętetur genitrix talis filii
[2b] Italia exultet alitrix tanti iuvenis
[3a] Et gallię trina divisio sacro certet litigio cuius esse debeat pręsul
[3b] Sed pariter habere se patrem omnes gaudeant turoni soli eius corpus foveant
[4a] Huic francorum atque germanię plebs omnis plaudat
[4b] Quibus videndum invexit dominum in sua veste
[5a] Hic celebris est egypti patribus grecię quoque cunctis sapientibus
[5b] Qui impares se martini meritis sentiunt atque eius medicamini
[6a] Nam febres sedat demonesque fugat paralitica membra glutinat
[6b] Et mortuorum sua prece trium reddit corpora vitę pristinę
[7a] Hic ritus sacrilegos destruit et ad christi gloriam dat ignibus idola
[7b] Hic nudis misteria brachiis conficiens pręditus est cęlesti lumine
[8a] Hic oculis ac manibus in cęlum et totis viribus suspensus terrena cuncta respuit
[8b] Eius ori numquam christus abfuit sive iustitia vel quicquid ad veram vitam pertinet
[9a] Igitur te cuncti poscimus o martine ut qui multa mira hic ostendisti
[9b] Etiam de cęlo gratiam christi nobis supplicatu tuo semper infundas

*

[1a] Let the whole Church at universal peace in every realm sing of the priest of Christ, of Martin!
[1b] Yet let every pallid heretic flee in fright from the name of this one!
[2a] Pannonia, his motherland, should celebrate a son such as this,
[2b] And Italy, who nursed him, should exult at such a youth;
[3a] And let Gaul, divided by three, contend in sacred dispute concerning whose bishop he should be;
[3b] Yet, while the citizens of Tours alone cherish his body, let people the world over rejoice to consider him their father.
[4a] All the peoples of France and Germany should applaud him,
[4b] Those for whom he wrapped the Lord in his own cloak, that He might appear.
[5a] He is known among the Egyptian Fathers, as well as among all the wise men of Greece,
[5b] Who recognize that they are cannot equal Martin in acts of service and cures:
[6a] For he calmed fevers, scattered demons, and restored withered limbs to use,
[6b] And through his prayer he brought again the bodies of three dead souls to life.
[7a] He destroyed those rites that profaned the sacred, and to the glory of Christ put fire to idols.
[7b] When celebrating the sacred mysteries with unclothed arms he was wrapped in a celestial light.
[8a] With eyes and hands, indeed with all his strength, raised to Heaven, he renounced all things of earth.
[8b] Christ, justice, or that which pertains to the life of truth, were never absent from his voice.
[9a] Thus to you, O Martin, we all pray, that you, who revealed many miracles on earth:
[9b] Even in Heaven through your supplication might continually fill us with the grace of Christ.

DISTINCTIVE VARIANTS

Rn 1343 [6b] *pares* for *Impares.* There are some unusual variants with respect to the final of individual phrases. For example, The Nonantolan sources end [6] on a and move back to D. In MOd 7 [6]–[8] remain on a; in PCsa 65 [8] is on a. Phrase 8 is the most unstable among the Italian concordances. See Brunner, "The Sequences of Verona 107," 2:111.

MELODIC VARIANTS

Rn 1343 [1a] *cunc(ta)* b(a); *or(bem)* aa~; *Al(lelu)ia* CF(G)' ... FEGFEDEDGGFD; [1b] *no(men)* aa~; *(here)ti(cus)* EE~; *(pal)li(dus)* FF~; [2a] *(Panno)ni(a)* FE; [2b] *I(ta)li(a)* a' FE; [3a] *cu(ius)* aa~; [3b] *(pa)ri(ter)* bb~; [4a] *(germa)nię* cb'bb~; [4b] *(do)mi(num)* cb; [5a] *quo(que)* aa~; [5b] *pares* G'E; *(meri)tis* aa~; *at(que)* aa~; [6a] *se(dat)* cc~; *fu(gat)* aa~; *mem(bra)* b(a); [6b] *(mortu)o(rum)* dd~; *tri(um)* aa~; *(vi)tę* aa~; [7a] *ri(tus)* FF~; *(sacrile)gos* EE~; *chris)ti* DD~; [7b] *est* EE~; [8a] *(cę)lum* GG~; *(sus)pen(sus)* DD(C); *(cunc)ta* DD~; [8b] *chris(tus)* EE~; *(iustiti)a* GG~; *quic(quid)* DD~; [9a] *cunc(ti)* d(c); *mi(ra)* GG~; *(osten)di(sti)* GG~; [9b] *no(bis)* aa~; *(in)fun(das)* G(F). **Bu 2824** [1a] *cunc(ta)* b(a); *per* aa~; *Al(lelu)ia* CF(G)' ... FEGFECEGGFD; [1b] *no(men)* aa~; *(pal)li(dus)* FF~; [2a] *(Panno)ni(a)* FE; [2b] *I(ta)li(a)* a' FE; [3a] *cu(ius)* aa~; [4a] *(germa)niae* cb'bb~; [5a] *quo(que)* aa~; [5b] *(meri)tis* aa~; *at(que)* aa~; [6a] *se(dat)* cc~; *fu(gat)* aa~; *mem(bra)* b(a); [6b] *tri(um)* aa~; *(vi)tę* aa~; [7a] *ri(tus)* FF~; *(sacrile)gos* EE~; *(chris)ti* DD~;

[7b] *(confici)ens* DD~; *est* EE~; [8a] *(ce)lum* GG~; *(sus)pen(sus)* DD(C); *(cunc)ta* DD~; [8b] *chris(tus)* EE~; *(iustiti)a* GG~; *quic(quid)* DD~; *(vi)tam* DD~; [9a] *cunc(ti)* d(c); *mira* GG~'EE~; *(osten)di(sti)* GG~; [9b] *no(bis)* aa~; *(in)fun(das)* G(F).

34. Deus in tua virtute

Sources

Rc 1741 fols. 124r–125r Seq<uentia>
Rn 1343 fols. 47v–48r Seq<uentia>
Bu 2824 fols. 90r–91v Seq<uentia>

Italian Concordances

Bu 2748 (pp. 215–17); BV 39 (178v–179r); BV 40 (141v–142r); MOd 7 (182r–182v); PAc 47 (222r–223r); PAs 697 (60bis r–60bis v); Ra 123 (259r–259v); Rvat 10645 (79v, incomplete); SEz 2 (11v–12r); VEcap 107 (117v–118r).

References

AH 53:210; Brunner, "The Sequences of Verona 107," 2:56; Brunner, "Catalogo," 224; de Goede, *Utrecht Prosarium*, 107; von den Steinen, *Notker der Dichter*, 1:431–33, 601, 2:131.

Text Commentary

This is a ninth-century text probably by a contemporary of Notker's at St. Gall, whom von den Steinen calls the "Andreasdichter." The text is based on a few references to St. Andrew's life as a fisherman turned apostle and martyr (he is thought to have been crucified at Patras). For specific references, see von den Steinen (*Notker der Dichter*, 1:601).

Text and Translation

[1] Deus in tua virtute sanctus andreas gaudet et lętatur eandem comitatus
[2a] Piscatio nati tui ipse primus factus piscator populorum Mirmidones idolatras diu fluctivagos recti cępit fidei
[2b] Is legibus achaiam tuis deus victor illius subiugavit Et tropheum christi tui fixit ibi bonum se ostentans militem
[3a] Miraculis virtutibus doctrinis quacumque quęsita spolia tibi o rex attulit
[3b] Atque suo cruore triumphi inscripsit titulos tui regum domine
[4a] Istum crucis socium et regni credimus
[4b] Christi filii tui atque fraterculum
[5a] Nos igitur peccatis nostris gravati te deus poscimus
[5b] Ut illius quod tua semper sectatus pręcepta tibi placet
[6] Nos intercessione tuearis in ęternum

*

[1] God, Holy Andrew rejoices in Your goodness, which he follows gladly.
[2a] Your Son's fishing: he was made the first fisherman of people; in the net of the proper faith he seized the heathen Myrmidons long since thrown around by the waves.
[2b] Victorious he brought the Greek under Your laws, O God, and proving himself to be a good soldier he firmly fixed the triumphal sign of Christ, Your Son.
[3a] All the spoils obtained through miracles, virtues, teachings, he has brought to You, O King.
[3b] And with his own blood he has written the title of Your triumph, O Lord of kings.
[4a] We believe that he is sharing the cross and the kingdom,
[4b] And that he is a little brother of Christ, your Son.
[5a] Burdened by our sins, we therefore pray to You, O God,
[5b] That for his sake, he who always followed your commands,
[6] You might deign to protect us in eternity.

Distinctive Variants

Rn 1343 [2b] *His* for *Is*. **Bu 2824** [2b] *His* for *Is*.

Melodic Variants

Rn 1343 [1] *(lę)ta(tur)* aa~; *(comi)ta(tus)* aa~; *(Allelu)ia* cdcbaa~G . . . aa~G; [2a] *(pis)ca(tor)* aa~; *(ce)pit* dd~; [2b] *de(us)* dd~; *(il)li(us)* aa~; *(osten)tans* dd~; [3a] *rex* dd~; *tri(umphi)* d; *(re)gum* dd~; [5a] *(nos)tris* dd~; [5b] *(sem)per* dd~; *(pla)cet* G; [6] *(ę)ter(num)* F(E). **Bu 2824** [1] *(lę)ta(tur)* aa~; *(comi)ta(tus)* aa~; *(Allelu)ia* cdcbaa~G . . . aa~G; [2a] *(pis)ca(tor)* aa~; *(ce)pit* dd~; [2b] *de(us)* dd~; *(il)li(us)* aa~; *(osten)tans* dd~; [3a] *rex* dd~; *tri(umphi)* d; *(re)gum* dd~; [5a] *(nos)tris* dd~; [5b] *(sem)per* dd~; *(pla)cet* G; [6] *(ę)ter(num)* F(E).

35. Ad templi huius limina

Sources

Rc 1741 fols. 125v–127r In dedic<atione> eccl<esi>e Seq<uentia>
Rn 1343 fols. 32r–32v Seq<uentia> In dedicatione te<m>pli

Italian Concordances

Bu 2748 (pp. 148–52); BV 35 (105v–106v); BV 38 (87r–87v): BV 39 (83v–84v); BV 40 (65r–66r); IV 60 (89v–90r); MCa 318 (p. 284*); MOd 7 (133r–133v); Mza 77 (169r–169v, conclusion 165r); PAc 47 (170v–171v); PCsa 65 (248v); PS 121 (77v–78v); Tn 18 (138v–139r);

Tn 20 (179v–180r); VEcap 107 (117v–118r); VO 39 (41v–42r).

References

AH 7:243; 53:402; Brunner, "The Sequences of Verona 107," 1:115–19, 2:66; Brunner, "Catalogo," 208; Crocker, "Repertoire," 2:10; Damilano, "Sequenze," 19; Hughes, *Sequelae*, 25.

Text Commentary

This text, for the Dedication of the Church, exits in two related versions that share the same incipit, one being an arrangement of the other. For a discussion of some of the problems associated with these texts, see Brunner, "The Sequences of Verona 107," 1:116. An interesting aspect of the two Nonantolan sources is that the melody stays with G final through phrase [6] and then moves to a final. The other two Nonantolan settings of "Eia turma" (i.e., *Haec sunt sacra festa*, no. 6, and *Eia recolamus*, no. 14) are more typical in that use G final through [5], then shift to d final from [6] on. Maintaining G final in Rc 1741 produces a direct leap of a tritone in both [6a] and [6b].

Text and Translation

[1]   Ad templi huius limina dedicata
[2a] Gaudiorum laudes ovans plebs devota persultat
[2b] Hodierna die quia adest festa annua
[3a] Fundata enim est domus ista supra montium cacumina
[3b] Et exaltata est supra omnes colles structura deifica
[4a] Nam hęc est magna hierusalem civitas scilicet illa superna
[4b] Ex auro mundo circumtectis gemmis ac rutilans muris per ampla
[5a] Hęc est illa cęlestis aula angelorum patria
[5b] Aecclesia firma quę petra eternaque regia
[6a] Dicta est quę pacis visio urbs hierusalem celsa
[6b] Ex vivis quę petris struitur beatorum animae
[7a] Qua deus quoque summus rex super omnes unus celsiora in sede presidet illa
[7b] Sunt maiestates coram virtutes atque prestant felicique quiete munera plena
[8a] Indefessa voce laudes persultant agmina
[8b] Gloria et regnum illi depromunt per secla
[9a] Veneranda est ergo aula noscitura ubi preesse numina talia
[9b] Adoranda est persona summa imperans cęlum et terram cunctaque maria
[10a] Sol luna et stellę illi dant gloriam
[10b] Cuncta creatura quę reptat per arva
[11a] Nosque summam ac pręcelsam flagitemus nunc personam
[11b] Paradisi ianuam reseret nobis fulgidam
[12] Merentem vitam eternam

*

[1]   At the consecrated door of this sacred place
[2a] The faithful people leap about singing praises of joy,
[2b] For today the annual feast is here.
[3a] This house is founded above the mountain peaks,
[3b] And this sacred construction is elevated above all the hills.
[4a] And it is called the great Jerusalem, that heavenly city,
[4b] Large and glittering with pure gold and gems around the walls.
[5a] This is the heavenly palace, home of the angels,
[5b] This is the Church, the firm rock and the eternal kingdom.
[6a] It is called "the vision of peace," the heavenly city, Jerusalem.
[6b] It is built up from living stones of the souls of the saints.
[7a] There God, the highest King, presides alone on His heavenly throne above all.
[7b] In front of him stand the celestial powers and offer their gifts filled with holy peace.
[8a] With unwearied voices their troops sing praises,
[8b] They sing "Gloria" and "Regnum" forever.
[9a] Worthy of veneration is this hall where such divine powers are to be known.
[9b] Worthy of adoration is the highest Person who reigns over heaven and earth, and all seas.
[10a] The sun, the moon, and the stars glorify Him,
[10b] And all creatures that crawl on the ground.
[11a] Now let us beseech the highest and the divine Person,
[11b] That he may open to us the shining door of paradise,
[12] Which brings the reward of life eternal.

Distinctive Variants

Rn 1343 [2b] *dies* for *die*; [6a] *animas* for *animę*; [10a] *stellas* for *stellę*; [10b] *reptant* for *reptat*; [11b] *fulgida* for *fulgidam*; [12] *Ferentem* for *merentem*.

Melodic Variants

Rn 1343 [2b] *die* F'FG; [3a] *do(mus)* a; *(su)pra* b; [3b] *col(les)* c(b); *(structu)ra* cc~b; [4b] *mun(do)* FF(E); *rutilans* b'a'G; *(mu)ris* GG~; [5a] *il(la)* F(E); *(an)gelorum* ab'a'GG~; [5b] *(e)ter(naque)* ab; *(re)gi(a)* G; [6a] *(hie)ru(salem)* ab; [6b] *(be)atorum* ab'aG'GG~; [7a] *deus* c'ba; *u(nus)* dd~; *in* c(b); *(persi)det* aa~; [7b] *pre(stant)* dd~; [8a] *(vo)ce* GG~; *(persul)tant* aa~; [8b] *et* aa~; *reg(num)* GG~; *(pro)munt* aa~; [9a] *(nosci)tu(ra)* dd~; *(prees)se* c; *(numi)na* a; [9b] *(cunc)taque* cc~b'a; *(ma)ri(a)* a; [10b] *rep(tat)* cc~b; [11a] *(per)so(nam)* a; [11b] *(para)di(si)* GG~; *(ful)gi(da)* a; [12] *(vi)tam* bcdd~c.

36. Benedicta semper sancta

SOURCES

Rc 1741 fols. 127v–129r Seq<uentia>
Rn 1343 fols. 51r–51v Seq<uentia>
Bu 2824 fols. 91v–93v Seq<uentia> i<n> s<ancte> Trinitate

ITALIAN CONCORDANCES

Bu 2748 (pp. 217–19); BV 34 (213v–214v); BV 35 (136v–137r); BV 38 (119v–120v): BV 39 (136r–137r); BV 40 (106r–107r); MCa 318 (p. 284*); Mod7 (202r–203r); Mza 76 (161r–162r); Mza 77 (167r–167v, conclusion 162r–163r); PAc 47 (246r–246v); PAs 697 (64r–64v); Pn 1669 (133r–134v); PCsa 65 (247v–248r); PS 121 (52v–53v); Ra 123 (263v–264v); Rv 52 (160v–161v); Tn 18 (158v–159v); VCd 146 (113v–114r); VCd 161 (131v–132r); VCd 162 (196r–19v7r); VEcap 90 (77r–77v); VEcap 107 (96r–97r); VO 39 (37v).

REFERENCES

AH 7:108; 53:139; Brunner, "Catalogo," 216; Crocker, "Repertoire," 2:20; Drinkwelder, *Sequentiar,* 38; de Goede, *Utrecht Prosarium,* 44, Hughes, *Sequelae,* 28; Moberg, *Schwedishen Sequenzen,* n. 16a; Schubiger, *Sängerschule,* 23; von den Steinen, "Anfänge," 41:152–53; von den Steinen, *Notker der Dichter,* 2:134.

TEXT COMMENTARY

This text to the Holy Trinity is included in the late ninth-century source (VEcap 90). Von den Steinen ("Anfänge") points both to West-Frankish traits, in the predominance of a-assonance and the tendency toward the general ceremony, as well as to East-Frankish ones, in the focus on the theme of the Trinity. The sequence has broad distribution throughout Europe, but particularly strong in Italy and Germany; a determination of its origin, however, remains elusive.

TEXT AND TRANSLATION

[1]   Benedicta semper sancta sit trinitas deitas scilicet unitas coequalis gloria
[2a] Pater filius sanctus spiritus tria sunt nomina omnium et eadem substantia
[2b] Deus genitor deus genitus ab utroque sacer deus spiritusque dominus
[3]   Non tres tamen dii sunt deus verus unus est sic pater dominus filius spiritusque dominus
[4a] Proprietas in personis unitas est et in essentia
[4b] Maiestas par et potestas decus honor eque per omnia
[5a] Sidera maria continens arva simul et universa condita
[5b] Quam tremunt impia tartara colit quoque quem et habyssus infirma
[6a] Hinc omnis vox atque lingua fateantur hanc laude debita
[6b] Quam laudant sol atque luna dignitas adorat angelica
[7a] Et nos voce precelsa omnes modulemur organica cantica dulci melodia
[7b] Eia et eia nunc una simul iubilemus altithrono domino laudes in excelsis
[8a] O admiranda trinitas
[8b] O veneranda unitas
[9a] Per te sumus creati vera eternitas
[9b] Per te sumus redempti summa tu caritas
[10a] Populum cunctum tu protege salva libera eripe et emunda
[10b] Te adoramus omnipotens tibi canimus tibi laus et gloria

*

[1]   Blessed be the Sacred Trinity at all times, the Deity that is unity, coequal in glory.
[2a] Father, Son, and Holy Spirit: all three names are the same in substance.
[2b] God the creator, God the created and from both God the Holy Spirit and the Lord.
[3]   Yet they are not three gods: but one true God, as the Father and Lord, the Son, and the Spirit and Lord.
[4a] Their character is in their persons, and their unity in their essence;
[4b] Their majesty and power identical, their glory and honor in all things equal. (read *quem*)
[5a] Holding together the stars, the sea, with the earth and all things created,
[5b] The godless inhabitants of the underworld fear Him, and even the lowest abyss offers Him honor. (read *Quem tremunt*)
[6a] Therefore let every voice and tongue acknowledge the Trinity with worthy acclamation,
[6b] Which the sun and moon praise and is dignified by the angelic ranks.
[7a] And let us all as well at higher pitch unfold measured songs with sweet melody.
[7b] Let us all now in concert rejoice: Eia and Eia! Praises in the highest to the Lord enthroned on high!
[8a] O Trinity to be worshipped!
[8b] O Unity to be adored!
[9a] Through you we are created, O eternal reality!
[9b] Through you we are redeemed, O highest love!
[10a] Protect all your people. Save them, free them, deliver and purify them!
[10b] You, O omnipotent One! You we adore, to you we sing, to you be praise and glory.

DISTINCTIVE VARIANTS

Bu 2824 [2a] *et* omitted; [2b] *filius* for *deus*; [4a] *atque* for *eque*; [5b] *Contremunt* for *Quam fremunt*; [6a] *hunc* for *hanc*.

MELODIC VARIANTS

Rn 1343 [2b] *(u)tro(que)* a; [5b] *im(pia)* d; [9a] *(ve)ra* b. **Bu 2824** [2a] *(pa)ter* bb~; [2b] *(de)us*¹ bb~; *(de)us*² bb~; *filius* F'G'G; *que* GG~; [3] *(ta)men* bb~; *(ve)rus* bb~; *(spiritus)que* GG~; [4a] *(po)tes(tas)* bb~; *atque* cc'~a; [6a] *lin(gua)* b(a); [6b] *lu(na)* bb~; *(ado)rat* aa~; [9a] *(e)ter(nitas)* b(a); [9b] *(re)dempti sum(ma)* e(d)'d'd(c); [10a] *(cunc)tum* dd~; *(prote)ge* a; [10b] *(glo)ri(a)* ba.

37. Stans a longe

SOURCES

Rc 1741 fols. 131r–131v Dom<inica> xi Seq<uentia>
Rn 1343 fols. 50r Dom<inica> xi Seq<uentia>
Bu 2824 fols. 99r–99v Seq<uentia>

ITALIAN CONCORDANCES

BV 35 (158v); BV 38 (159r): BV 40 (165v, incomplete); MOd 7 (192v–193r); Mza 76 (149v); NV 1 (202v); PAc 47 (234r–234v); PAs 697 (64v–65r); PCsa 65 (247r–247v); PS 121 (51r–51v); Ra 123 (262r–262v); Rv 9 (167); Rv 52 (160r–160v); Tn 18 (143r–143v); Tn 20 (149r–149v); VCd 146 (115r); VCd 161 (134v); VCd 162 (190v); VEcap 107 (118v); VO 39 (37v).

REFERENCES

AH 7:254; 53:158; Brunner, "The Sequences of Verona 107," 2:68; Brunner, "Catalogo," 263; Brunner, "The Tao of Singing"; Crocker, "Repertoire," 2:74; Crocker, "The Sequence (*Gattung*)," 286–87; de Goede, *Utrecht Prosarium*, 115; Hughes, *Sequelae*, 70; von den Steinen, "Anfänge," 41:136–39.

TEXT COMMENTARY

This text concerns the publican's lament from the Gospel of Luke (18:13–14). The sequence takes its incipit, both text and music, from an antiphon now assigned to Lauds on the tenth Sunday after Pentecost. Since the piece was mentioned by Hucbald, it can be dated at least back to ca. 850. The text is discussed by von den Steinen ("Anfänge"), who considers it a prototype of the lyric sequence. Crocker refers to *Stans a longe* as a Gospel-song that he ranks as "one of the classic accomplishments of the first generation of sequences" ("The Sequence (*Gattung*)," 287).

TEXT AND TRANSLATION

[1]   Stans a longe
[2a] Publicanus lavit se fide lacrimosa
[2b] Fidem docens quę valet perpetrare tanta
[3a] Nolebat alta conspectare cęli sidera
[3b] Sed pectus tundens hęc promebat voce lacrimosa
[4a] Deus propicius michi peccatori esto
[4b] Et mea omnia pius dele facinora
[5a] Hac voce benignam promeruit clementiam
[5b] Necnon et iustificatus venit in domum suam
[6a] Cuius nos sacra sequentes exempla dicamus deo
[6b] Deus benigne nobis miserere laxans debita
[7]   Pius et nos iustifica

*

[1]   Standing at a distance
[2a] The publican cleansed himself in tears of faith
[2b] Teaching faith which has the power to accomplish so much.
[3a] He refused to gaze upon the lofty stars of heaven,
[3b] But pounding his chest he exclaimed in a tearful voice:
[4a] "O God, be merciful to me, a sinner,
[4b] And abolish all my sins, O merciful One."
[5a] Through this word he obtained beneficent mercy
[5b] And came back to his home forgiven.
[6a] Following his holy example, let us sing to God:
[6b] "O God, in your kindness have mercy on us and release our debts
[7]   And forgive us, O loving One."

DISTINCTIVE VARIANTS

Rn 1343 [6a] *huius* for *cuius*. **Bu 2824** [3a] *dolebat* for *nolebat*; [6a] *huius* for *cuius*. Later addition, twelfth century, in northern Italian notation.

MELODIC VARIANTS

Rn 1343 [2b] *do(cens)* EE~; [3a] *al(ta)* F(E); [3b] *tun(dens)* F(E); [4a] *es(to)* EE~; [6a] *(ex)em(pla)* E(D); [6b] *(be)nig(ne)* aa(G); [7] *(iusti)fi(ca)* ED. **Bu 2824** [1] *(publi)ca(nus)* EE~; [2b] *do(cens)* EE~; [3a] *al(ta)* F(E); [3b] *tun(dens)* F(E); [4a] *es(to)* EE~; [4b] *(om)ni(a)* FE; [5a] *(be)nig(nam)* cc~; [6a] *(sa)cra* G~; *(ex)em(pla)* E(D); [6b] *(be)nig(ne)* aa(G); [7] *(iusti)fi(ca)* ED.

38. Laeta mente

SOURCES

Rc 1741 fols. 131v–132r Dom<minica> xiii Seq<uentia>
Rn 1343 fols. 49v tercia decima dom<inica> Seq<uentia>
Bu 2824 fols. 98v–99r Seq<uentia>

ITALIAN CONCORDANCES

None.

REFERENCES

AH 53:103; Brunner, "Catalogo," 239; Brunner, "The Tao of Singing"; Hughes, *Sequelae,* 41; Schubiger, *Sängerschule,* 19; von den Steinen, *Notker der Dichter,* 1:221–22, 551, 2:48.

TEXT COMMENTARY

Notker's text draws its central images from Ps. 80:8, 11, and 17 (Ps. 81 in the English numbering). *Mesraim* [4] is the Hebrew name for Egypt used in the Vulgate. Von den Steinen discusses both text and melody (see *Notker der Dichter,* 1:221–22, 548, 551). Interestingly, the Nonantolan manuscripts are the only surviving sources from Italy that contain *Laeta mente.*

TEXT AND TRANSLATION

[1] Leta mente canamus deo nostro
[2] Qui defectam peccatis semper novat ęcclesiam
[3] Et eam pallidulam de radio veri solis illuminat
[4] Et terrę de mesraim eduxit fornacibus ignitis
[5] Quique in omni tribulatione eam exaudit
[6] Insuper cęlesti nutrit pane et cultum docet suum
[7] Qui de petra melle dulci eam adimplet

*

[1] With a joyous mind let us sing to our God,
[2] Who always renews the Church when weakened through sins,
[3] And who illuminates her, though pale, with the ray of the true sun
[4] And who led her forth from the fiery furnaces of the land of Mesriam,
[5] And He listens to her in all her tribulation,
[6] And nourishes her with celestial bread
[7] And teaches her to worship Him.
[8] He who fills her with sweet honey from the rock.

DISTINCTIVE VARIANTS

Bu 2824 later addition, twelfth century, in northern Italian notation.

MELODIC VARIANTS

Rn 1343 [1] *(Allelu)ia* dccdf...; [4] *(igni)tis* ee~; [5] *(tribulati)o(ne)* ee~; *(ex)au(dit)* e(d); [9] *Qui de petra me(le)* f'g'a'g'ff(e). **Bu 2824** [1] *(Alle)luia* cd'dccdf...; [4] *(igni)tis* ee~; [5] *(tribulati)o(ne)* ee~; *(ex)au(dit)* e(d); [9] *Qui de petra me(le)* f'g'a'g'ff(e).

39. *O quam mira*

SOURCES

Rc 1741 fols. 132r–132v Dom<minica> xvii Seq<uentia>
Rn 1343 fols. 49v–50r Dom<minica> xviiii Seq<uentia>
Bu 2824 fols. 94v–95r Seq<uentia>

ITALIAN CONCORDANCES

Ra 123 (221v).

REFERENCES

AH 53:118; Brunner, "Catalogo," 250; Schubiger, *Sängerschule,* 22; von den Steinen, *Notker der Dichter,* 1:551, 2:54.

TEXT COMMENTARY

Notker used the image of Joseph in this sequence as a miracle worker and as representing Christ, although Joseph's name does not appear in the text. Notker draws on Ps. 104:17–23 (Ps. 105 in the English Bible). The silver vase in [5–6] is a reference to Gen. 44. Von den Steinen explores these references and images in some detail (*Notker der Dichter,* 1:223–24, 548).

TEXT AND TRANSLATION

[1] O quam mira sunt deus tua portenta
[2] Qui spretum suis et extraneis odiosum
[3] Utrisque et amandum et valde terribilem fecisti
[4] Ex pręcognita fame et erogatione frumenti
[5] Qui fratris minimi causa per vas argenteum
[6] Cognitus est fratribus
[7] Qui nos ad terram promissę mansionis
[8] Pharao perducat extincto

*

[1] How marvelous are your powers, O God!
[2] You who made Him, rejected by his own and hated by strangers,
[3] To be loved and feared greatly by both,
[4] Because he had foreknowledge of the famine and had distributed wheat.
[5] You who for the sake of his youngest brother,
[6] Was recognized by his brothers through a silver vase.
[7] You who led us to the land of the promised home
[8] After the Pharaoh was destroyed.

DISTINCTIVE VARIANTS

Rn 1343 [7] "Q" of *Qui* omitted; [8] "P" of *Pharao* omitted.

Melodic Variants

Rn 1343 [1] *(por)ten(ta)* GG~; [2] *su(is)* FF~; *(odi)o(sum)* DD~; [3] *(a)man(dum)* DD(C); [4] *fa(me)* EE~; [6] *(cogni)tus* FF~; [8] *(ex)tinc(to)* FF(E). **Bu 2824** [2] *su(is)* FF~; *(odi)o(sum)* DD~; [3] *(a)man(dum)* DD(C); [4] *fa(me)* EE~; [8] *(ex)tinc(to)* FF(E).

40. *Almiflua caelorum*

Sources

Rc 1741 fols. 133r–134r Dom<minica> xxii Seq<uentia>

Rn 1343 fols. 50r–50v Dom<minica> xxii Seq<uentia>

Bu 2824 fols. 100v–101v Seq<uentia>

Italian Concordances

VO 39 (57r–57v).

References

AH 34:92; Brunner, "Catalogo," 213.

Text Commentary

This text is placed on the Twenty-second Sunday after Pentecost, although it is edited in *AH* as a generic piece to the Virgin Mary. The text is very general and rather undistinguished. Apparently written along with the melody in northern Italy, it survives only in a single source outside of Nonantola (VO 39).

Text and Translation

[1] Almiflua cęlorum turba
[2a] Individuę trinitati laudes concinit in astris
[2b] Nos quoque in arvis gratulantes ipsius misteria
[3a] Nisibus ex totis per longa recitemus devote tempora
[3b] Exultant cernendo regis obtutum celsi sanctorum agmina
[4a] Iubilet et in huius diei festa populorum caterva
[4b] Poplite flexo christi solamen poscens paradisi gaudia
[5a] Ut queant iter post carnis mortem vite scandere supernę
[5b] Qua dei genitrix cum civibus almis consistit maria
[6a] Quę meruit in tantum conditoris ęterni fore conspectibus placita
[6b] Ut humani generis factorem gererent casta sui corporis viscera
[7a] O virgo clausa per ęvum et per te cunctis est patefacta altithroni ianua
[7b] Quapropter veniam servulis quęsumus prece sedula
[8] Quo perfrui tecum mereamur gloria per eum qui regnat incuncta secula

*

[1] The multitude of Heaven flowing with grace
[2a] Sings praises amid the stars to the indivisible Trinity.
[2b] Let us on earth as well rejoice over its mystery
[3a] And with all our strength sing faithfully at length.
[3b] The crowd of saints rejoices discerning the eyes of the exalted King.
[4a] May the troop of peoples rejoice as well in this day's feast
[4b] Beseeching you, Christ, on bended knee, for consolation, for the joys of paradise,
[5a] So that they, after the body's death, can ascend the path of celestial life,
[5b] Where God's Mother Mary resides together with the holy citizens,
[6a] She who deserved to be so pleasing in the sight of the eternal Creator,
[6b] That the chaste womb of her body brought forth the creator of humankind.
[7a] O Virgin, through you the eternally closed door to the One enthroned on high was opened for all.
[7b] Therefore, we beseech you with diligent prayers, to have mercy on us servants,
[8] So that we may deserve to enjoy the glory together with you, through Him, who reigns for ever.

Distinctive Variants

Bu 2824 [5a] *At* for *Ut*.

Melodic Variants

Rn 1343 [1] *tur(ba)* ee(d); *(Alle)lu(ia)* ... e(d); [2a] *(trini)ta(ti)* ee~; [3a] *to(tis)* cc~; [3b] *(cer)nen(do)* cc~; [4b] *fle(xo)* ee~; [5a] *i(ter)* cc~; *(mor)tem* dd~; [5b] *(civi)bus* dd~; [6a] *tan(tum)* ee(d); *(ę)ter(ni)* e(d); [6b] *(corpo)ris* dd~; [7b] *ę(vum)* ee~; *pa(tefacta)* ee~; [8] *per eum qui reg(nat)* c'e'g'f'e; *secu(la)* f'e. **Bu 2824** [6b] *(corpo)ris* dd~.

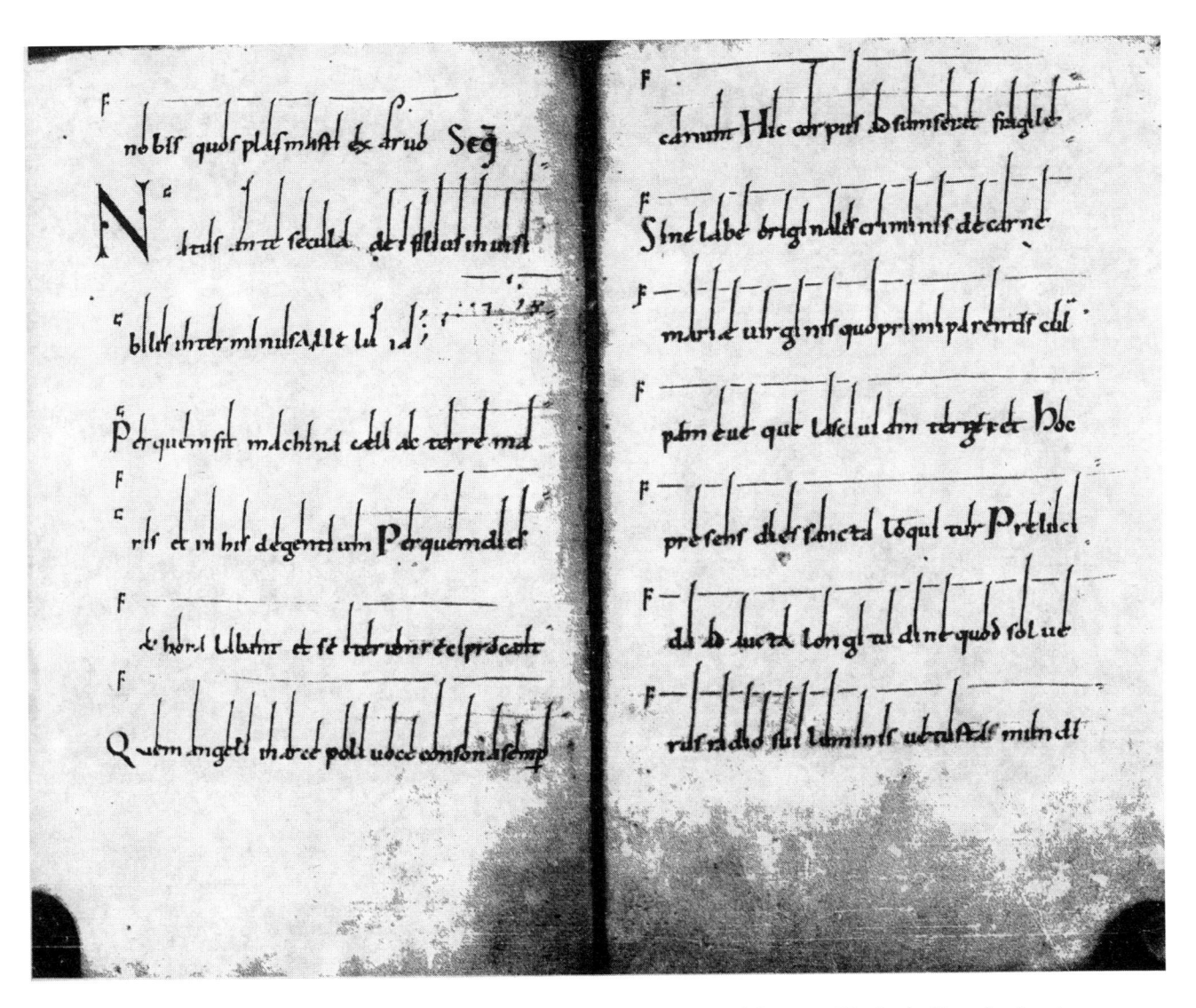

Plate 1. Bologna, Biblioteca Universitaria, MS 2824, fols. 24v–25r, including the beginning of *Natus ante saecula* (no. 2).

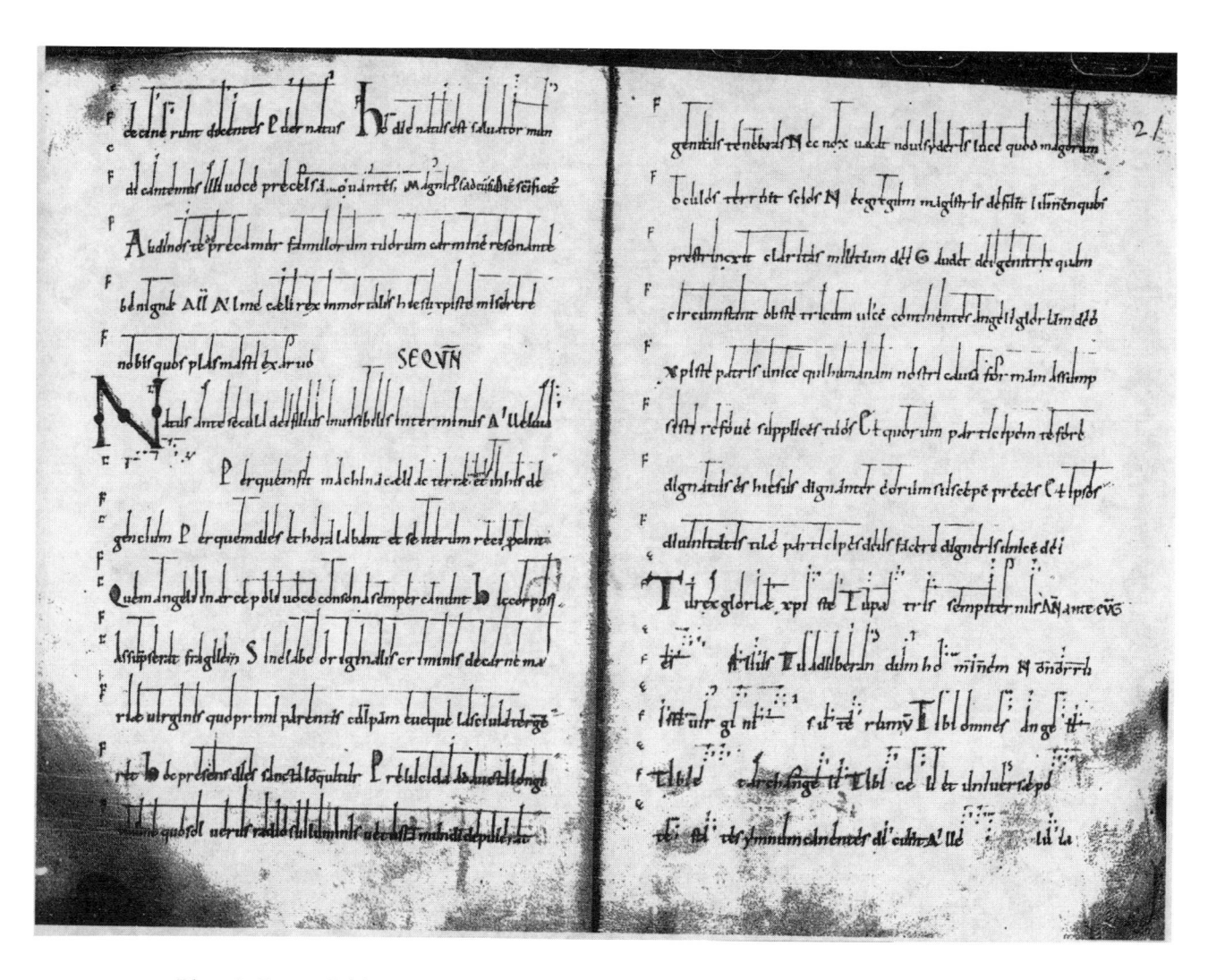

Plate 2. Rome, Biblioteca Nazionale, MS 1343 (*olim* Sessoriano 62), fols. 20v–21r, including all of *Natus ante saecula* (no. 2).

1. Christi hodiernae pangimini

Bu 2824

[1] Chris- ti ⟨h⟩o- di- er- ne pa- gi- mi- ni om- nis u- na Al-

-le- lu- ia [2a] Vo- ce si- mul con- so- na na- ti- vi- ta- tis

mag- ne [2b] Quod ver- bum ca- ro fac- tum ex- ib- er- e se vo- lu- it

[3a] Mun- do quam re- de- mit iam ve- ne- rat de se- de pa- tris do- mi- nus

[3b] Nun- ci- at an- ge- lus pas- to- ri- bus in- gen- ti cur- rent gau- di- o

[4a] Pre- se- pi- o pu- e- rum ma- ri- a po- su- it in sta- bu- lum

[4b] Va- gi- ens in- fan- tu- lum a quo re- gi- tur om- nis mun- dus

[5a] Vi- gi- lan- tes pas- to- res au- di- unt cho- rum An- ge- li- cum in cæ- lis

psal- len- tes glo- ri- a laus de- cus in ex- cel- sis de- o [5b] Quem pro- phe- te

cunc- ti pre- di- ca- ve- runt o- lim Iam ap- pa- ret for- ma quam in- du- it

do- mi- nus quem vir- go ma- ter pan- nis te- git [6a] Ex- i- gu- o

te- gi- tur di- ver- so- ri- o qui ar- va con- di- dit et po- lum

[6b] Non os- trum e- le- git non au- ri- fi- cum non ru- ti- lum ve- nit in lo- cum

[7a] Ma- ri- a ge- ni- trix que ex- ul- ta- bat in- con- ta- mi- na- to

al- vo e- ni- xa est auc- to- rem om- ni- um do- mi- num

[7b] Io- seph val- de se si- mul re- co- la- bat am- mi- ran- do

re- trac- ta- bat quod re- i ac- ta hu- ius- ce- mo- di ve- ni- ret

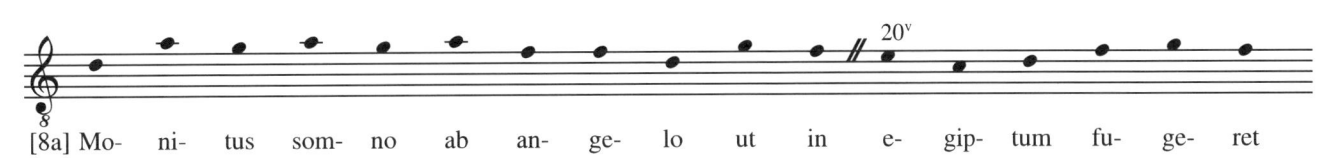

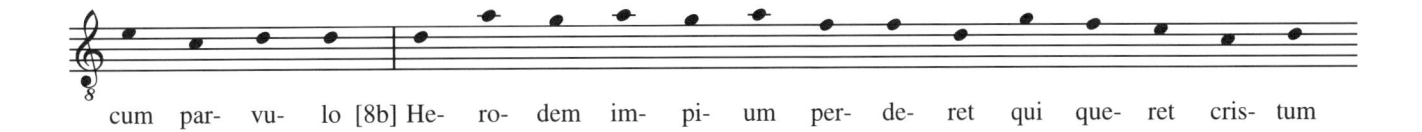

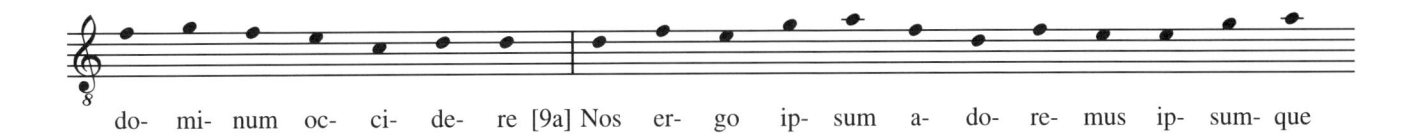

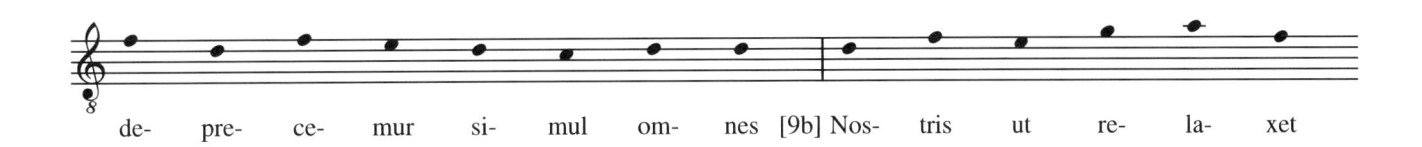

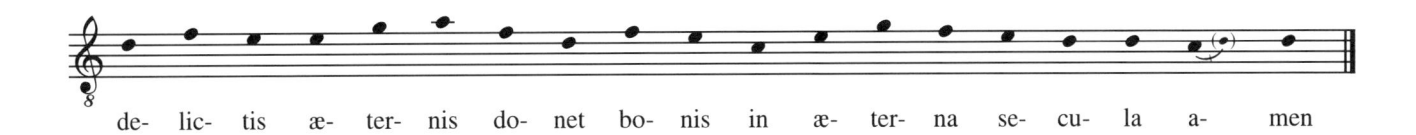

[8a] Mo- ni- tus som- no ab an- ge- lo ut in e- gip- tum fu- ge- ret cum par- vu- lo [8b] He- ro- dem im- pi- um per- de- ret qui que- ret cris- tum do- mi- num oc- ci- de- re [9a] Nos er- go ip- sum a- do- re- mus ip- sum- que de- pre- ce- mur si- mul om- nes [9b] Nos- tris ut re- la- xet de- lic- tis æ- ter- nis do- net bo- nis in æ- ter- na se- cu- la a- men

2. Natus ante saecula

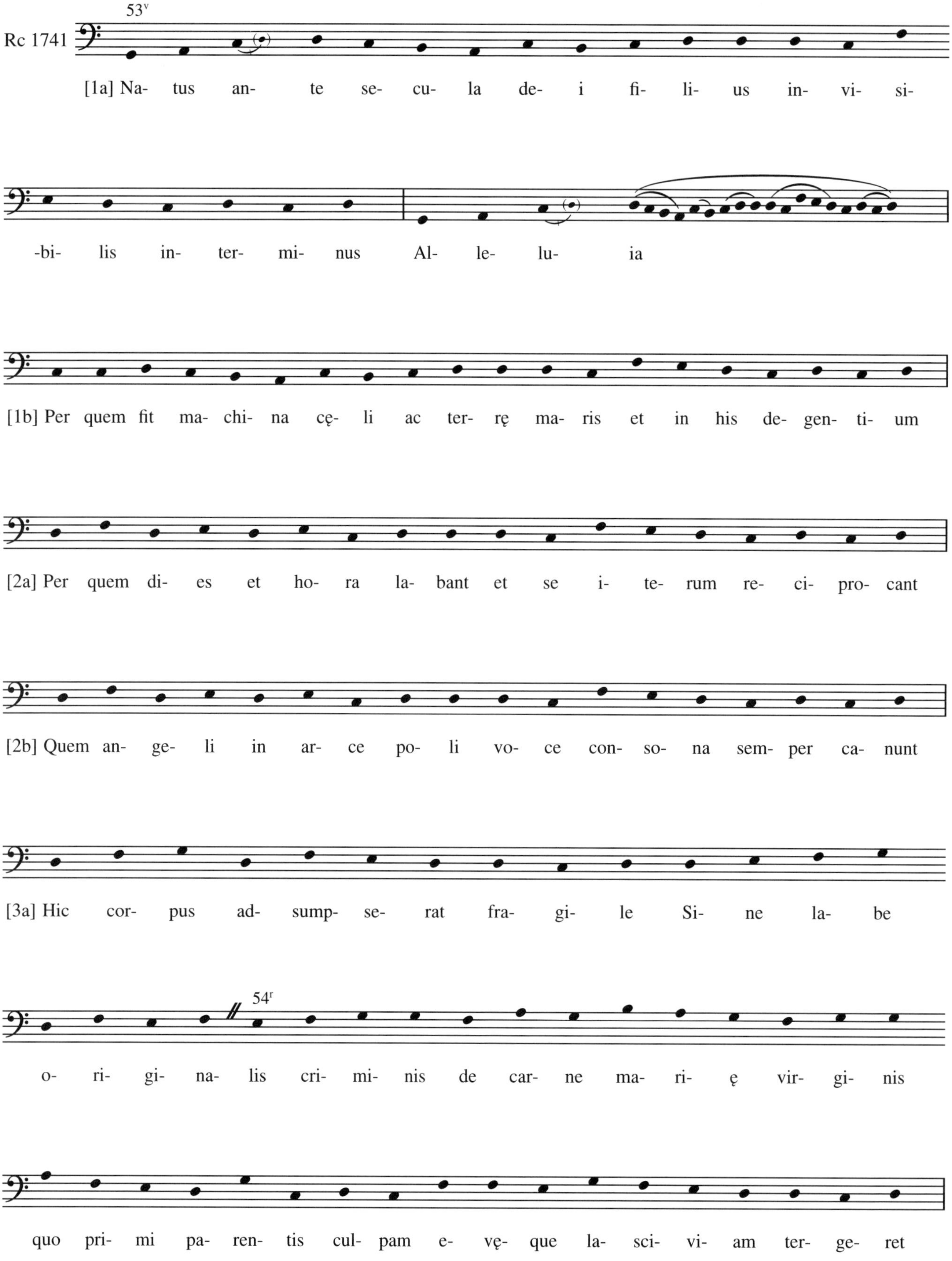

Rc 1741

[1a] Natus ante secula dei filius invisibilis interminus Alleluia

[1b] Per quem fit machina cęli ac terrę maris et in his degentium

[2a] Per quem dies et hora labant et se iterum reciprocant

[2b] Quem angeli in arce poli voce consona semper canunt

[3a] Hic corpus adsumpserat fragile Sine labe originalis criminis de carne marię virginis

quo primi parentis culpam evęque lasciviam tergeret

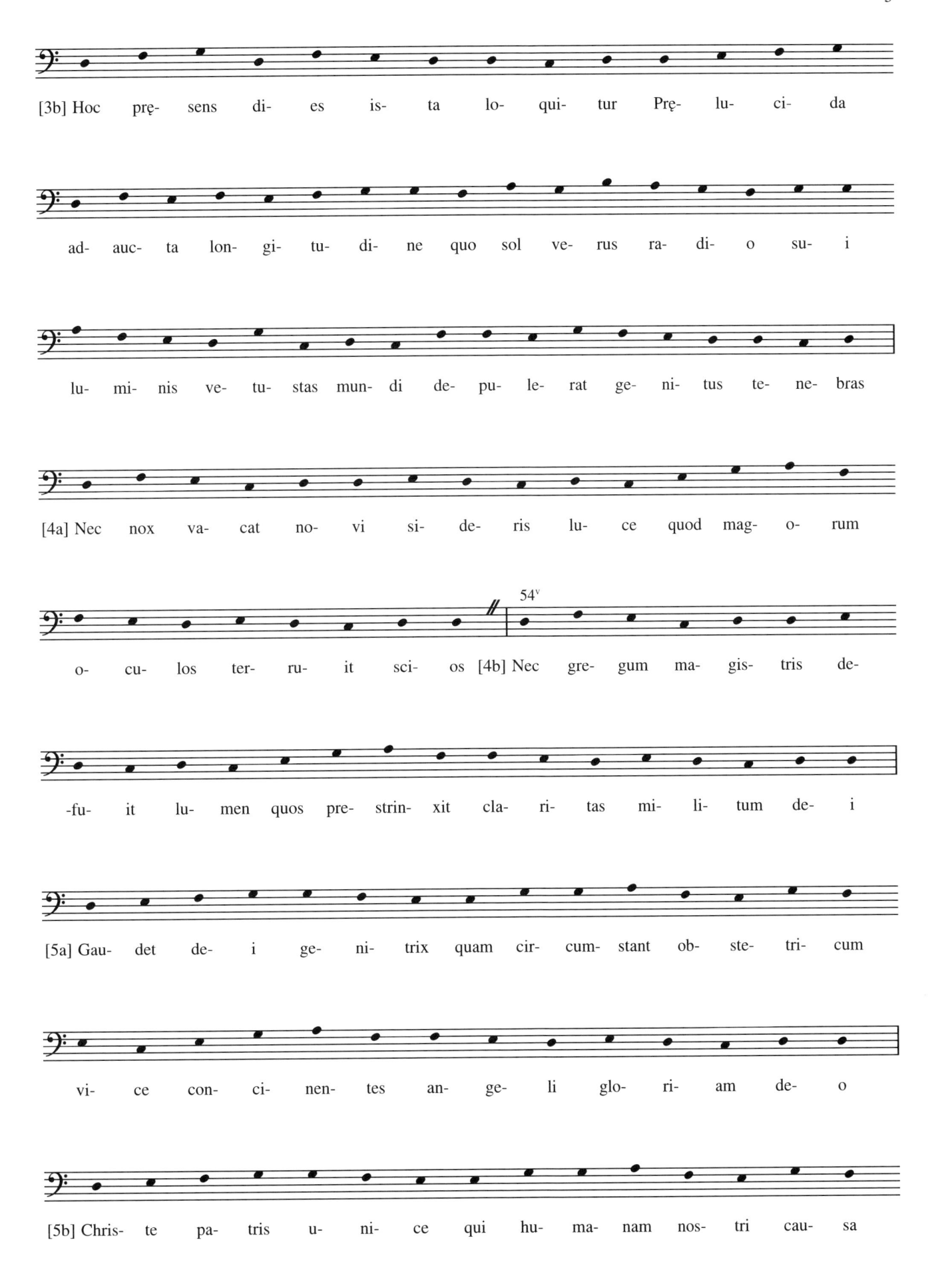

[3b] Hoc pręsens dies ista loquitur Pręlucida adaucta longitudine quo sol verus radio sui luminis vetustas mundi depulerat genitus tenebras

[4a] Nec nox vacat novi sideris luce quod magorum oculos terruit scios [4b] Nec gregum magistris defuit lumen quos prestrinxit claritas militum dei

[5a] Gaudet dei genitrix quam circumstant obstetricum vice concinentes angeli gloriam deo

[5b] Christe patris unice qui humanam nostri causa

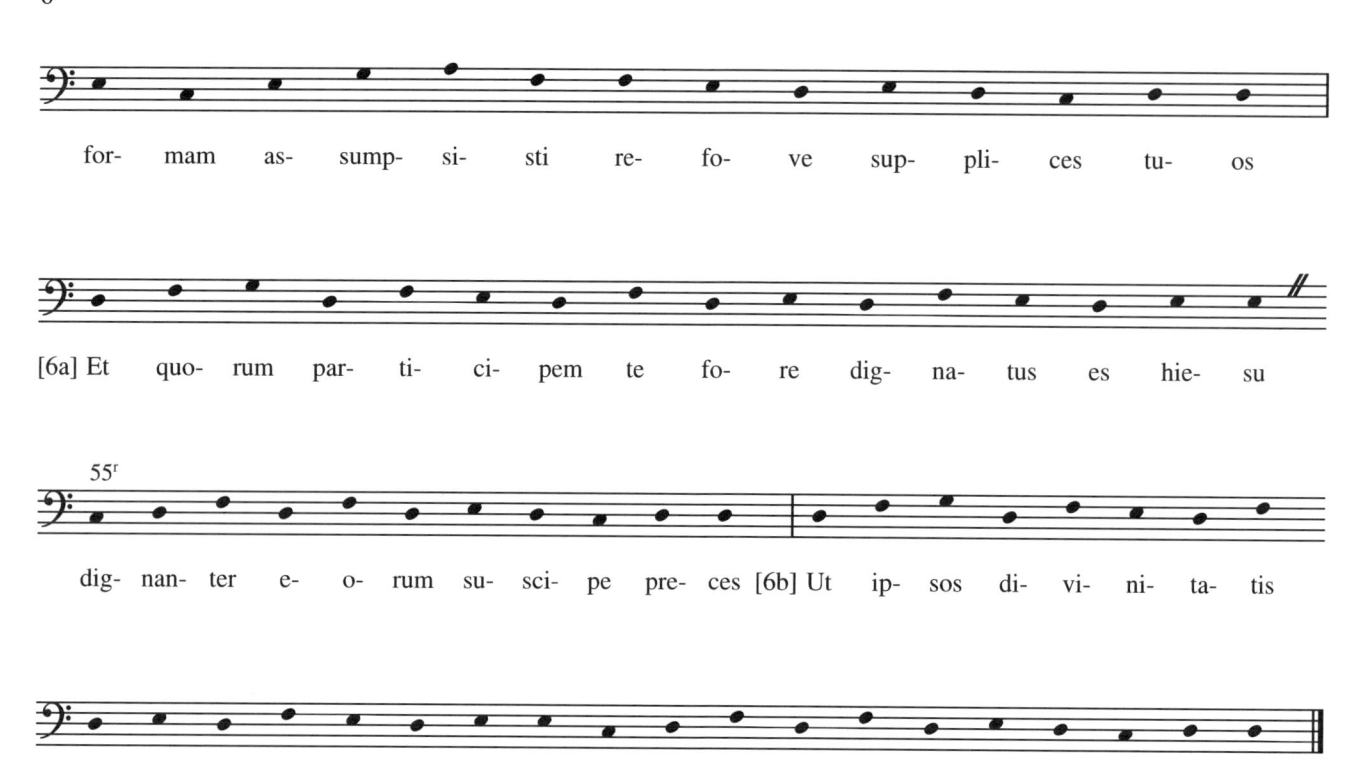

for- mam as- sump- si- sti re- fo- ve sup- pli- ces tu- os

[6a] Et quo- rum par- ti- ci- pem te fo- re dig- na- tus es hie- su

dig- nan- ter e- o- rum su- sci- pe pre- ces [6b] Ut ip- sos di- vi- ni- ta- tis

tuę par- ti- ci- pes de- us fa- ce- re dig- ne- ris u- ni- ce de- i

3. Hanc concordi

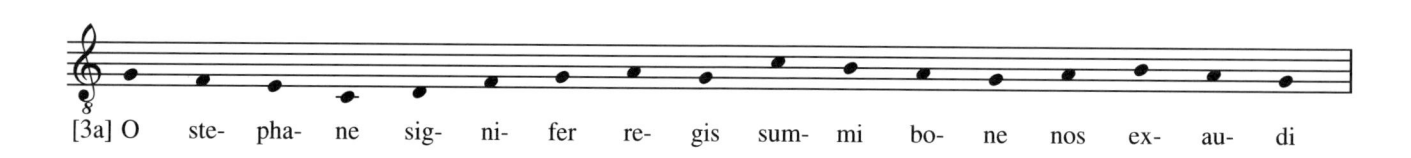

Rc 1741

[1] Hanc con- cor- di fa- mu- la- tu co- la- mus sol- lem- ni- ta- tem

Al- le- lu- ia [2a] Auc- to- ris il- li- us ex- em- plo

doc- ti be- nig- no [2b] Pro per- se- cu- to- rum pre- can- tis frau- de su- o- rum

[3a] O ste- pha- ne sig- ni- fer re- gis sum- mi bo- ne nos ex- au- di

[3b] Pro- fi- cu- ę qui es pro tu- is ex- au- di- tus in- i- mi- cis

[4a] Pau- lus tu- is pre- ci- bus ste- pha- ne te quon-dam per- se- cu- tus chris- to cre- dit

[4b] Et te- cum tri- pu- di- at in reg- no cu- i nul- lus per- se- cu- tor ap- pro- pin- quat

[5a] Nos pro- in- de nos sup- pli- ces ad te cla- man- tes et pre- ci- bus te pul- san- tes

[5b] O- ra- ti- o sanc- tis- si- ma nos tu- a sem- per con- ci- li- et de- o nos- tro

[6a] Te pe- trus chris- ti mi- ni- strum sta- tu- it Tu pe- tro nor- mam cre- den- di a- stru- is

ad dex- tram sum- mi pa- tris os- ten- den- do quem plebs fu- rens cru- ci- fi- xit

[6b] Te si- bi chris- tus e- le- git ste- pha- ne Per quem fi- de- les su- os cor- ro- bo- rat

se ti- bi in- ter ro- ta- tus sax- o- rum so- la- ci- o ma- ni- fe- stans

[7] Nunc in- ter in- cli- tas mar- ty- rum pur- pu- ras co- rus- cas co- ro- na- tus

4. Iohannes Iesu Christo

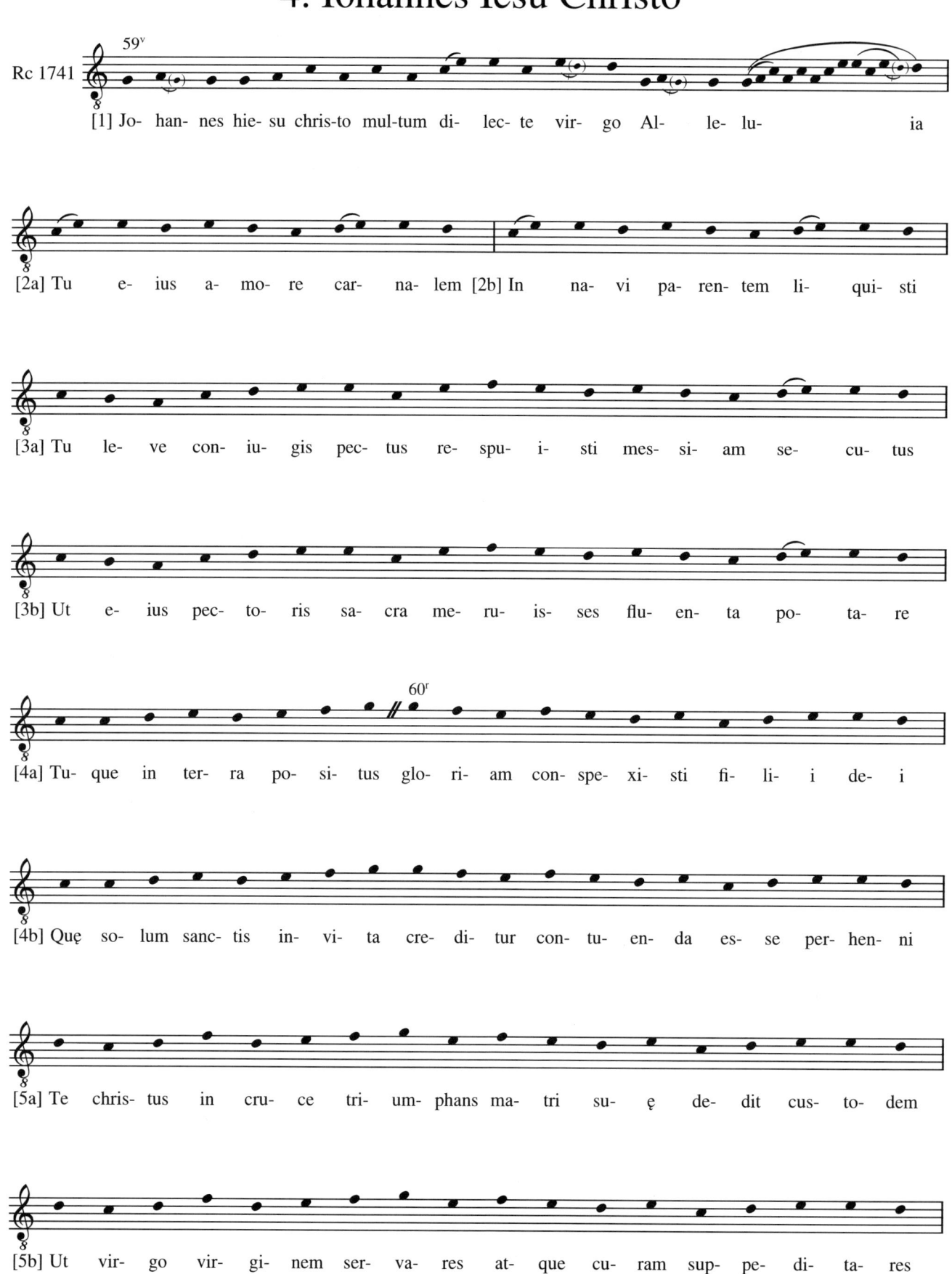

Rc 1741

[1] Johannes hiesu christo multum dilecte virgo Alleluia

[2a] Tu eius amore carnalem [2b] In navi parentem liquisti

[3a] Tu leve coniugis pectus respuisti messiam secutus

[3b] Ut eius pectoris sacra meruisses fluenta potare

[4a] Tuque in terra positus gloriam conspexisti filii dei

[4b] Quę solum sanctis invita creditur contuenda esse perhenni

[5a] Te christus in cruce triumphans matri suę dedit custodem

[5b] Ut virgo virginem servares atque curam suppeditares

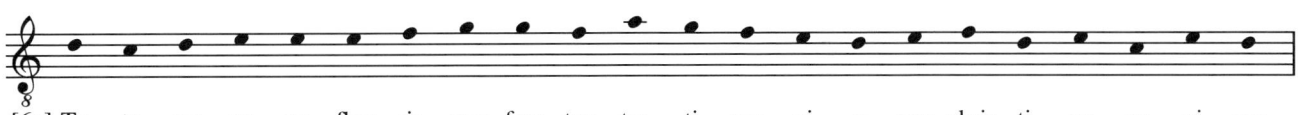

[6a] Tu te car-ce- re flag-ris- que frac-tus tes- ti- mo- ni- o pro chris- ti es ga- vi- sus

[6b] I- dem mor- tu- os su- sci- tas in- que hie-su no- mi- ne ve- ne- num

for- te vin- cis [7a] Ti- bi sum- mus ta- ci- tum ce- te- ris ver- bum

su- um pa- ter re- ve- lat [7b] Tu nos om- nes se- du- lis pre- ci- bus

a- pud de- um sem- per com- men- da [8] Jo- han- nes chris- ti ca- re

5. Laus tibi Christe cui sapit

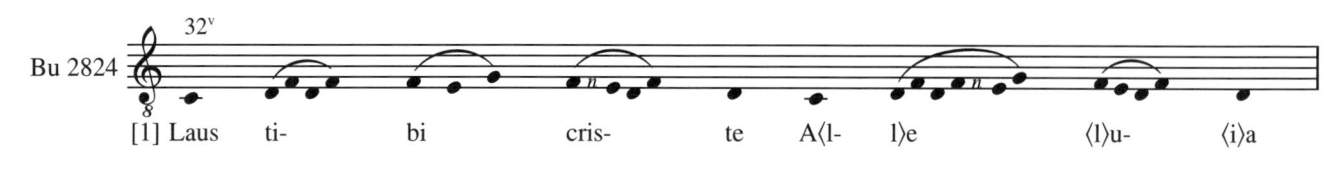

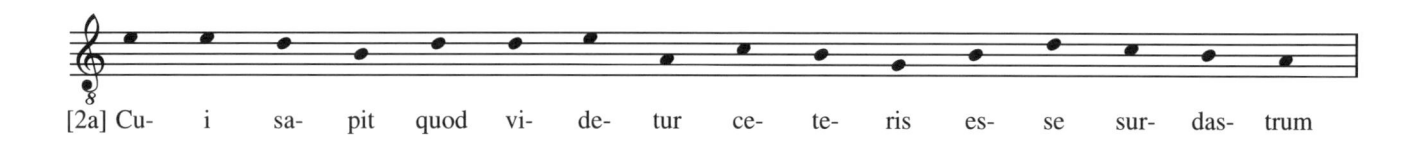

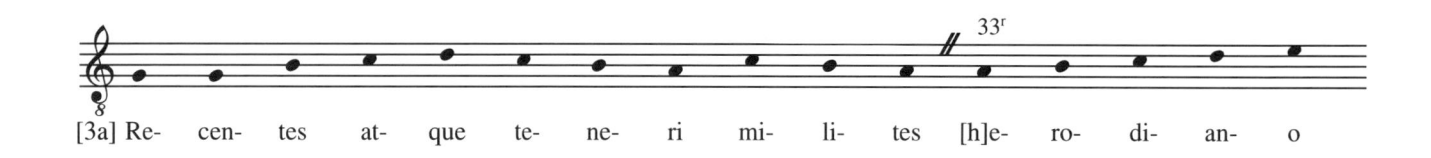

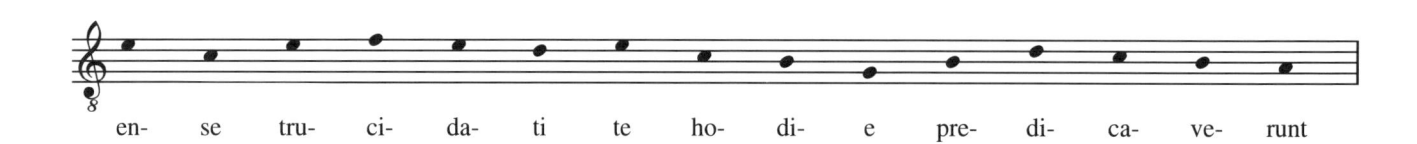

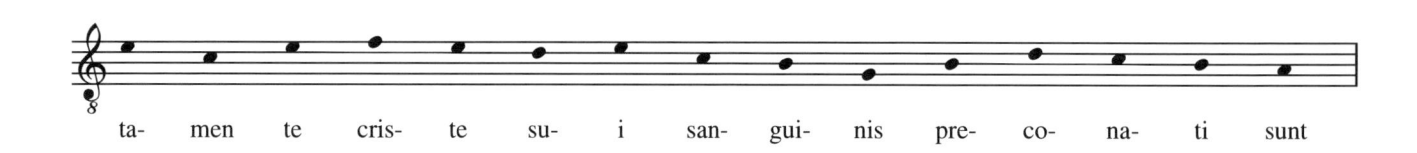

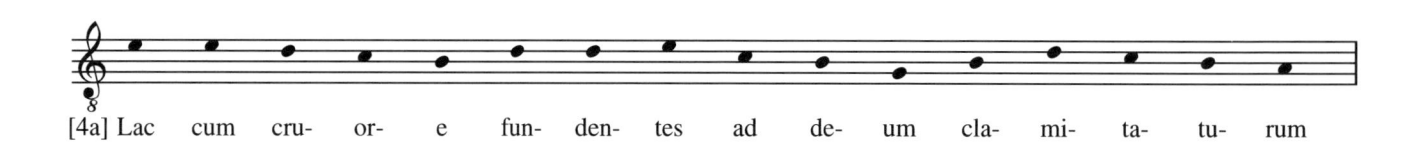

[1] Laus ti- bi cris- te A⟨l- l⟩e ⟨l⟩u- ⟨i⟩a

[2a] Cu- i sa- pit quod vi- de- tur ce- te- ris es- se sur- das- trum

[2b] Fa- mu- la- tum cu- ius om- nis com- pe- tit se- xus et e- tas

[3a] Re- cen- tes at- que te- ne- ri mi- li- tes [h]e- ro- di- an- o en- se tru- ci- da- ti te ho- di- e pre- di- ca- ve- runt

[3b] Li- cet nec- dum po- tu- e- runt li- gu- la ef- fu- si- o- ne ta- men te cris- te su- i san- gui- nis pre- co- na- ti sunt

[4a] Lac cum cru- or- e fun- den- tes ad de- um cla- mi- ta- rum

[4b] Ut apud illi quem gena miseret et innocentes

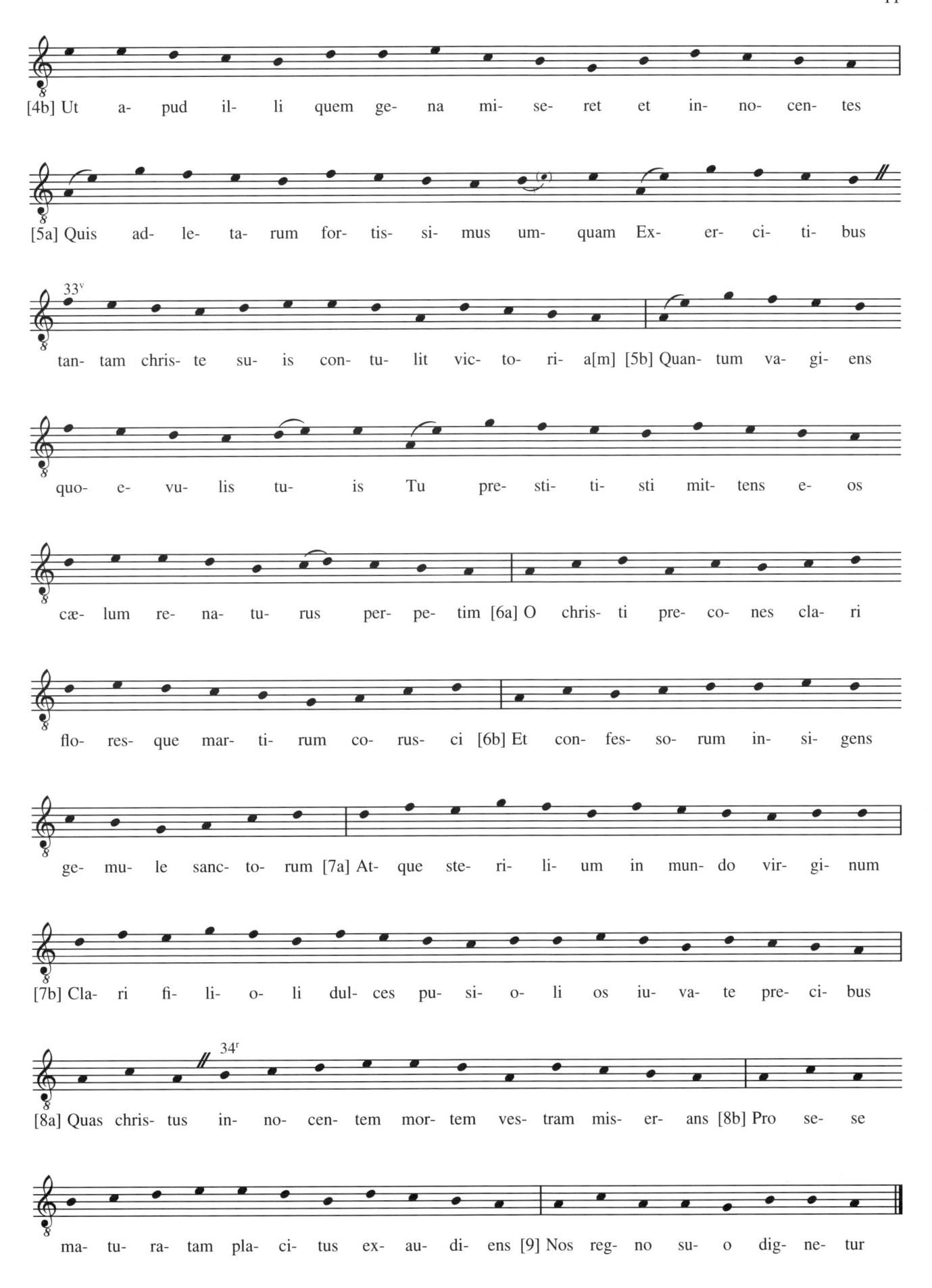

[5a] Quis ad letarum fortissimus umquam Exercitibus tantam christe suis contulit victoria[m] [5b] Quantum vagiens quo evulis tuis Tu prestitisti mittens eos cælum renaturus perpetim [6a] O christi precones clari floresque martirum corusci [6b] Et confessorum insigens gemule sanctorum [7a] Atque sterilium in mundo virginum [7b] Clari filioli dulces pusioli os iuvate precibus [8a] Quas christus innocentem mortem vestram miserans [8b] Pro se se maturatam placitus exaudiens [9] Nos regno suo dignetur

6. Haec sunt sacra festa

Rc 1741

[1] Hęc sunt sa- cra fes- ta lau- di- bus mag- nis dig- na Al- le- lu- ia

[2a] No- stra hac di- e car- mi- na pe- ne- trent temp- la pre- ci- bus si- de- re- a

[2b] Sanc- ti sil- ve- stri me- ri- tis me- ri- ta no- bis im- plo- re- mus pro- spe- ra

[3a] In- ter e- the- re- os ci- ves tu- os post de- lic- ta nos sanc- te sil- ves- ter re- vo- ca

[3b] Tu- a- rum o- vi- um mar- ga- ri- ta pre- ci- o- sa tu gem- ma ple- bis ful- gi- da

[4a] Tu dux gre- gis lę- ta io- cun- dę prę- vi- di- sti tu- is vi- tę pa- bu- la

[4b] Ser- vans cus- tos o- vi- um cau- las ef- fe- ras ab- e- gi- sti in- si- di- as

[5a] Nunc a- li- as te- nens pa- tri- as an- ge- lo- rum de- li- ci- as

[5b] Ter- ram e- den ru- ra pin- gui- a mag- nis de- li- ci- is ple- na

[6a] Ne nos te quę-su-mus de- se- ras ba- iu- lans- que o- ves tu- as

[6b] Dis- per- sas pe- ti- mus re- vo- ca sub- le- va- que pre- ce tu- a

[7a] Ne sit pro cul tu- a cu- ra ne si- mus hos- tis prę- da mor- tis te- la vi- o- lent men- tis a- ni- mam [7b] Fran- gi- mur bel- li pug- na dex- te- ra si- ne tu- a tu- a sit vic- to- ri- a chris- ti gra- ti- a [8a] Iu- di- cem pos- tu- la de- le- at nos- tra cri- mi- na [8b] Quę- su- mus im- pe- tra re- mis- si- o- nis ve- ni- am [9a] Pas- tor tu- am fa- mi- li- am sanc- te sil- ves- ter gu- ber- na [9b] At- que de- o ut mu- ne- ra hos- ti- am quo- que re- pre- sen- ta [10] Ut dig- ni fru- a- mur glo- ri- a

7. Laude mirandum

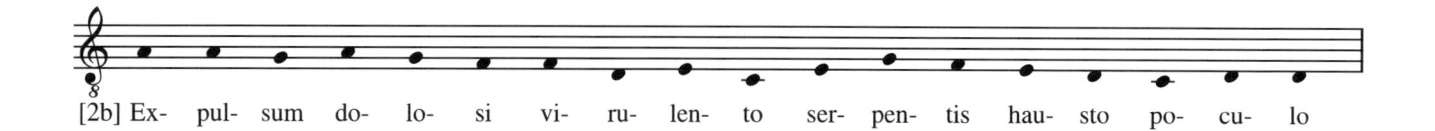

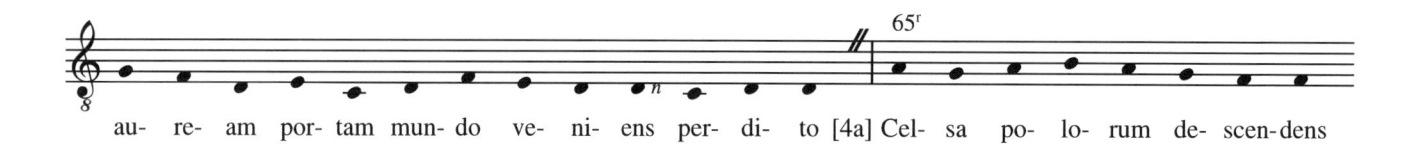

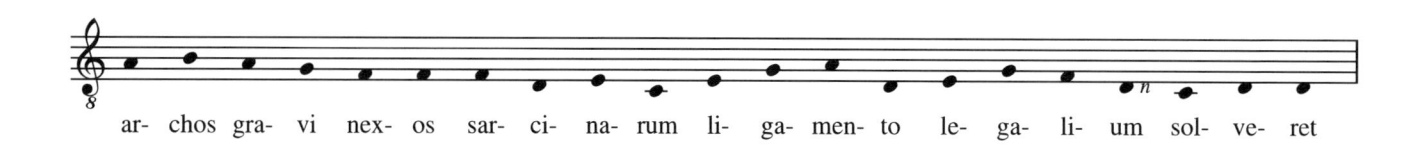

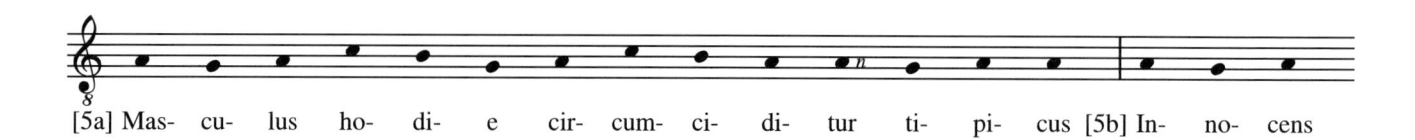

Rc 1741

[1] Lau- de mi- ran- dum dig- na pro- se- qua- mur re- gem Al- le- lu- ia

[2a] Qui pri- mum fron- do- sa pa- ra- di- si pa- ren- tem se- de mi- se- rans

[2b] Ex- pul- sum do- lo- si vi- ru- len- to ser- pen- tis hau- sto po- cu- lo

[3a] Hu- ma- no na- sci pro- ge- ne- re vo- lu- it [3b] Per vir- gi- na- lis au- lę

au- re- am por- tam mun- do ve- ni- ens per- di- to [4a] Cel- sa po- lo- rum de- scen- dens

ar- ce sum- mus tu- lit mem- bra ser- vi- li- a do- mi- nus [4b] Ut nos le- gis la- tor

ar- chos gra- vi nex- os sar- ci- na- rum li- ga- men- to le- ga- li- um sol- ve- ret

[5a] Mas- cu- lus ho- di- e cir- cum- ci- di- tur ti- pi- cus [5b] In- no- cens

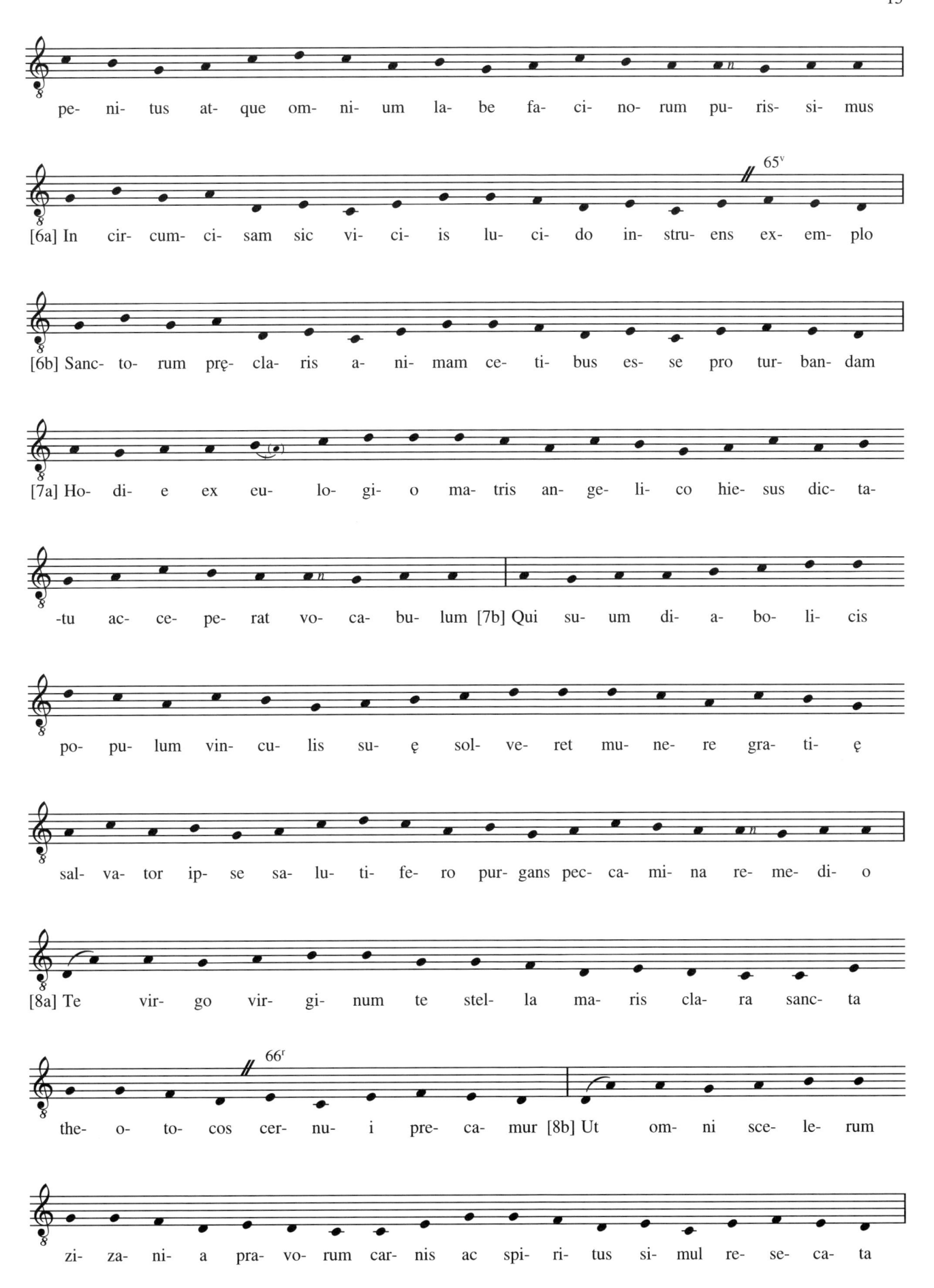

pe- ni- tus at- que om- ni- um la- be fa- ci- no- rum pu- ris- si- mus

[6a] In cir- cum- ci- sam sic vi- ci- is lu- ci- do in- stru- ens ex- em- plo

[6b] Sanc- to- rum prę- cla- ris a- ni- mam ce- ti- bus es- se pro tur- ban- dam

[7a] Ho- di- e ex eu- lo- gi- o ma- tris an- ge- li- co hie- sus dic- ta-

-tu ac- ce- pe- rat vo- ca- bu- lum [7b] Qui su- um di- a- bo- li- cis

po- pu- lum vin- cu- lis su- ę sol- ve- ret mu- ne- re gra- ti- ę

sal- va- tor ip- se sa- lu- ti- fe- ro pur- gans pec- ca- mi- na re- me- di- o

[8a] Te vir- go vir- gi- num te stel- la ma- ris cla- ra sanc- ta

the- o- to- cos cer- nu- i pre- ca- mur [8b] Ut om- ni sce- le- rum

zi- za- ni- a pra- vo- rum car- nis ac spi- ri- tus si- mul re- se- ca- ta

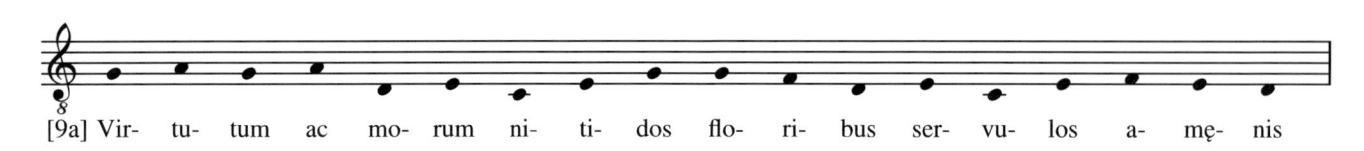

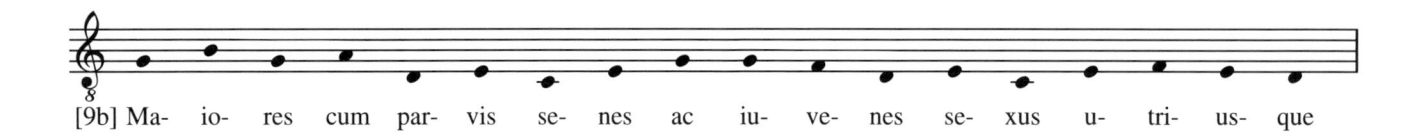

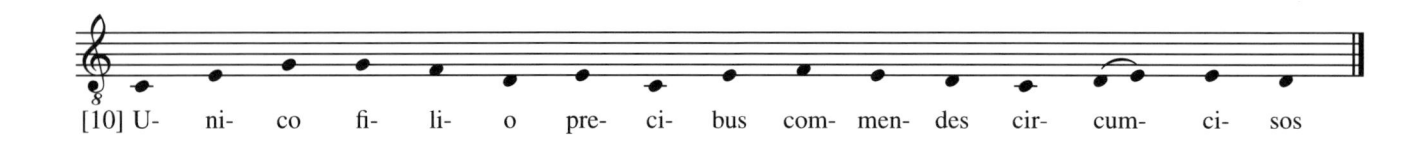

[9a] Virtutum ac morum nitidos floribus servulos amęnis

[9b] Maiores cum parvis senes ac iuvenes sexus utriusque

[10] Unico filio precibus commendes circumcisos

8. Festa christi

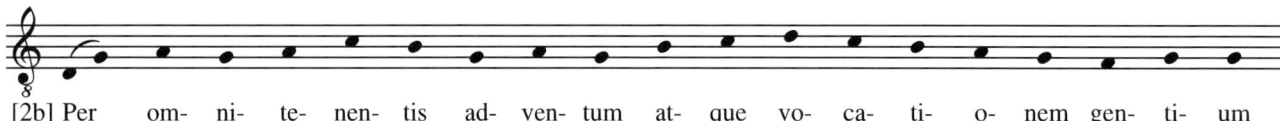

Rc 1741

[1] Festa christi omnis christianitas celebret Alleluia

[2a] Quę miris sunt modis ornata cunctisque veneranda populis

[2b] Per omnitenentis adventum atque vocationem gentium

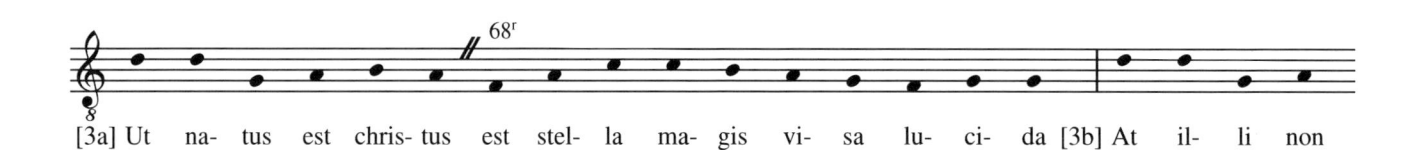

[3a] Ut natus est christus est stella magis visa lucida [3b] At illi non

cassam putantes tanti signi gloriam [4a] Secum munera deferunt par- vu- lo of- fe- runt ut re- gi cę- li quem si- dus pre- di- cat [4b] At- que au- re- o

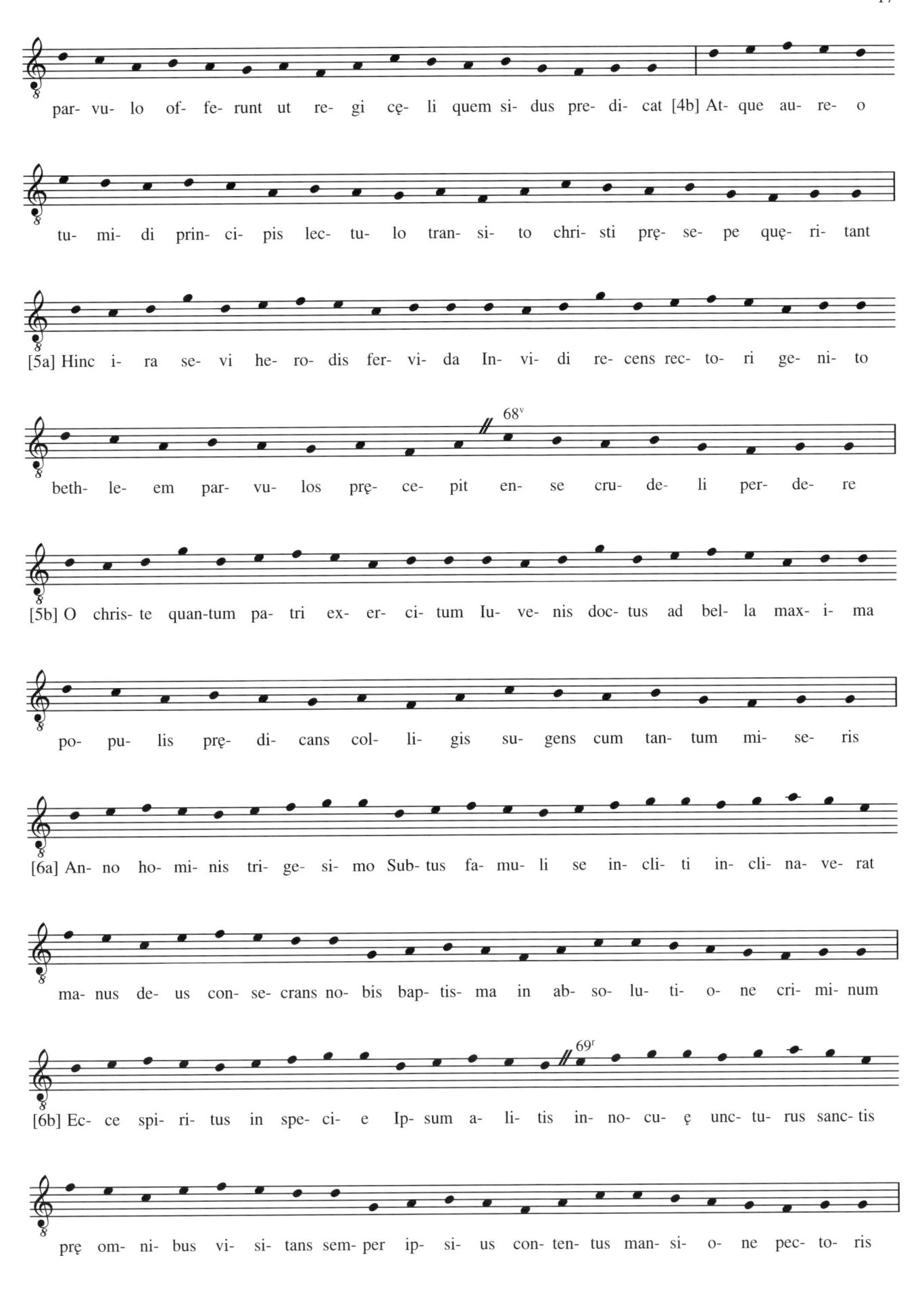

tu- mi- di prin- ci- pis lec- tu- lo tran- si- to chri- sti pre̜- se- pe quę- ri- tant

[5a] Hinc i- ra se- vi he- ro- dis fer- vi- da In- vi- di re- cens rec- to- ri ge- ni- to

beth- le- em par- vu- los prę- ce- pit en- se cru- de- li per- de- re

[5b] O chri- ste quan- tum pa- tri ex- er- ci- tum Iu- ve- nis doc- tus ad bel- la max- i- ma

po- pu- lis prę- di- cans col- li- gis su- gens cum tan- tum mi- se- ris

[6a] An- no ho- mi- nis tri- ge- si- mo Sub- tus fa- mu- li se in- cli- ti in- cli- na- ve- rat

ma- nus de- us con- se- crans no- bis bap- tis- ma in ab- so- lu- ti- o- ne cri- mi- num

[6b] Ec- ce spi- ri- tus in spe- ci- e Ip- sum a- li- tis in- no- cu- ę unc- tu- rus sanc- tis

prę om- ni- bus vi- si- tans sem- per ip- si- us con- ten- tus man- si- o- ne pec- to- ris

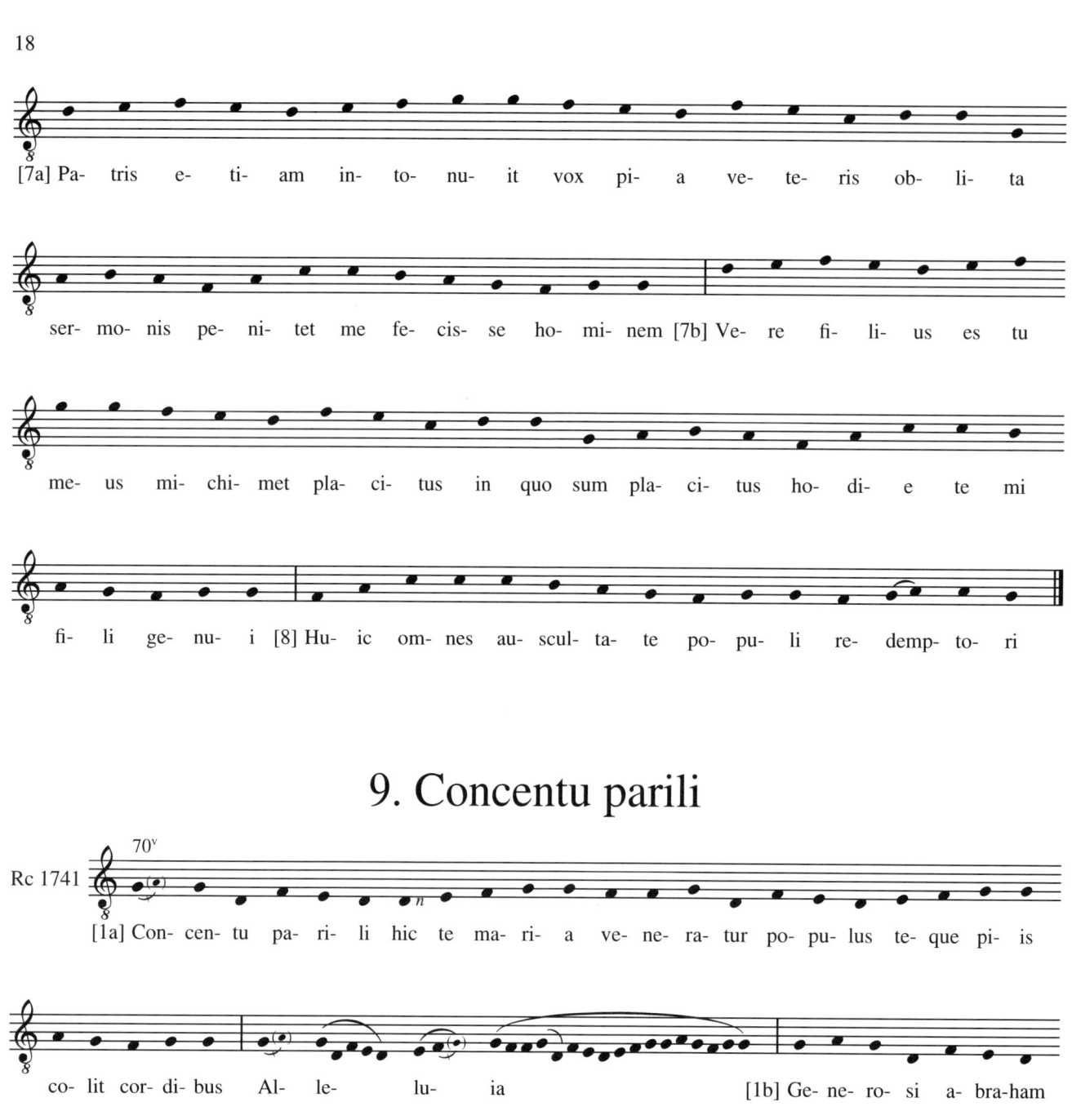

[7a] Patris etiam intonuit vox pia veteris oblita sermonis penitet me fecisse hominem [7b] Vere filius es tu meus michimet placitus in quo sum placitus hodie te mi fili genui [8] Huic omnes auscultate populi redemptori

9. Concentu parili

Rc 1741

[1a] Concentu parili hic te maria veneratur populus teque piis colit cordibus Alleluia [1b] Generosi abraham tu filia veneranda regia de davidis stirpe genita

[2a] Lętare mater et virgo nobilis gabrihelis archangeli quoque oraculo credita genuisti clausa filium

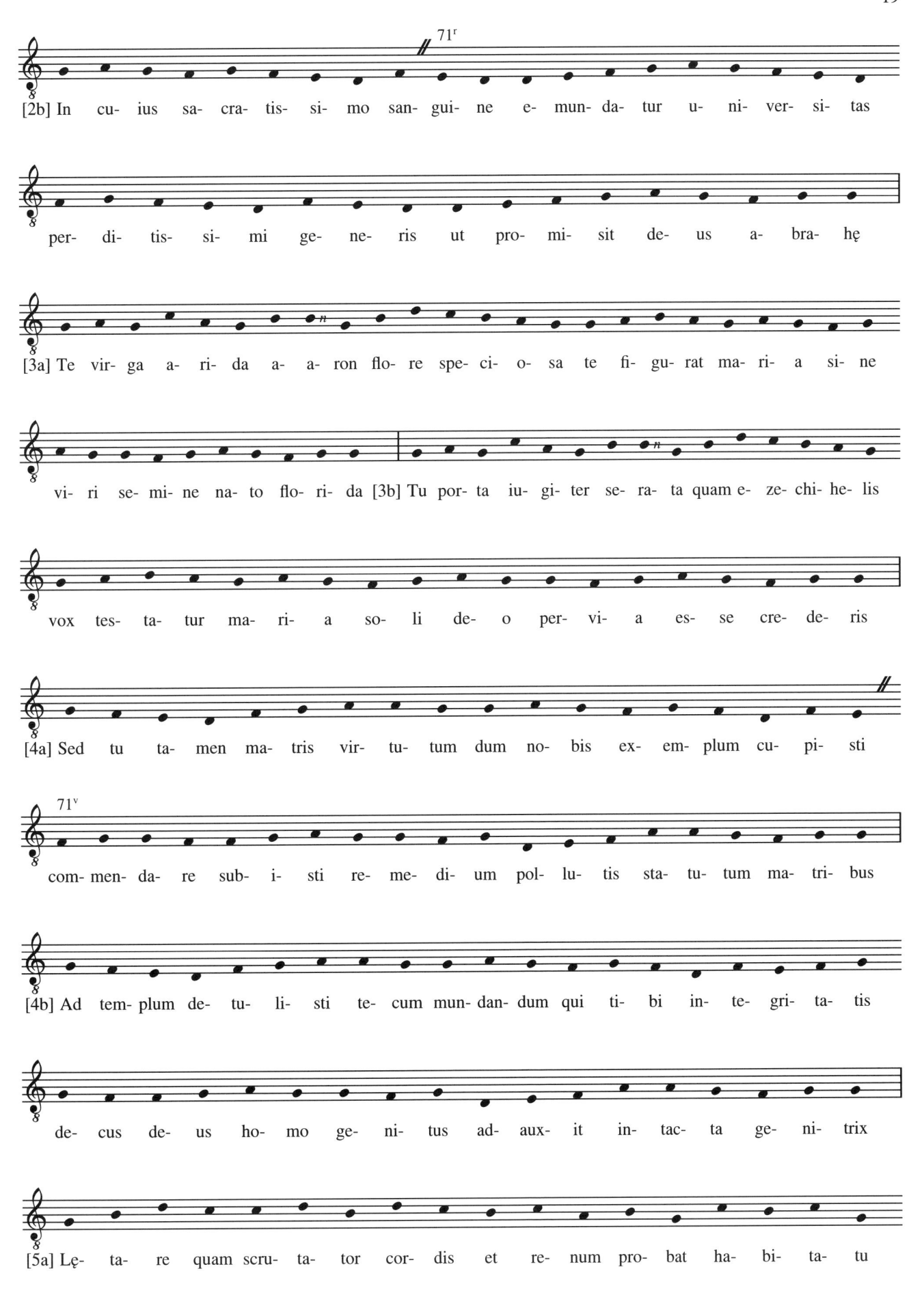

[2b] In cuius sacratissimo sanguine emundatur universitas perditissimi generis ut promisit deus abrahę

[3a] Te virga arida aaron flore speciosa te figurat maria sine viri semine nato florida

[3b] Tu porta iugiter serata quam ezechihelis vox testatur maria soli deo pervia esse crederis

[4a] Sed tu tamen matris virtutum dum nobis exemplum cupisti commendare subisti remedium pollutis statutum matribus

[4b] Ad templum detulisti tecum mundandum qui tibi integritatis decus deus homo genitus adauxit intacta genitrix

[5a] Lętare quam scrutator cordis et renum probat habitatu

pro- pri- o sin- gu- la- ri- ter dig- nam sanc- ta ma- ri- a

[5b] Ex- ul- ta cu- i par- vus ar- ri- sit tum ma- ri- a qui lę- ta- ri

om- ni- bus et con- si- ste- re su- o nu- tu tri- bu- it

[6a] Er- go qui- que co- li- mus fe- sta par- vu- li chris- ti prop- ter

nos fac- ti e- ius- que pi- ę ma- tris ma- ri- ę [6b] Si non de- i

pos- su- mus tan- tam ex- se- qui tar- di hu- mi- li- ta- tem

for- ma sit no- bis e- ius ge- ni- trix [7a] Laus pa- tri glo- ri- ę

qui su- um fi- li- um gen- ti- bus et po- pu- lo re- ve- lans

is- ra- hel nos so- ci- at [7b] Laus e- ius fi- li- o qui su- o

san- gui- ne nos pa- tri con- ci- li- ans su- per- nis so- ci- a- vit

ci- vi- bus [8] Laus quo- que sanc- to spi- ri- tu- i sit per ę- vum

10. Virginis venerandae

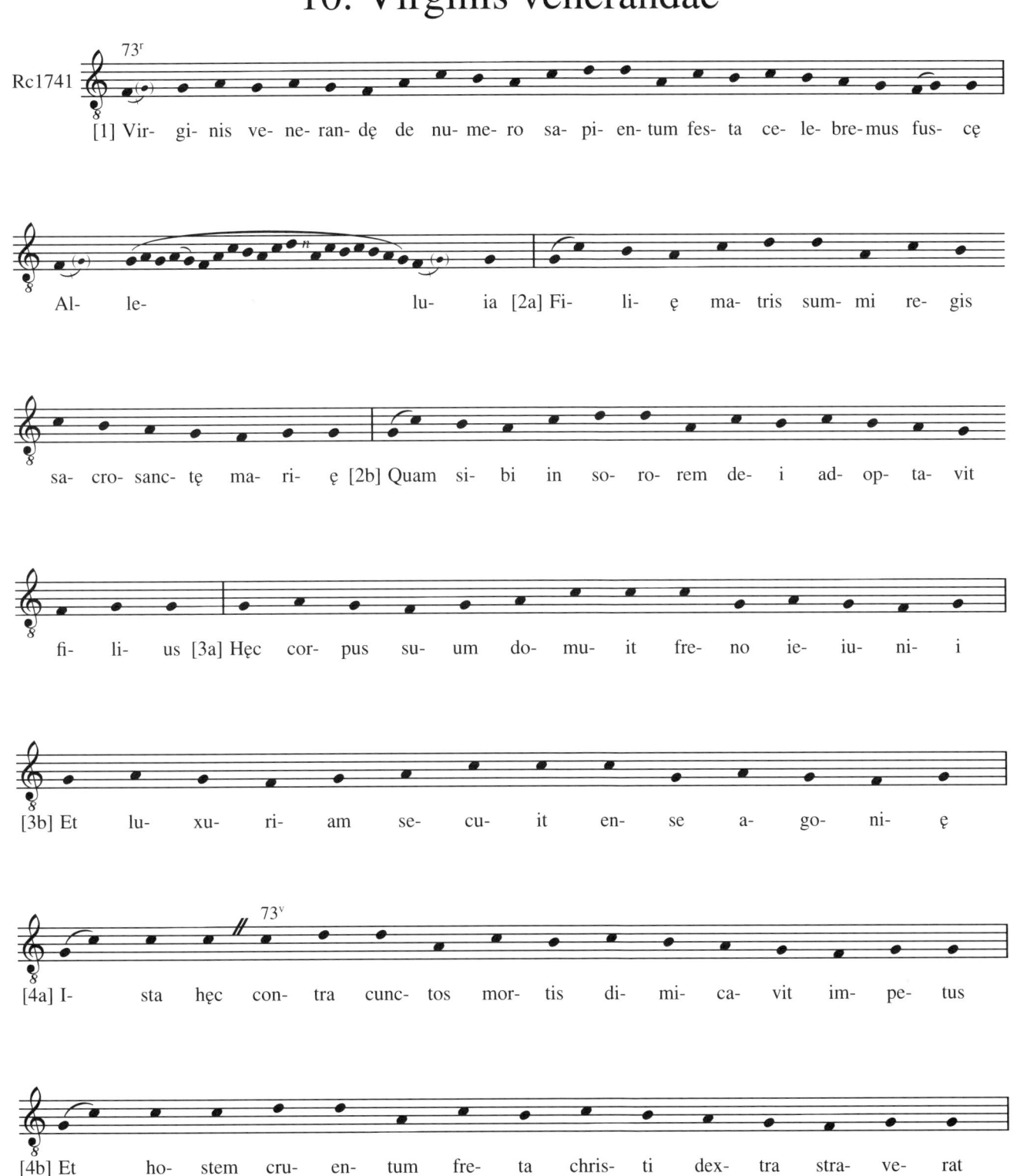

Rc1741

[1] Virginis venerandę de numero sapientum festa celebremus fusce

Alleluia [2a] Filię matris summi regis sacrosanctę marię [2b] Quam sibi in sororem dei adoptavit filius [3a] Hęc corpus suum domuit freno ieiunii

[3b] Et luxuriam secuit ense agonię

[4a] Ista hęc contra cunctos mortis dimicavit impetus

[4b] Et hostem cruentum freta christi dextra straverat

[5a] Hęc sponsum ab aula cęli sese invisentem alacris

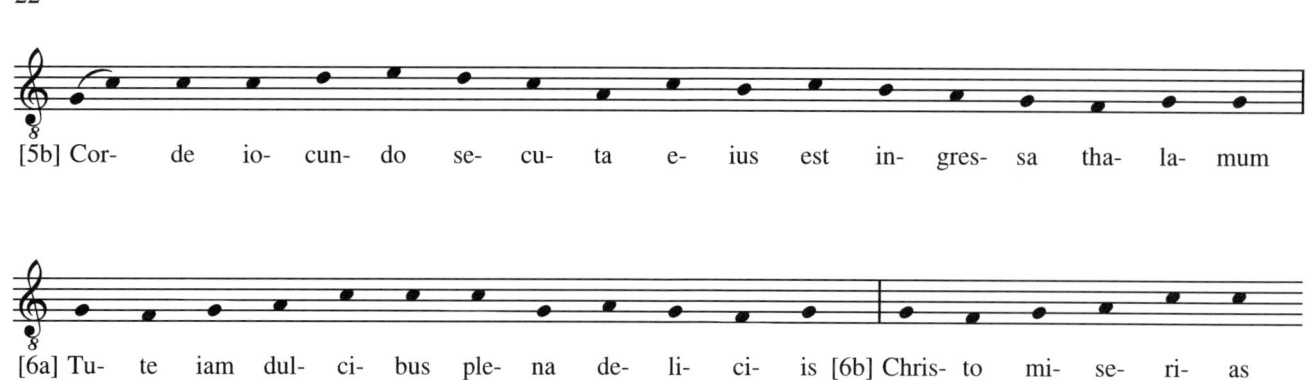

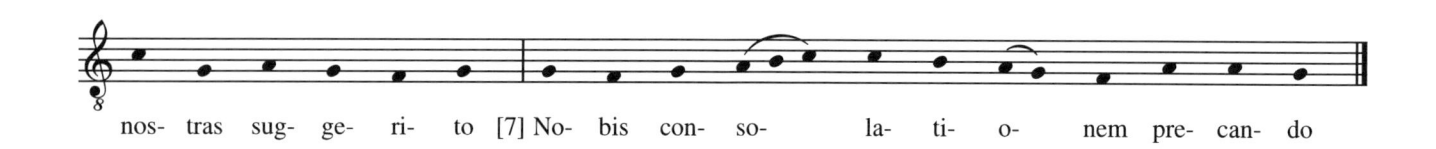

[5b] Cor- de io- cun- do se- cu- ta e- ius est in- gres- sa tha- la- mum

[6a] Tu- te iam dul- ci- bus ple- na de- li- ci- is [6b] Chris- to mi- se- ri- as

nos- tras sug- ge- ri- to [7] No- bis con- so- la- ti- o- nem pre- can- do

11. Ecce vicit

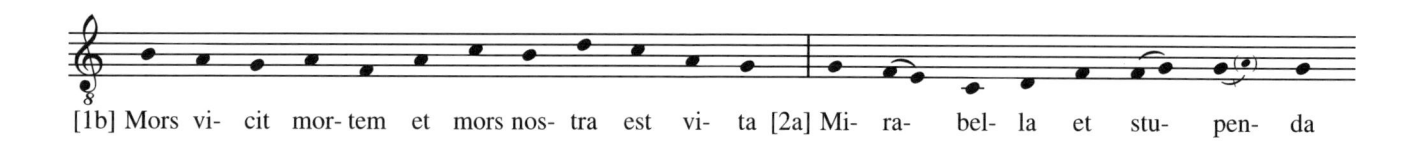

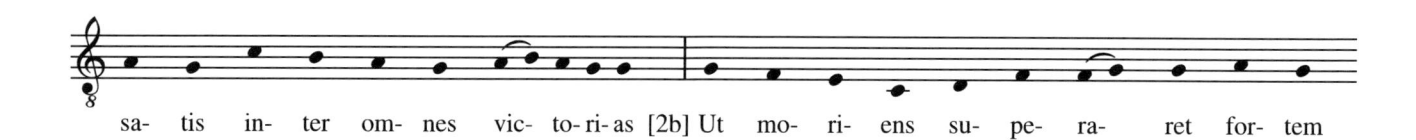

Rc 1741

[1] Ec- ce vi- cit ra- dix da- vid le- o de tri- bu iu- da Al- le- lu- ia

[1b] Mors vi- cit mor- tem et mors nos- tra est vi- ta [2a] Mi- ra- bel- la et stu- pen- da

sa- tis in- ter om- nes vic- to- ri- as [2b] Ut mo- ri- ens su- pe- ra- ret for- tem

cum cal- li- da ver- su- ti- a [3a] Do- mum e- ius in- gres- sus est rex ę- ter- nus

et a- ver- ni con- fre- git va- sa [3b] Drag- mam se- cum quę pe- ri- e- rat por- ta- vit et pa- te- fe- cit reg- ni claus- tra [4a] Pa- ra- di- si por- tam quę clau- sa

fu- e- rat [4b] Per lig- num ve- ti- tum et cul- pam lę- ta- lem in hoc ę- vo

[5a] Quam com- mi- sit pro- to- pla- stus re- se- ra- vit dex- tra per sti- pi- tem e- the- re- a

[5b] Su- sce- pe- rat mors in- dem-nem quem te- ne- re num-quam po- tu- e- rat prop- ter cul- pam

[6a] Dum am- bi- it in- li- ci- ta quę te- ne- bat iu- ste per- di- dit ad- qui- si- ta

[6b] Am- pli- a- re vo- lu- e- rat in suc- ces- sus sed re- man- sit e- va- cu- a- ta

[7a] In se re- fu- sa de- fe- cit ex- tre- mi- tas ut qui- bus ad vi- tam fu- e- rat lar- gi- tus

in- gres- sus do- na- ret et re- gres- sus ad per- ci- pi- en- dam ve- ni- am

[7b] Hic ve- rus est ag- nus le- ga- lis qui mul- tis se ma- ni- fe- sta- vit fi- gu- ris tan- dem se

pro mun- do ho- sti- am de- dit pa- tri ut re- di- me- ret plas- ma su- um

[8a] Hic la- pis est an- gu- la- ris quem re- pro- ba- ve- runt ę- di- fi- can- tes

[8b] Iam fac- tus est in ca- put an- gu- li su- per om- nes in ex- cel- so

[9] Reg- num e- ius mag- num et po- tes- tas e- ius pri- ma per se- cu- la

12. Clara gaudia

Rc 1741

[1] Cla- ra gau- di- a fe- sta pas- cha- li- a Al- le- lu- ia

[2a] Con- gau- det ce- tus per om- ni- a [2b] Dul- ce de- can- tans al- le- lu- ia

[3a] In qua chris- tus per cru- cem re- de- mit a- ni- mas in- fer- no de- di- tas

[3b] A pro- to- pla- sto quot- quot in hoc se- cu- lo pro ge- ni- tę fu- e- rant

[4a] Pa- tri- ar- cha- rum om- ni- um- que si- mul pro- phe- ta- rum re- gum pon- ti- fi- cum

[4b] De- ti- ne- ban- tur clau- stro tar- ta- re- o mor- tis cru- o- re re- tru- sę

[5a] Do- nec vic- tor mor- tis do- mi- nus om- ni- um at- que sanc- tus sanc- to- rum

[5b] Cum cru- cis tro- phe- o in- fer- num pe- ne- trans ab- e- git clau- stra se- va

[6a] Quis es de- mo- nes u- lu- lant lu- ci- fer qui no- stra ut de- us sol- vis

vin- cu- la cunc- ta [6b] Fu- ga- tis te- ne- bris ful- get at the- a- tra- lis

or- ror ru- ti- lo lu- mi- ne per- lu- stra- tus [7a] Cla- ma- bant sanc- ti ad- ve- ni- sti o

iam do- mi- ne re- gum rex a- ve [7b] Quem o- lim va- tes ce- ci- ne- re iam

nos ha- bes re- demp- tos rex a- ve [8a] Tunc hie- sus cum lę- ta sanc- to- rum

glo- ri- a pro- ces- sit mor- te vic- ta [8b] Cu- i psal- le- re lau- des sub om- ni

car- mi- ne non ces- set om- nis ę- tas [9] De- can- tans al- le- lu- ia

13. Dic nobis

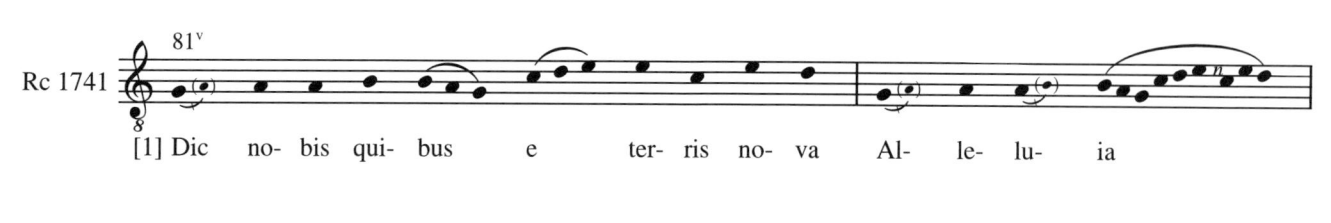

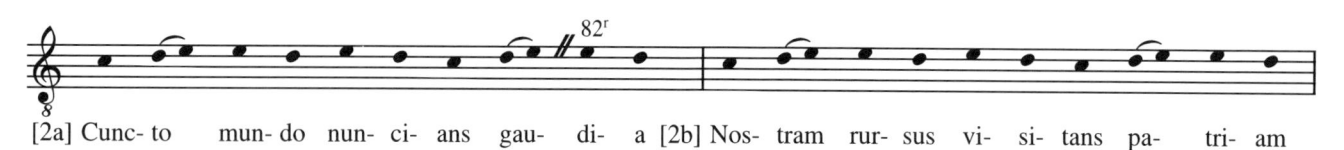

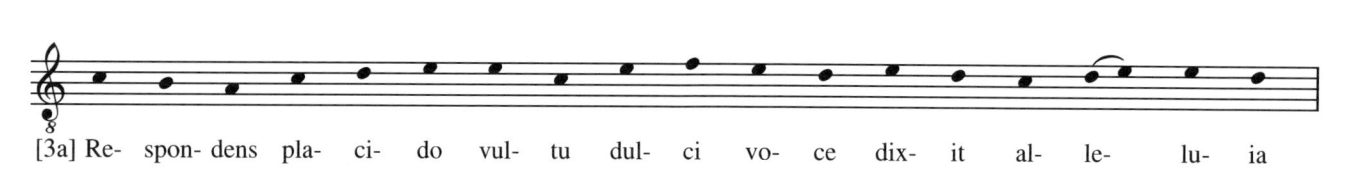

Rc 1741

[1] Dic no- bis qui- bus e ter- ris no- va Al- le- lu- ia

[2a] Cunc- to mun- do nun- ci- ans gau- di- a [2b] Nos- tram rur- sus vi- si- tans pa- tri- am

[3a] Re- spon- dens pla- ci- do vul- tu dul- ci vo- ce dix- it al- le- lu- ia

[3b] An- ge- lus mi- chi de chris- to nun- ci- a- vit pi- a mi- ra- cu- la

[4a] Re- sur- re- xis- se do- mi- num sy- de- ra ce- ci- ne- runt vo- ce lau- dan- da

[4b] Mox e- go pen- nas vo- lu- cris va- cu- as di- ri- gens lę- ta per au- ras

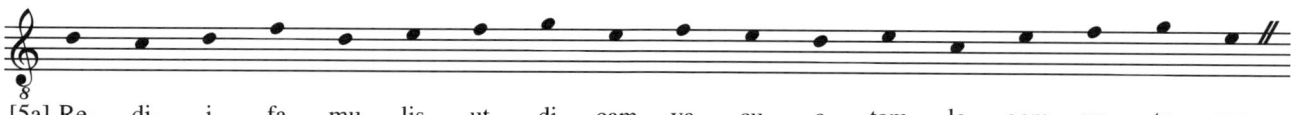

[5a] Re- di- i fa- mu- lis ut di- cam va- cu- a- tam le- gem ve- te- rem

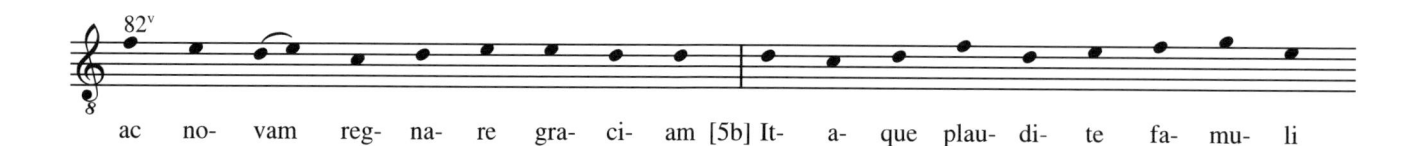

ac no- vam reg- na- re gra- ci- am [5b] It- a- que plau- di- te fa- mu- li vo- ce cla- ra chris- tus ho- di- e re- de- mit nos a mor- te di- ra

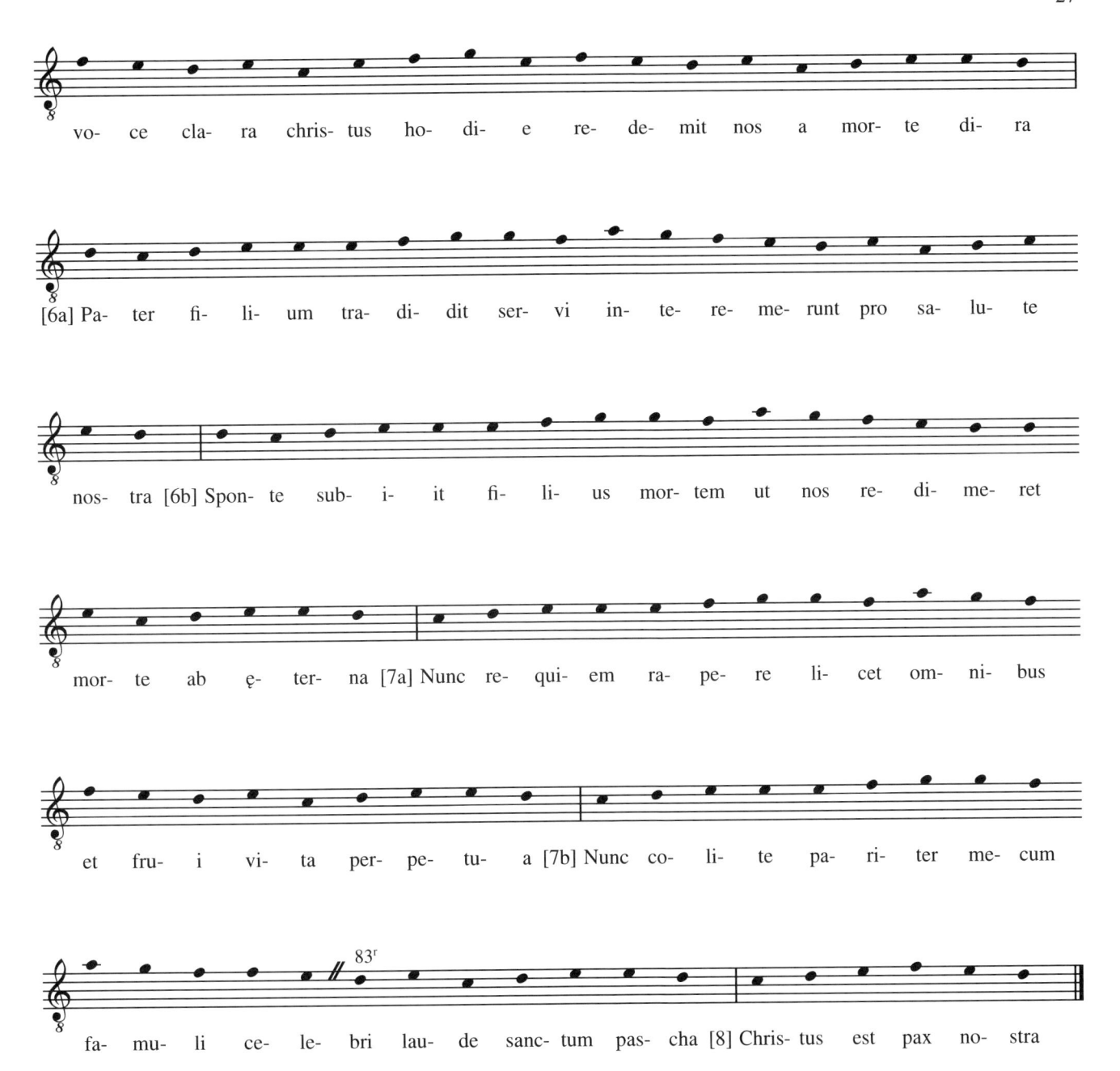

[6a] Pa- ter fi- li- um tra- di- dit ser- vi in- te- re- me- runt pro sa- lu- te

nos- tra [6b] Spon- te sub- i- it fi- li- us mor- tem ut nos re- di- me- ret

mor- te ab ę- ter- na [7a] Nunc re- qui- em ra- pe- re li- cet om- ni- bus

et fru- i vi- ta per- pe- tu- a [7b] Nunc co- li- te pa- ri- ter me- cum

fa- mu- li ce- le- bri lau- de sanc- tum pas- cha [8] Chris- tus est pax no- stra

14. Eia recolamus

Rc 1741

[1] E- ia re- co- la- mus lau- di- bus pi- is dig- na Al- le- lu- ia

[2a] Hu- ius di- e- i car- mi- na in qua no- bis lux o- ri- tur gra- tis- si- ma

[2b] Noc- tis in- te- rit ne- bu- la per- e- unt nos- tri cri- mi- nis um- bra- cu- la

[3a] Ho- di- e se- cu- lo stel- la ma- ris est e- nix- a no- vę sa- lu- tis gau- di- a

[3b] Quem tre- munt ba- ra- tra mors cru- en- ta pa- vet ip- sa a quo per- i- bit mor- tu- a

[4a] Ge- mit cap- ta pes- tis an- ti- qua co- lu- ber li- vi- dus per- dit spo- li- a [4b] Ho- mo lap- sus o- vis ab- duc- ta re- vo- ca- tur ad ę- ter- na gau- di- a [5a] Gau- dent in hac di- e ag- mi- na an- ge- lo- rum cę- le- sti- a [5b] Qui- a e- rat drag- ma de- ci- ma per- di- ta et est in- ven- ta [6a] O cul- pa ni- mi- um be- a- ta ac

re- demp- ta na- tu- ra [6b] De- us qui cre- a- vit om- ni- a na- sci- tur ex fe- mi- na

[7a] Mi- ra- bi- lis na- tu- ra mi- ri- fi- ce in- du- ta as- su- mens quod non e- rat

ma- nens quod e- rat [7b] In- du- i- tur na- tu- ra di- vi- ni- tas hu- ma- na quis

au- di- vit ta- li- a dic ro- go fac- ta [8a] Quę- re- re ve- ne- rat pa- stor pi- us

quod per- i- e- rat [8b] In- du- i- tur ga- le- a cer- tat ut mi- les ar- mis ar- ma

[9a] Pro- stra- tus in su- a pro- pri- a ru- it ho- stis spi- cu- la au- fe- run- tur

te- la [9b] In qui- bus fi- de- rat di- vi- sa sunt il- li- us spo- li- a cap- ta

prę- da su- a [10a] Chri- sti pug- na for- tis- si- ma sa- lus no- stra est ve- ra [10b] Qui nos

su- am ad pa- tri- am dux- it post vic- to- ri- am [11] In qua si- bi laus ę- ter- na

15. Sanctae crucis celebremus

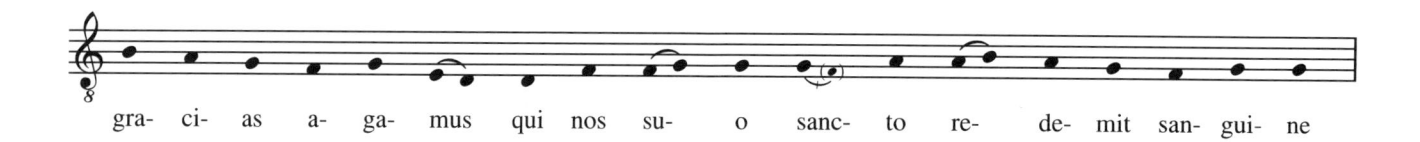

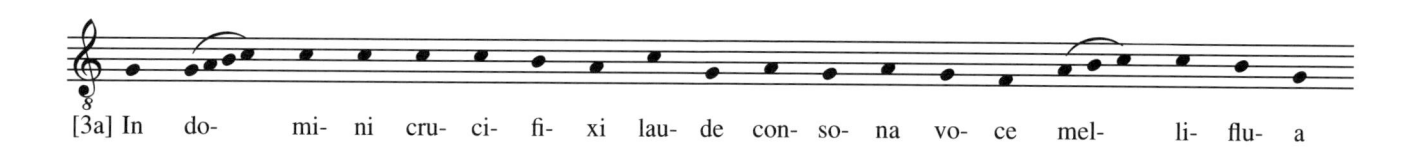

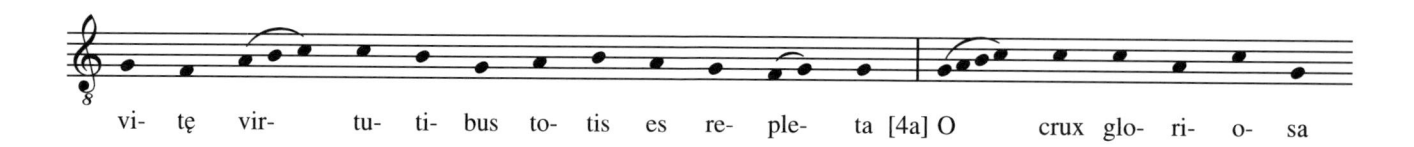

Rc 1741

[1a] Sancte crucis celebremus devotione veneranda Alleluia [1b] Signaculum triumphale per quod salutis sacramentum [2a] Sumpsimus culpa qui protoparentis heu eramus exules facti patrię [2b] Redempti ergo gracias agamus qui nos suo sancto redemit sanguine [3a] In domini crucifixi laude consona voce melliflua concinamus cantica [3b] O crux splendidissima salus perhennitas vitę virtutibus totis es repleta [4a] O crux gloriosa

o crux a- do- ran- da quę pre- ci- um mun- di fer- re tu me- ru- i- sti

[4b] Sal- va prę- sen- tem hu- mi- lem ple- bem in lau- de tu- a ho- di- e

con- gre- ga- tam [5] Quę so- la fu- i- sti por- ta- re dig- na ta- len- tum

16. Laus tibi Christe patris

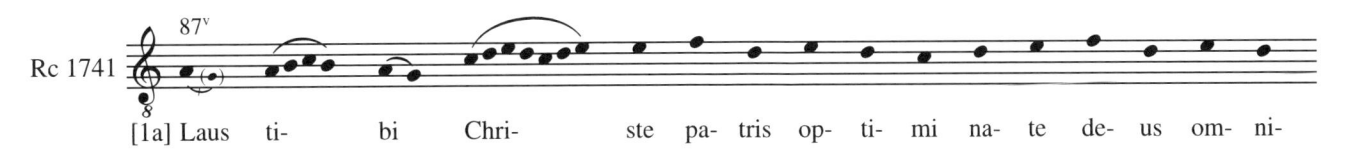

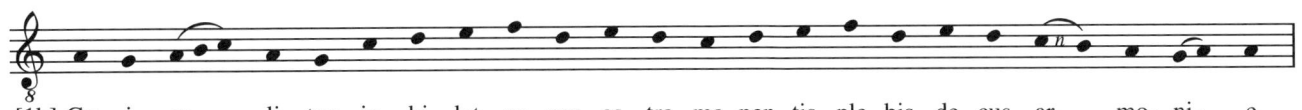

Rc 1741

[1a] Laus ti- bi Chri- ste pa- tris op- ti- mi na- te de- us om- ni-

-po- ten- ti- ę Al- le- lu- ia

[1b] Cu- i cę- li- tus iu- bi- lat su- per as- tra ma- nen- tis ple- bis de- cus ar- mo- ni- ę

[2a] Quem ag- mi- na mar- ty- rum so- no- ris hym- nis col- lau- dant e- the- ris in ar- ce

[2b] Quos im- pi- i ob no- mi- nis o- di- um tu- i mi- se- ro stra- ve- re vul- ne- re

[3a] Quos pi- e nunc re- mu- ne- ras in cę- lis chri- ste pro pę- nis ni- ti- de

[3b] So- li- ta u- sus gra- ci- a qui tu- os or- nas co- ro- nis splen- di- de

[4a] Quo- rum pre- ci- bus sa- cris de- le pre- ca- mur no- strę pi- e cri- mi- na vi- tę

[4b] Ut quos lau- di- bus tu- is re- se- ras no- bis is- tic do- nes cle- mens fa- ve- re

[5a] Il- lis ę- ter- nę dans lu- men glo- ri- ę [5b] No- bis ter- re- na con- ce- de vin- ce- re

[6] Ut li- ce- at se- re- nis ac- ti- bus ple- ni- ter ad- i- pi- sci do- na tu- ę gra- ci- ę

17. Summi trimphum

Rc 1741

[1] Sum- mi tri- um-phum re- gis pro- se- qua- mur lau- de Al- le- lu- ia

[2a] Qui ce- li qui ter- re re- git scep- tra in- fer- ni iu- re do- mi- to

[2b] Qui se- se pro no- bis re- di- men- dis per- mag- num de- dit pre- ci- um

[3a] Hu- ic no- men ex- tat con- ve- ni- ens i- di- thun [3b] Nam tran- si- li- vit om- nes stre- nu- e mon- tes col- li- cu- los- que be- thel [4a] Sal- tum de ce- lo de- dit in vir- gi- na- lem ven- trem in- de in pel- la- gus se- cu- li [4b] Post- quam il- lud su- o mi- ti- ga- vit po- ten- ta- tu te- tras fle- ge- ton- tis as- si- li- it te- ne- bras

[5a] Prin- ci- pis il- li- us dis- tur- ba- to im- pe- ri- o [5b] Ma- ni- plis plu- ri- mis in- de e- ru- tis mun- dum il- lu- strat su- o iu- ba- re [6a] Cap- ti- vi- ta- tem- que

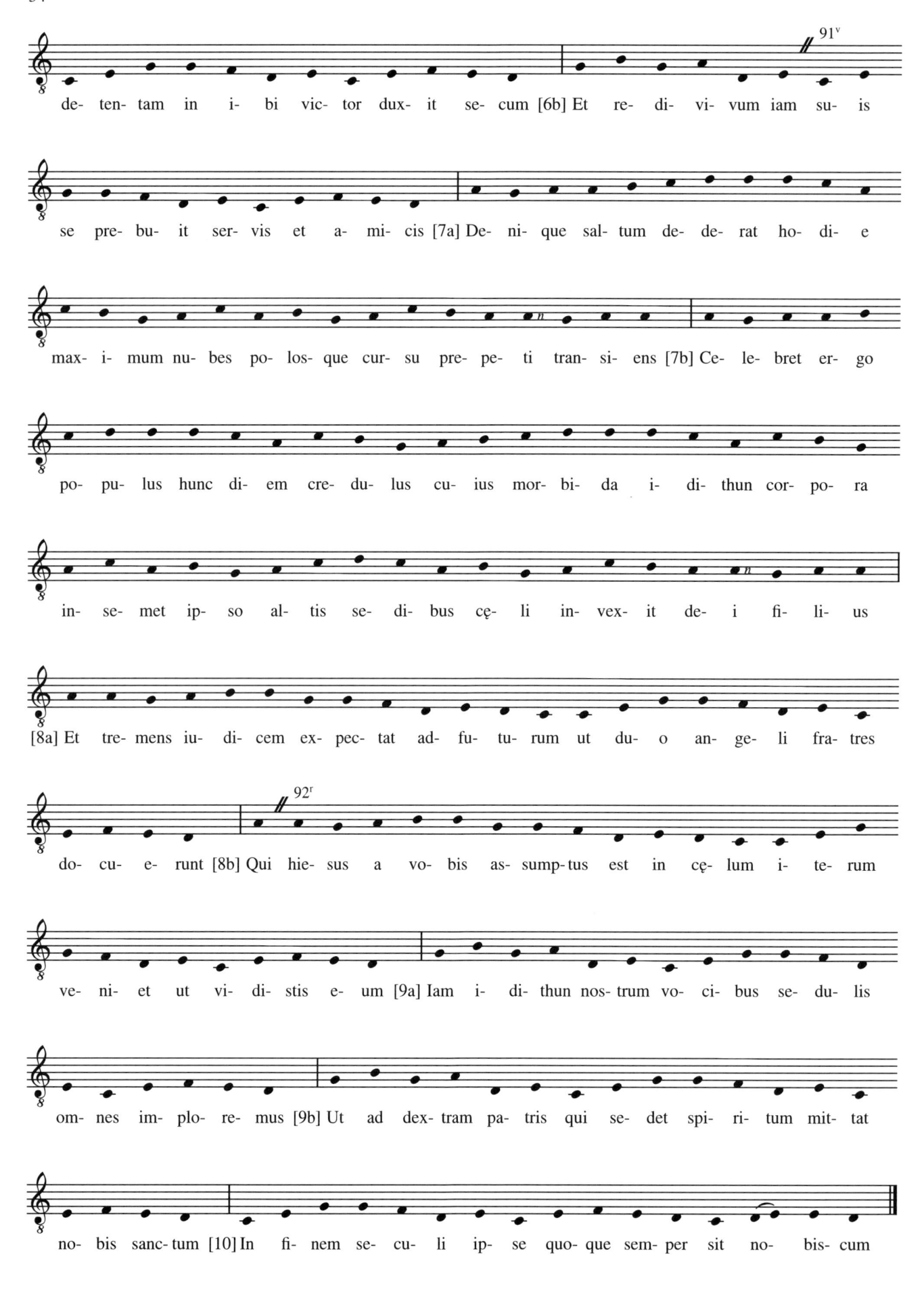

de- ten- tam in i- bi vic- tor dux- it se- cum [6b] Et re- di- vi- vum iam su- is

se pre- bu- it ser- vis et a- mi- cis [7a] De- ni- que sal- tum de- de- rat ho- di- e

max- i- mum nu- bes po- los- que cur- su pre- pe- ti tran- si- ens [7b] Ce- le- bret er- go

po- pu- lus hunc di- em cre- du- lus cu- ius mor- bi- da i- di- thun cor- po- ra

in- se- met ip- so al- tis se- di- bus cę- li in- vex- it de- i fi- li- us

[8a] Et tre- mens iu- di- cem ex- pec- tat ad- fu- tu- rum ut du- o an- ge- li fra- tres

do- cu- e- runt [8b] Qui hie- sus a vo- bis as- sump- tus est in cę- lum i- te- rum

ve- ni- et ut vi- di- stis e- um [9a] Iam i- di- thun nos- trum vo- ci- bus se- du- lis

om- nes im- plo- re- mus [9b] Ut ad dex- tram pa- tris qui se- det spi- ri- tum mit- tat

no- bis sanc- tum [10] In fi- nem se- cu- li ip- se quo- que sem- per sit no- bis- cum

18. Rex omnipotens

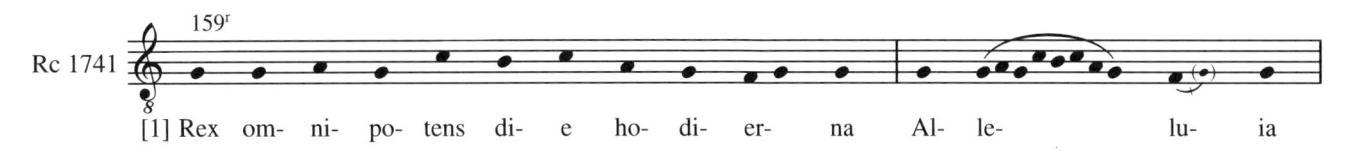

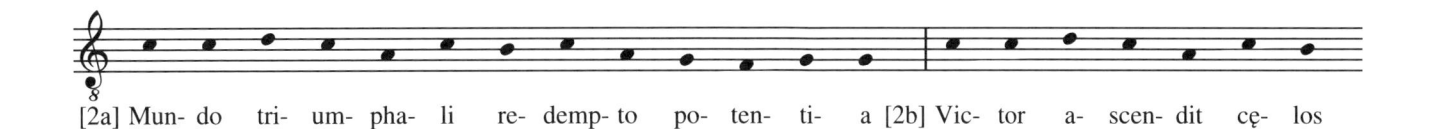

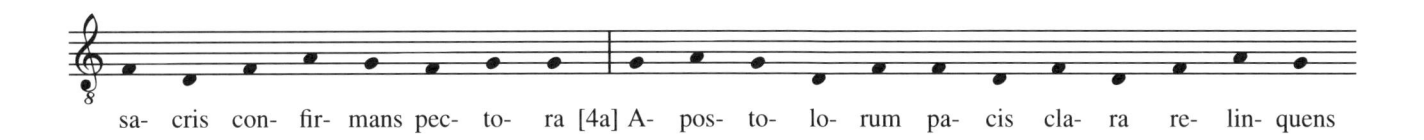

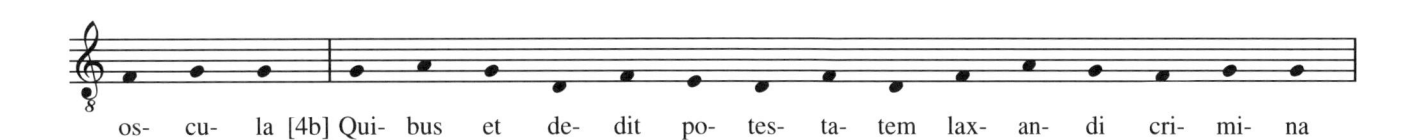

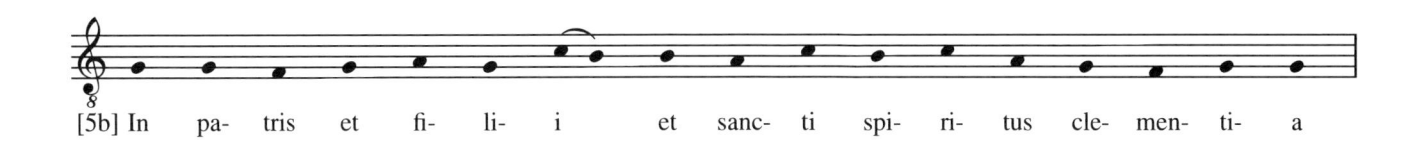

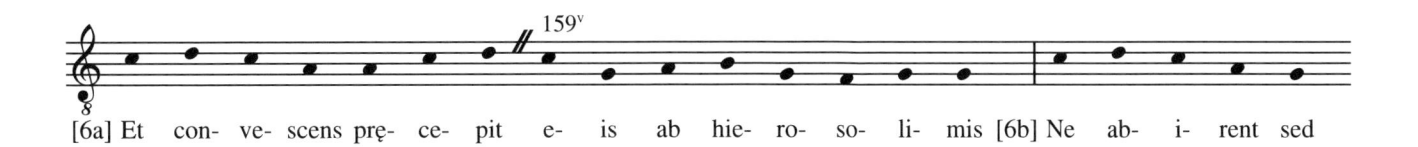

Rc 1741

[1] Rex om- ni- po- tens di- e ho- di- er- na Al- le- lu- ia

[2a] Mun- do tri- um- pha- li re- demp- to po- ten- ti- a [2b] Vic- tor a- scen- dit cę- los

un- de de- scen- de- rat [3a] Nam quad- ra- gin- ta post-quam sur- re- xe- rat [3b] Di- e- bus

sa- cris con- fir- mans pec- to- ra [4a] A- pos- to- lo- rum pa- cis cla- ra re- lin- quens

os- cu- la [4b] Qui- bus et de- dit po- tes- ta- tem lax- an- di cri- mi- na

[5a] Et mi- sit e- os in mun- dum bap- ti- za- re cunc- tas a- ni- mas

[5b] In pa- tris et fi- li- i et sanc- ti spi- ri- tus cle- men- ti- a

[6a] Et con- ve- scens pręce- pit e- is ab hie- ro- so- li- mis [6b] Ne ab- i- rent sed

ex- pec- ta- rent pro- mis- sa mu- ne- ra [7a] Non post mul- tos e- nim di- es mit- tam vo- bis spi- ri- tum pa- ra- cli- tum in ter- ris [7b] Et e- ri- tis mi- chi tes- tes in hie- ru- sa- lem iu- de- a si- ve sa- ma- ri- a [8a] Et cum hoc dix- is- set vi- den- ti- bus il- lis e- le- va- tus est et nu- bes cla- ra [8b] Sus- ce- pit e- um ab e- o- rum o- cu- lis in- tu- en- ti- bus il- lis a- e- ra [9a] Ec- ce ste- te- runt a- mic- ti du- o vi- ri in ve- ste al- ba [9b] Iux- ta di- cen- tes quid am- mi- ran- mi- ni cę- lo- rum al- ta [10a] Hie- sus e- nim hic qui as- sump- tus est a vo- bis ad pa- tris dex- te- ram [10b] Ut a- scen- dit i- ta ve- ni- et que- rens ta- len- ti com- mis- si luc- ra [11a] O de- us ma- ris poli arvę hominem quem creasti quam fraude subdola [11b] Hostis expulit paradiso et captivatum secum traxit ad tartara [12a] Sanguine proprio quem redemisti deus Illuc et redit unde primum corruit ad paradisi gaudia [12b] Iudex cum veneris iudicare sęculum Da nobis petimus sempiternam requiem in sanctorum patria [13] In qua tibi cantemus alleluia

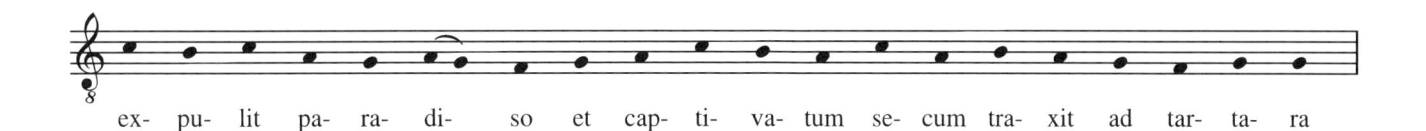

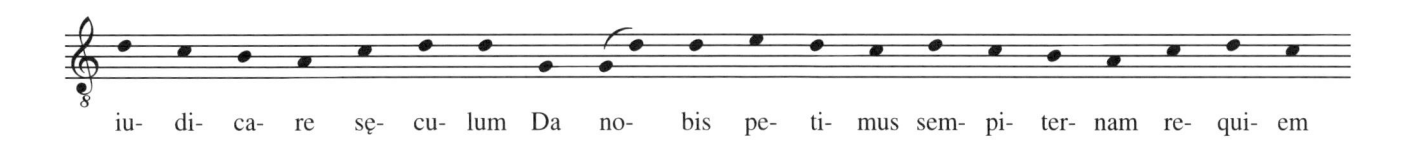

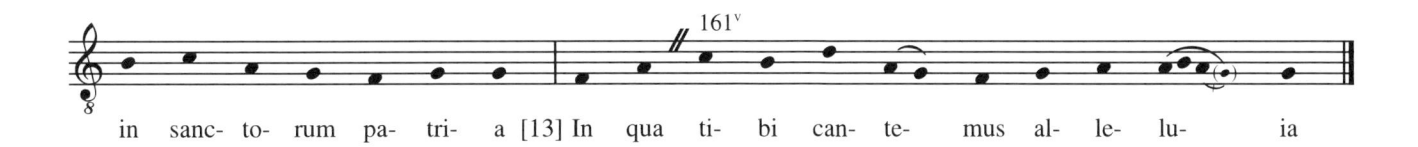

19. Sancti spiritus assit

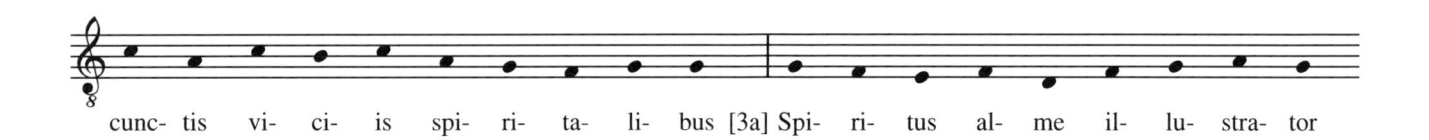

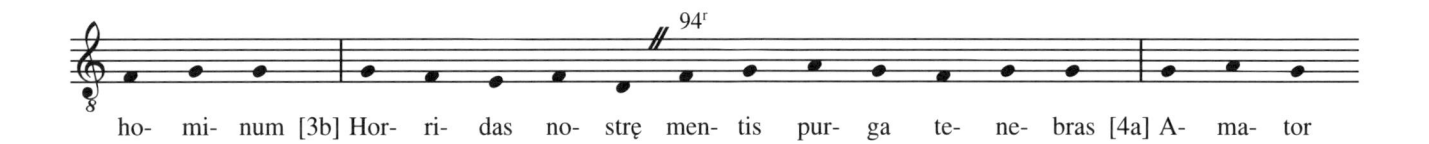

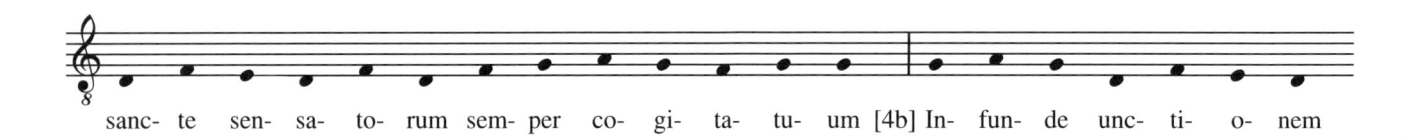

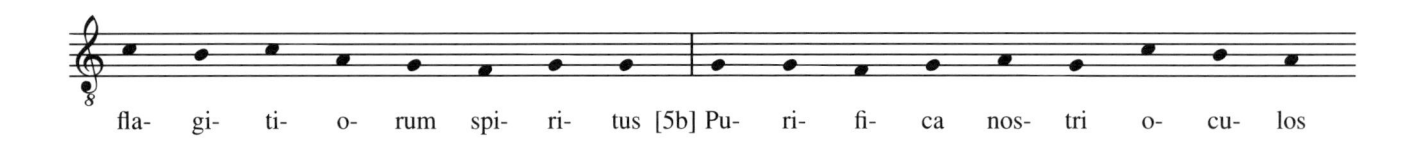

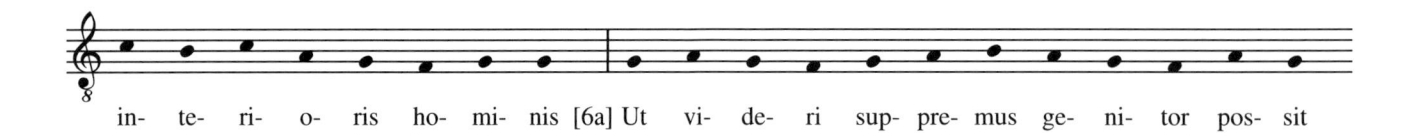

[1] Sancti spiritus adsit nobis gratia Alleluia
[2a] Quę corda nostra sibi faciat habitaculum [2b] Expulsis inde cunctis viciis spiritalibus [3a] Spiritus alme illustrator hominum [3b] Horridas nostrę mentis purga tenebras [4a] Amator sancte sensatorum semper cogitatuum [4b] Infunde unctionem tuam clemens nostris sensibus [5a] Tu purificator omnium flagitiorum spiritus [5b] Purifica nostri oculos interioris hominis [6a] Ut videri suppremus genitor possit

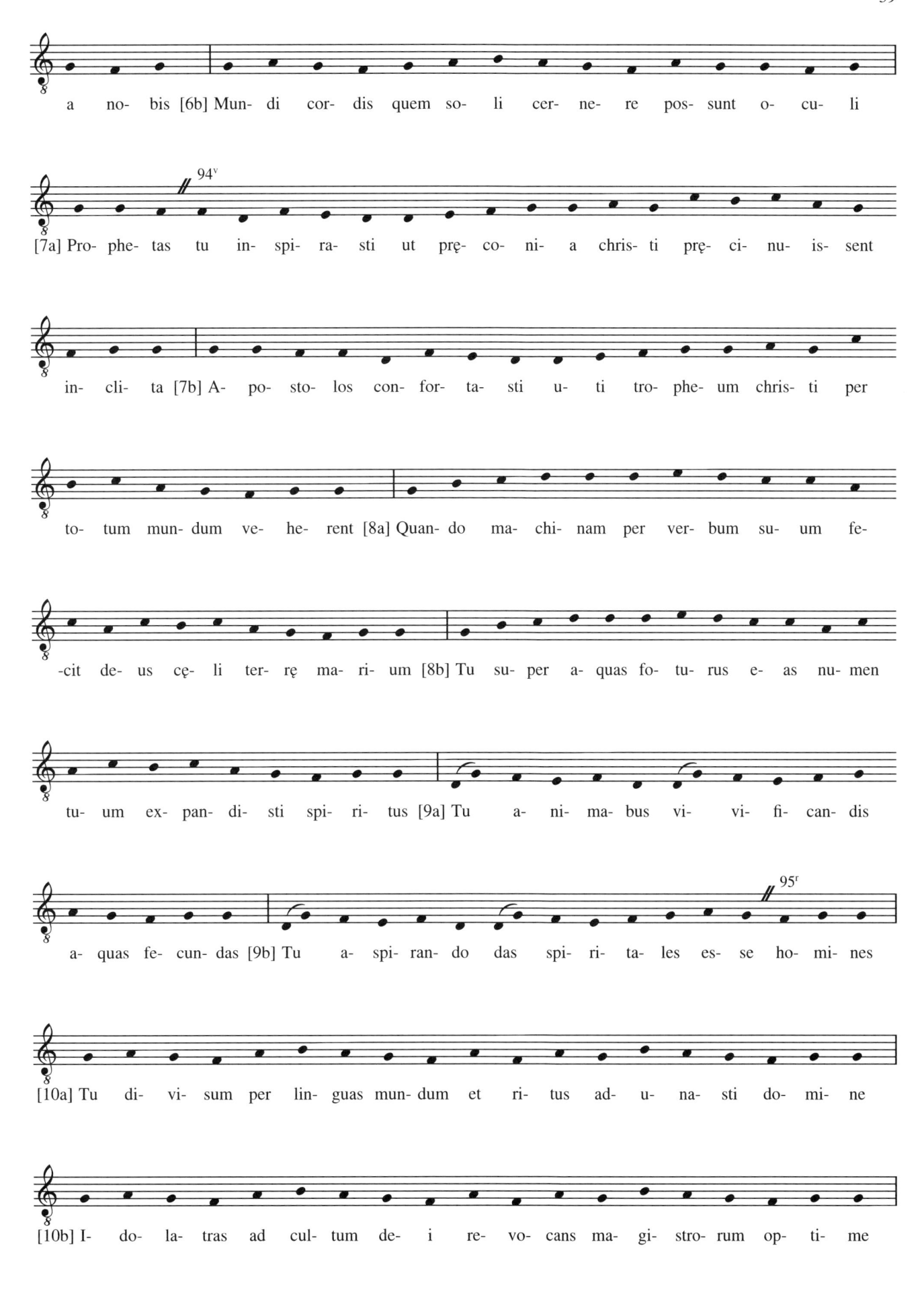

a no- bis [6b] Mun- di cor- dis quem so- li cer- ne- re pos- sunt o- cu- li

[7a] Pro- phe- tas tu in- spi- ra- sti ut pre- co- ni- a chris- ti pre- ci- nu- is- sent

in- cli- ta [7b] A- po- sto- los con- for- ta- sti u- ti tro- phe- um chris- ti per

to- tum mun- dum ve- he- rent [8a] Quan- do ma- chi- nam per ver- bum su- um fe-

-cit de- us ce- li ter- re ma- ri- um [8b] Tu su- per a- quas fo- tu- rus e- as nu- men

tu- um ex- pan- di- sti spi- ri- tus [9a] Tu a- ni- ma- bus vi- vi- fi- can- dis

a- quas fe- cun- das [9b] Tu a- spi- ran- do das spi- ri- ta- les es- se ho- mi- nes

[10a] Tu di- vi- sum per lin- guas mun- dum et ri- tus ad- u- na- sti do- mi- ne

[10b] I- do- la- tras ad cul- tum de- i re- vo- cans ma- gi- stro- rum op- ti- me

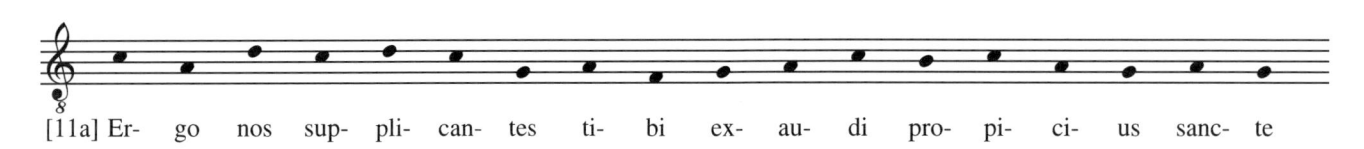

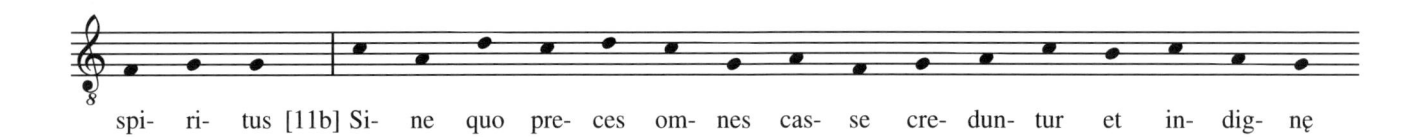

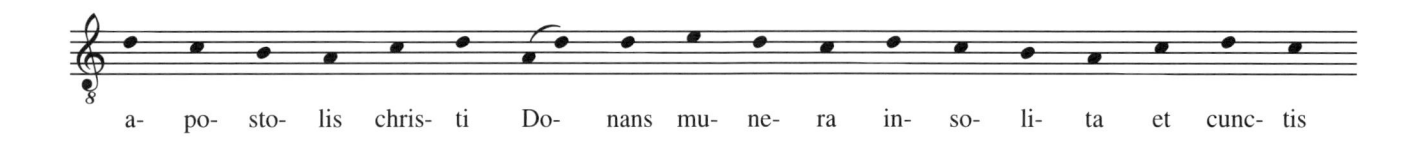

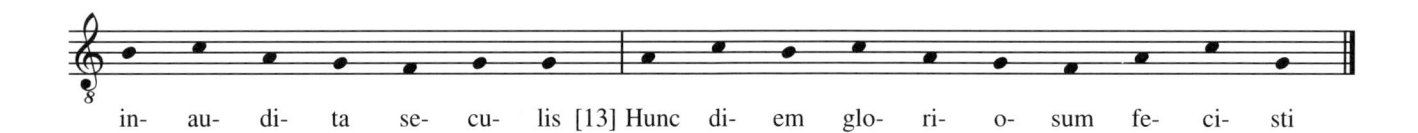

[11a] Ergo nos supplicantes tibi exaudi propicius sancte spiritus [11b] Sine quo preces omnes casse creduntur et indignę dei auribus [12a] Tu qui omnium seculorum sanctos Tui nominis docuisti instinctu amplectende spiritus [12b] Ipse hodie apostolis christi Donans munera insolita et cunctis inaudita seculis [13] Hunc diem gloriosum fecisti

20. Alme mundi rex

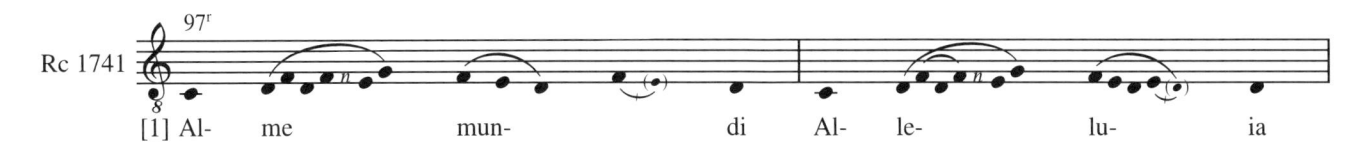

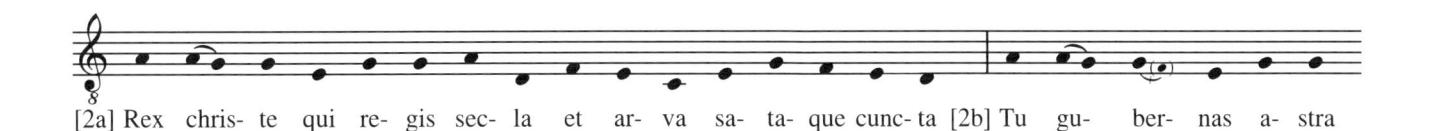

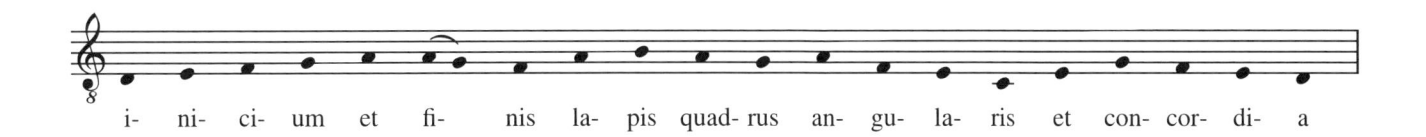

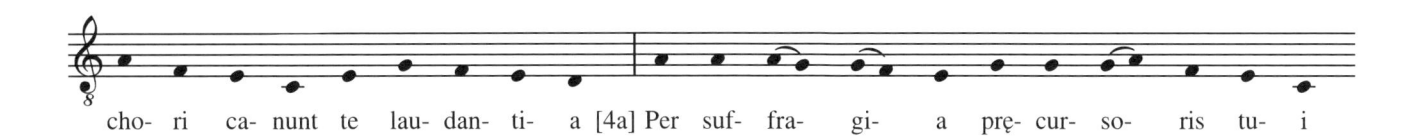

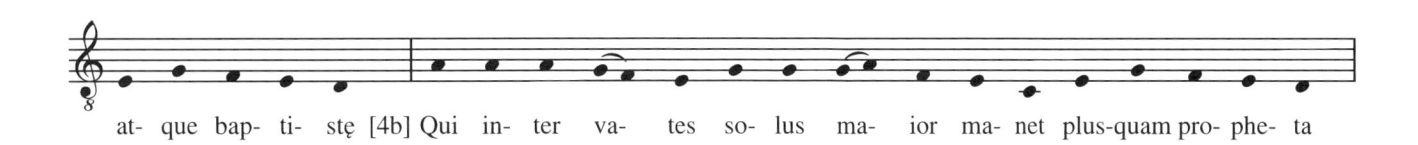

Rc 1741

[1] Al- me mun- di Al- le- lu- ia

[2a] Rex chris- te qui re- gis sec- la et ar- va sa- ta- que cunc- ta [2b] Tu gu- ber- nas a- stra su- pra ma- ris- que ha- bi- ta- cu- la [3a] Ip- se es qui vo- ca- ris al- pha et ω i- ni- ci- um et fi- nis la- pis quad- rus an- gu- la- ris et con- cor- di- a [3b] Qui fa- cis pri- sca no- bis prę- sen- ti- a quę- su- mus ut con- ce- das cu- i su- per- ni cho- ri ca- nunt te lau- dan- ti- a [4a] Per suf- fra- gi- a prę- cur- so- ris tu- i at- que bap- ti- stę [4b] Qui in- ter va- tes so- lus ma- ior ma- net plus-quam pro- phe- ta [5a] U- na cum il- lo an- ge- li- co ag- mi- ne Tu- um mi- ra- bi- le con- lau- da- re

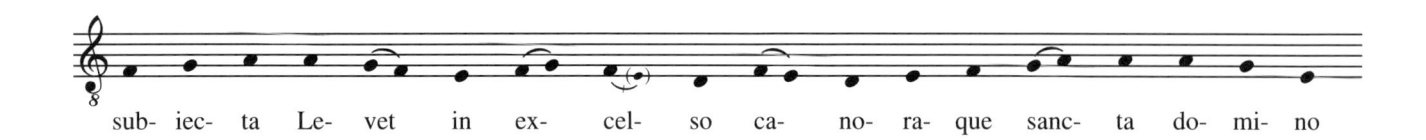

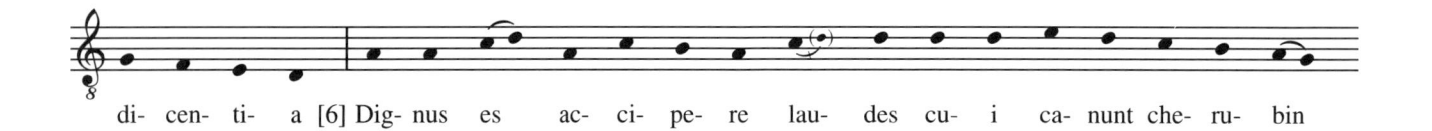

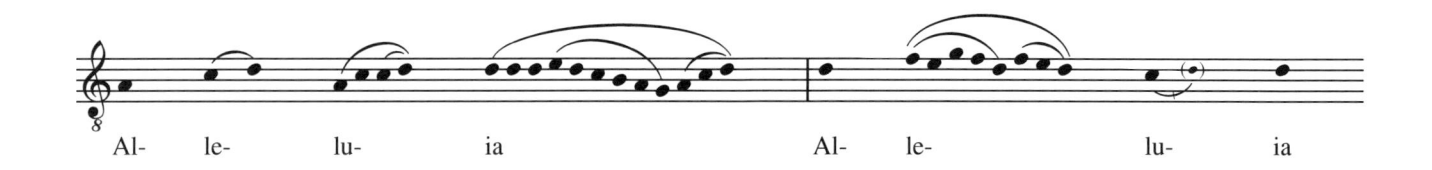

no-men Va-le-at fa-lanx no-stra [5b] Iam nunc om-nis tur-ba fi-de-i

sub-iec-ta Le-vet in ex-cel-so ca-no-ra-que sanc-ta do-mi-no

di-cen-ti-a [6] Dig-nus es ac-ci-pe-re lau-des cu-i ca-nunt che-ru-bin

Al- le- lu- ia Al- le- lu- ia

A- gi- e rex ę-ter-ne [7a] Qui so-lus reg-nas cum pa-tre et pa-ra-cli-to

[7b] Per im-mor-ta-li-a se-cu-lo-rum se-cu-la [8] A-men di-cant om-ni-a

21. Pretiosa sollemnitas

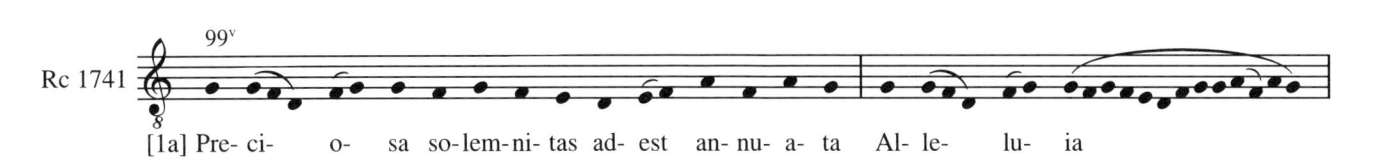

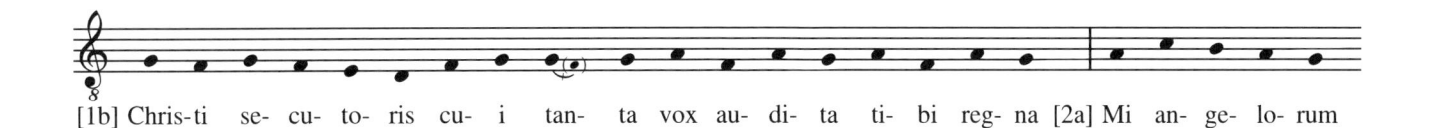

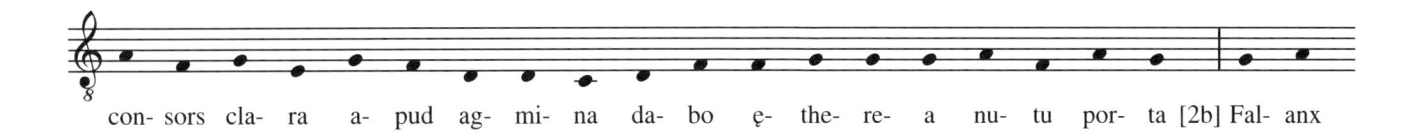

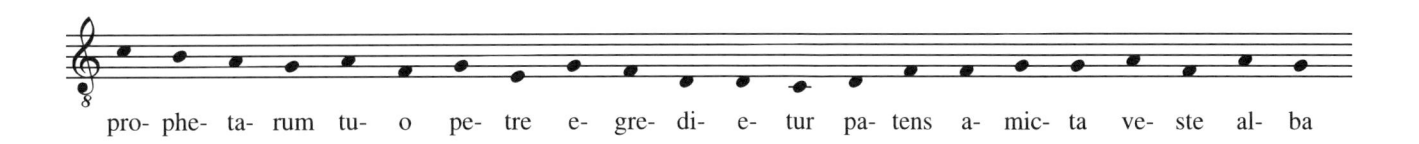

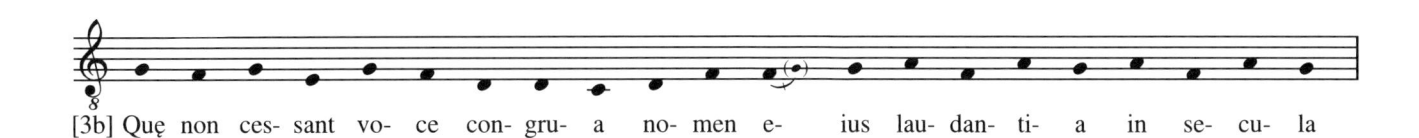

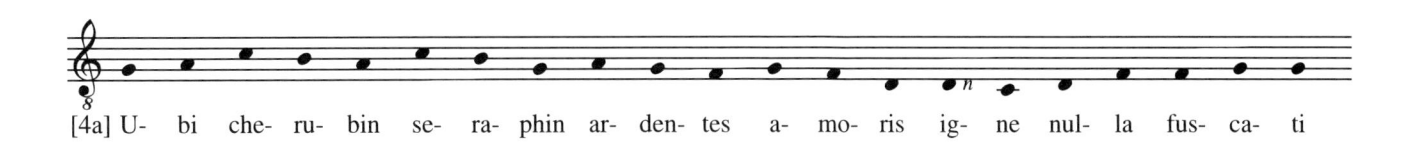

[1a] Pre- ci- o- sa so-lem-ni- tas ad- est an- nu- a- ta Al- le- lu- ia

[1b] Chris-ti se- cu- to- ris cu- i tan- ta vox au- di- ta ti- bi reg- na [2a] Mi an- ge- lo- rum

con- sors cla- ra a- pud ag- mi- na da- bo ę- the- re- a nu- tu por- ta [2b] Fal- anx

pro- phe- ta- rum tu- o pe- tre e- gre- di- e- tur pa- tens a- mic- ta ve- ste al- ba

cum co- ro- na [3a] U- bi ad- stant co- ram do- mi- no mil- le mi- li- a cla- man- ti- a

[3b] Quę non ces- sant vo- ce con- gru- a no- men e- ius lau- dan- ti- a in se- cu- la

[4a] U- bi che- ru- bin se- ra- phin ar- den- tes a- mo- ris ig- ne nul- la fus- ca- ti

ne- qui- ci- a [4b] Mu- rus re- ful- get or- na- tus a- sper- sa que gem- mis re- do- lent nec- tar o-le-um lac et u-na ro-ri-flu-a [5a] Cum qui-bus for-ti-tur col-la-ta cla-ve reg-ni cę-lo-rum pe-trus chris-ti ath-le-ta re-gens cunc-ta [5b] Ip-se-que pro no-bis in-ter-ce-de-re pa-trem po-lo-rum de-vo-ti-o-ne su-a at-que fi-de non de-sis-tat [6] U-ti dig-na car-mi-na pa-tri ac fi-li-o po-si-ta [7] Pro-fe-ra-mus per co-ę-ter-na se-cu-lo-rum se-cu-la

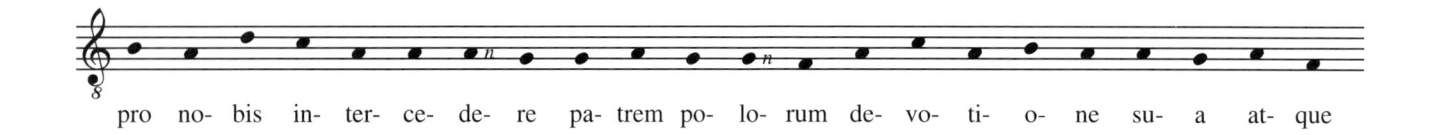

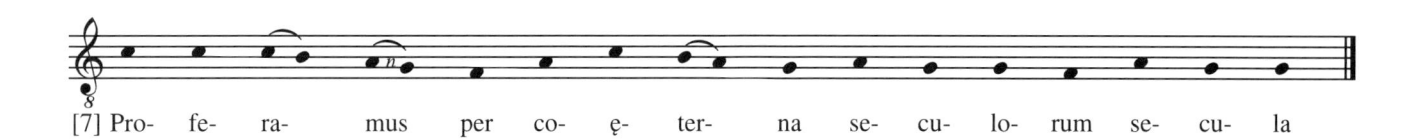

22. Petre summe

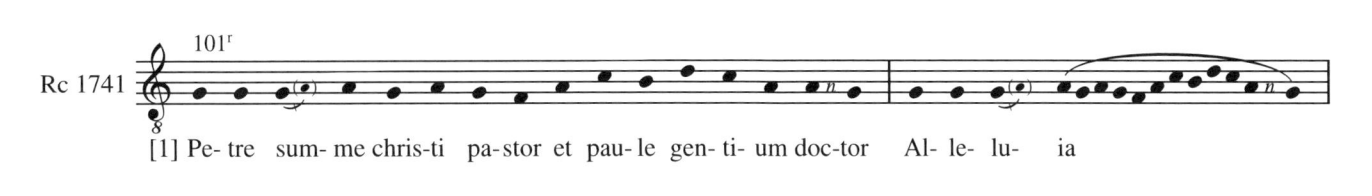

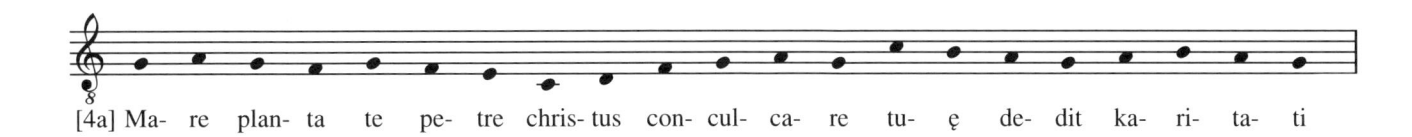

Rc 1741

[1] Petre summe christi pastor et paule gentium doctor Alleluia

[2a] Aecclesiam vestris doctrinis illuminatam [2b] Per circulum terrę precatus adiuvet vester [3a] Nam dominus petre cęlorum tibi claves dono dedit [3b] Armigerum beniamin christus texit suum vasque lectum

[4a] Mare planta te petre christus conculcare tuę dedit karitati

[4b] Umbra tui corporis infirmis debilibusque fecit medicinam

[5a] Spermologon philosophos te paule christus dat vincere sua voce

[5b] Multiplices victorias tu paule christo per populos adquisisti

[6a] Pos- tre- mo vic- tis om- ni- bus bar- ba- ris Ad ar- cem sum- mi per- gi- tis cul- mi- nis

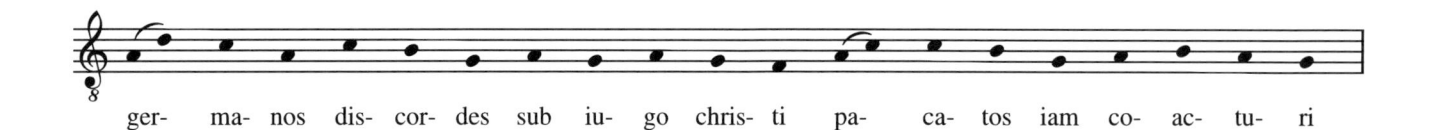

ger- ma- nos dis- cor- des sub iu- go chris- ti pa- ca- tos iam co- ac- tu- ri

[6b] I- bi ne- ro- nis fe- ri- tas prin- ci- pes A- po- sto- lo- rum pręliis plu- ri- mis

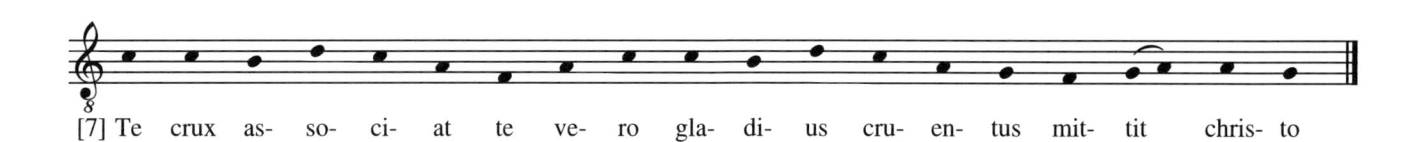

vic- to- res di- ver- sę te pe- tre et pau- le ad- dix- e- rat pe- nę mor- tis

[7] Te crux as- so- ci- at te ve- ro gla- di- us cru- en- tus mit- tit chris- to

23. Sancti merita Benedicti

Rc 1741

[1] Sancti merita benedicti inclita Alleluia

[2a] Venerande sanctitatis ac monachorum presulis [2b] Ad laudem hiesu christi organa nostra concrepent [3a] Nursia felix tulit natum genitrix [3b] Domina mundi roma fovit alitrix [4a] Hic ergo preventus optimo sancti spiritus dono [4b] Sophiam despexit humanam nactus et angelicam [5a] Hic fide subnixus integra redintegravit confracta [5b] Incendia carnis edomat cruce venenum effugat [6a] Vage mentis monachum reparat fontem rutilat [6b] Eius iussu de laci abdito

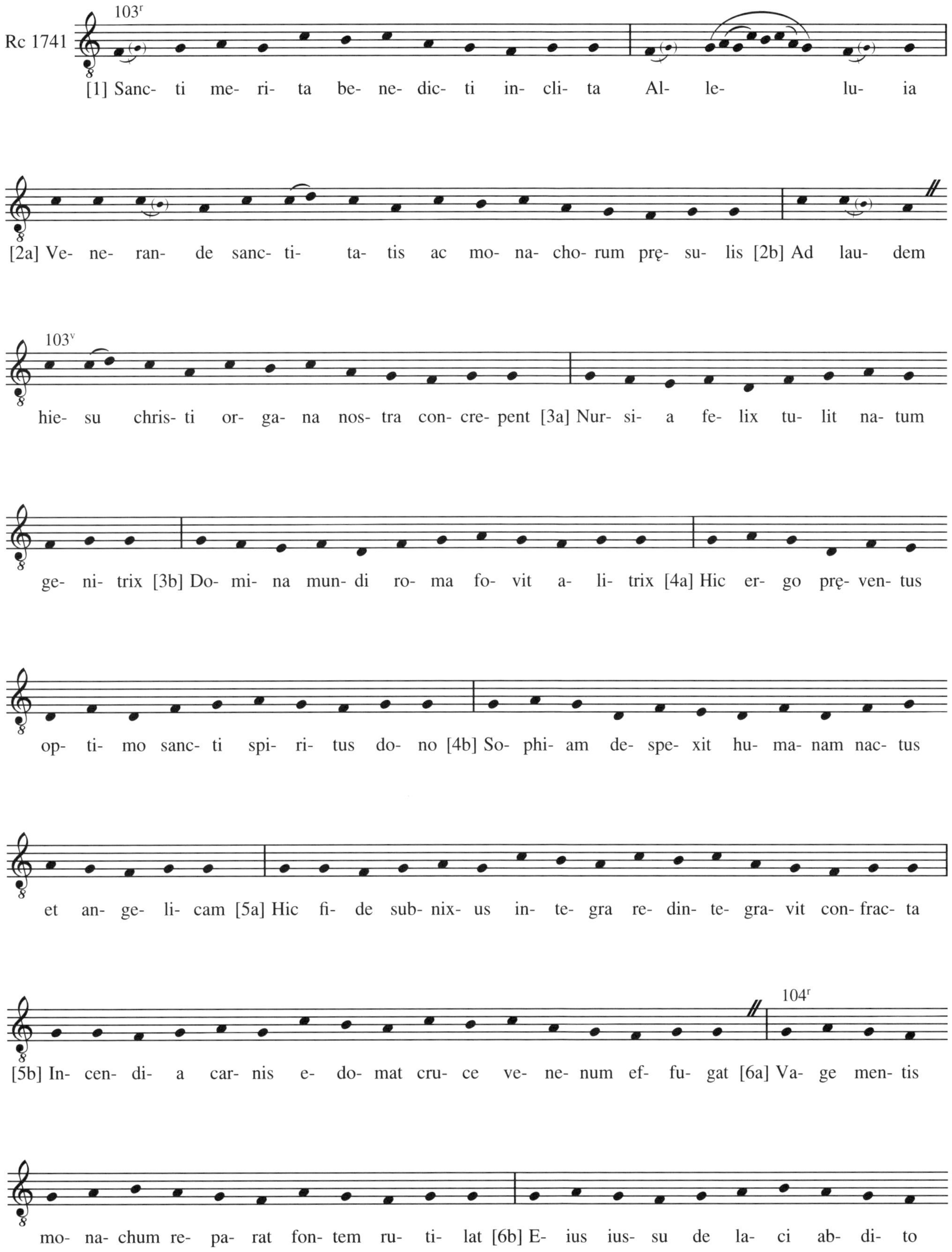

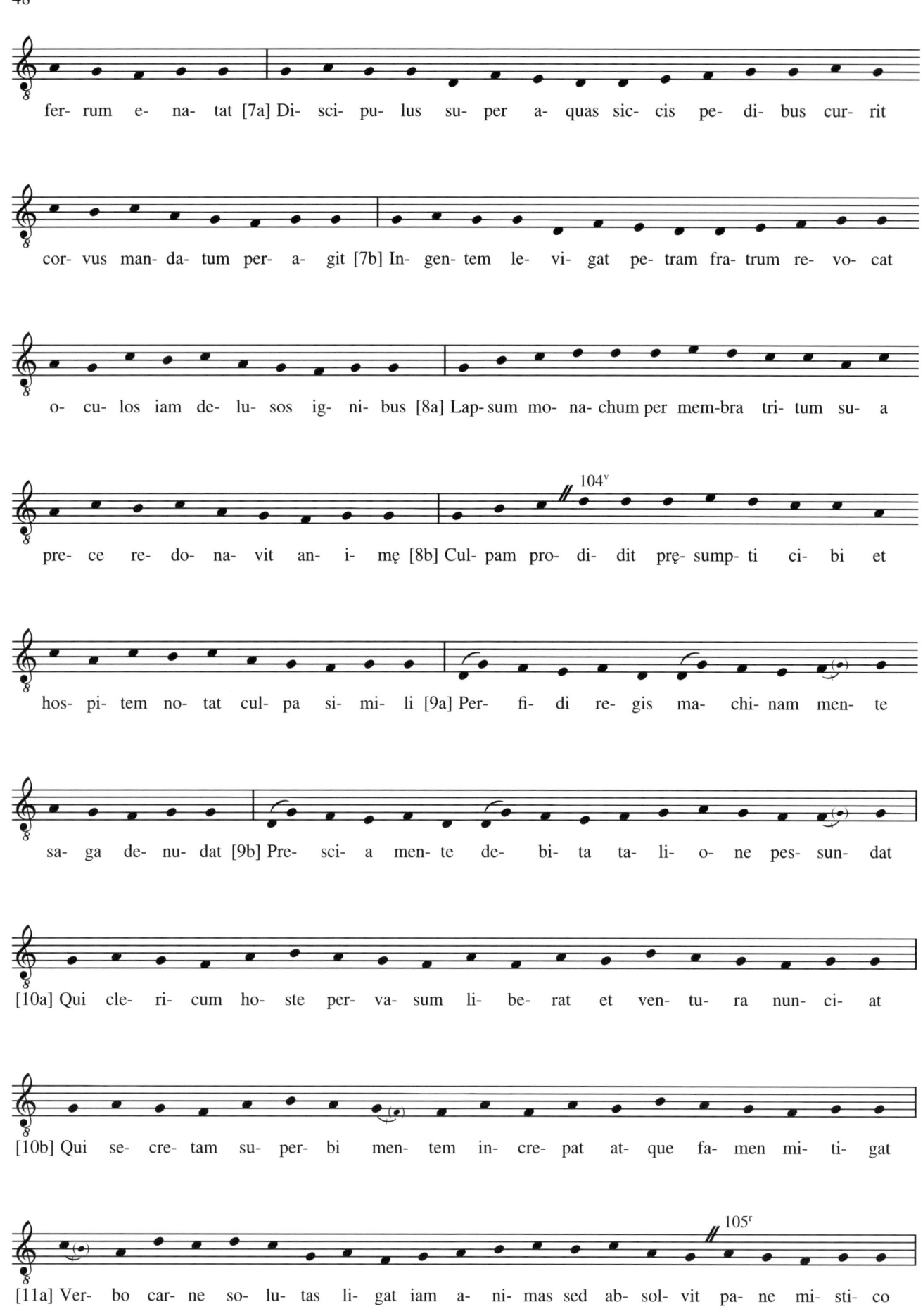

ferrum e- na- tat [7a] Di- sci- pu- lus su- per a- quas sic- cis pe- di- bus cur- rit

cor- vus man- da- tum per- a- git [7b] In- gen- tem le- vi- gat pe- tram fra- trum re- vo- cat

o- cu- los iam de- lu- sos ig- ni- bus [8a] Lap- sum mo- na- chum per mem- bra tri- tum su- a

pre- ce re- do- na- vit an- i- mę [8b] Cul- pam pro- di- dit prę- sump- ti ci- bi et

hos- pi- tem no- tat cul- pa si- mi- li [9a] Per- fi- di re- gis ma- chi- nam men- te

sa- ga de- nu- dat [9b] Pre- sci- a men- te de- bi- ta ta- li- o- ne pes- sun- dat

[10a] Qui cle- ri- cum ho- ste per- va- sum li- be- rat et ven- tu- ra nun- ci- at

[10b] Qui se- cre- tam su- per- bi men- tem in- cre- pat at- que fa- men mi- ti- gat

[11a] Ver- bo car- ne so- lu- tas li- gat iam a- ni- mas sed ab- sol- vit pa- ne mi- sti- co

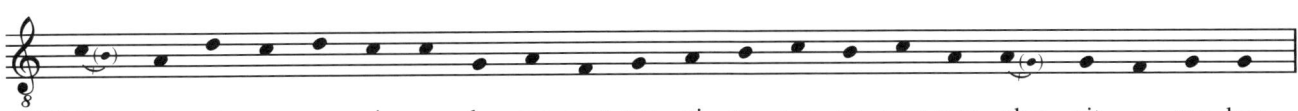

[11b] Cau- tes ab- sque pe- ri- cu- lo ser- vant vas vi- tre- um op- pres- sum plan- git e- mu- lum

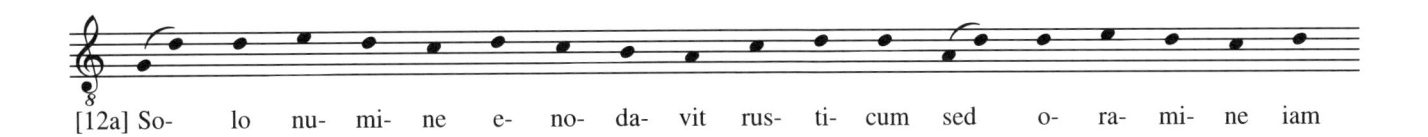

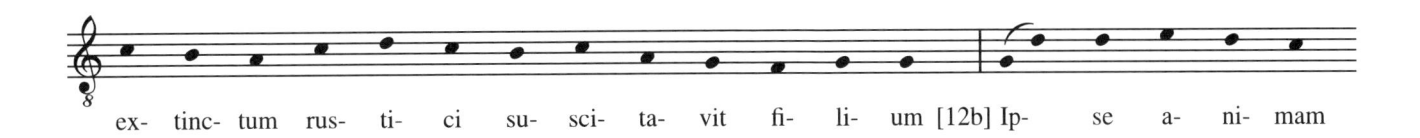

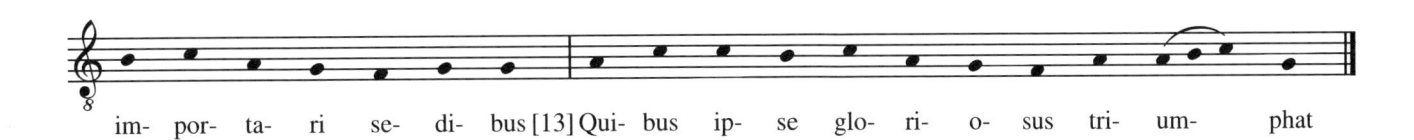

[12a] So- lo nu- mi- ne e- no- da- vit rus- ti- cum sed o- ra- mi- ne iam

ex- tinc- tum rus- ti- ci su- sci- ta- vit fi- li- um [12b] Ip- se a- ni- mam

ca- pu- a- ni prę- su- lis vi- dit lu- mi- ne in so- li- to su- per- nis

im- por- ta- ri se- di- bus [13] Qui- bus ip- se glo- ri- o- sus tri- um- phat

24. Candida contio melos

Rc 1741

[1a] Candida contio melos concrepa Alleluia

[1b] Tinnula cantibus iungas organa [2a] Benedictum caste resultet

liquido sonore simphonia [2b] Artifici plectro perita

sillabatim stringere neumata [3a] Fluxerat quondam sopor immania

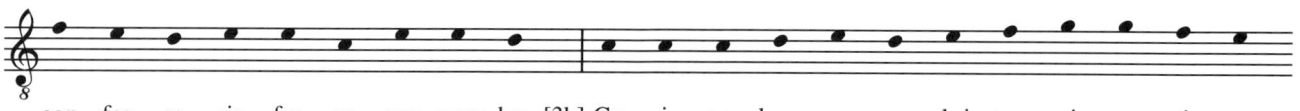

confessoris fessa per membra [3b] Cui prebens sacra christus viatica

intulit grata famina [4a] Care quid hesitas non est quod metuas

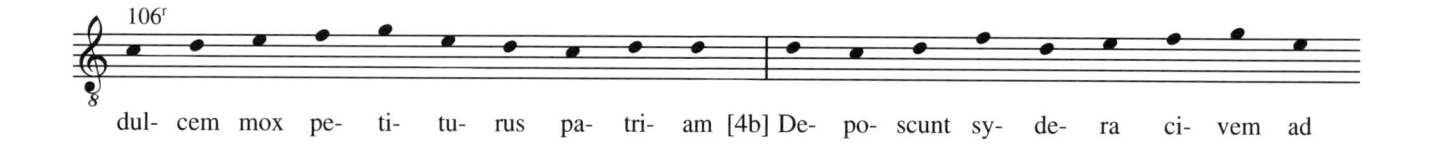

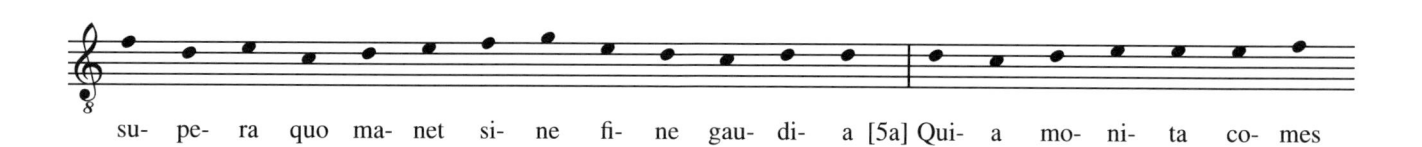

dulcem mox petiturus patriam [4b] Deposcunt sydera civem ad

supera quo manet sine fine gaudia [5a] Quia monita comes

excipit egrimonia membra carpens languida [5b] Die septima supera sequens cęli convexa felix scandit anima [6a] Plaudens gallia funus excipit ac inclita servat in aula [6b] Eius per sacra christe suffragia nostra guberna tempora [7] Amen dicant omnia

25. Laurenti David

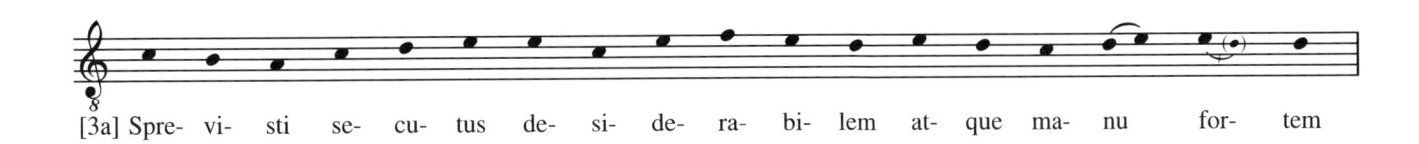

Rc 1741

[1] Laurenti david magni martyr milesque fortis Alleluia
[2a] Tu imperatoris tribunal [2b] Tu manus tortorum cruentas
[3a] Sprevisti secutus desiderabilem atque manu fortem

[3b] Qui solus potuit regna superare tyranni crudelis

[4a] Cuiusque sanctus sanguinis prodigos facit amor milites eius

[4b] Dum-mo-do illum liceat cernere dispendio vitę presentis

[5a] Cesaris tu fasces contemnis et iudicis minas derides [5b] Carnifex ungulas et ustor craticulam vane consumunt [6a] Dolet impius urbis prefectus victus a pisce assato christi cibo [6b] Gaudet domini conviva favo conresurgendi cum ipso saturatus [7a] O laurenti miles david invictissime regis ęterni [7b] Apud illum servulis ipsius deprecare veniam semper [8] Martir milesque fortis

26. Congaudent angelorum chori

Rc 1741

[1] Congaudent angelorum chori gloriosę virgini Alleluia

[2a] Quę sine virili commixtione genuit [2b] Filium qui suo mundum cruore medicat [3a] Nam ipsa lętatur quod cęli iam conspicatur principem [3b] In terris cui quondam sugendas virgo mamillas prębuit [4a] Quam celebris angelis maria hiesu mater creditur [4b] Qui filii illius debito se cognoscunt famulos [5a] Qua gloria in cęlis ista virgo colitur Quę domino cęli prębuit hospitum sui sanctissimi corporis [5b] Quam splendida polo stella maris rutilat Quę omnium lumen astrorum et hominum atque spirituum genuit

[6a] Te cę- li re- gi- na hęc ple- bi- cu- la pi- is con- ce- le- brat men- ti- bus

[6b] Te can- tu me- lo- dos su- per e- the- ra u- na cum an- ge- lis e- le- vat

[7a] Te li- bri vir- go con- ci- nunt pro- phe- ta- rum cho- rus iu- bi- lat sa- cer- do- tum a- po- sto- li chris- ti- que mar- ty- res prę- di- cant [7b] Te ple- bes se- xus se- qui- tur u- tri- us- que vi- tam di- li- gens vir- gi- na- lem cę- li- -co- las in cas- ti- mo- ni- a e- mu- lans [8a] Aec- cle- si- a er- go cunc- ta te cor- di- bus te que car- mi- ni- bus ce- le- brat [8b] Ti- bi su- am ma- ni- fe- stat de- vo- ti- o- nem Pre- ca- tu te sup- pli- ci im- plo- rans ma- ri- a [9] Ut si- bi aux- i- li- o cir- ca chris- tum do- mi- num es- se dig- ne- ris per ę- vum

27. Felix valde

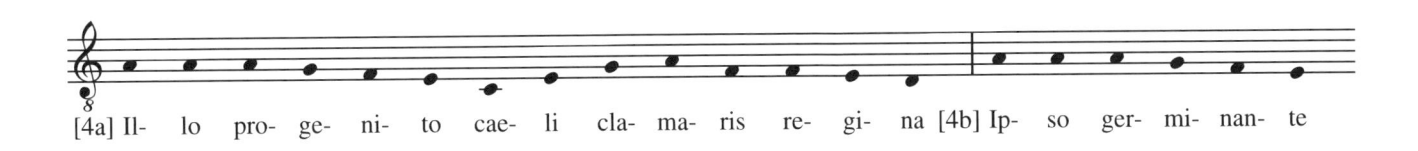

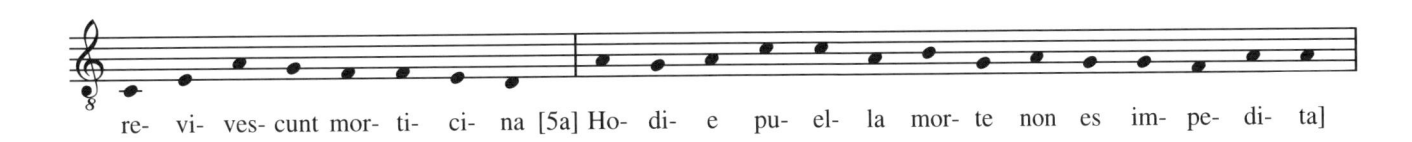

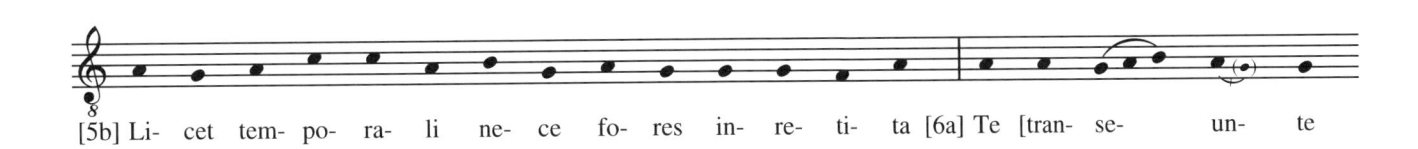

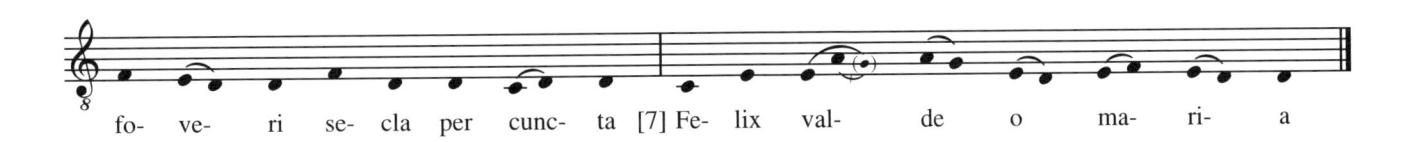

Rn 1343

[1] [Fe- lix val- de [2a] O ma- ri- a in- cor- rup- ta pu- er- pe- ra

[2b] Tu me- ri- to vo- ca- ris mun- di do- mi- na [3a] An- ge- li dic- tis o- be- dis- ti vir- go pu- di- ca [3b] Ver- nan- ti flo- re mox fu- i- sti vir- go praeg- na- ta

[4a] Il- lo pro- ge- ni- to cae- li cla- ma- ris re- gi- na [4b] Ip- so ger- mi- nan- te re- vi- ves- cunt mor- ti- ci- na [5a] Ho- di- e pu- el- la mor- te non es im- pe- di- ta]

[5b] Li- cet tem- po- ra- li ne- ce fo- res in- re- ti- ta [6a] Te [tran- se- un- te lae- ta- tur] po- lo- rum fors be- a- ta [6b] Te ad- iu- van- te pos- si- mus fo- ve- ri se- cla per cunc- ta [7] Fe- lix val- de o ma- ri- a

28. Summa stirpe

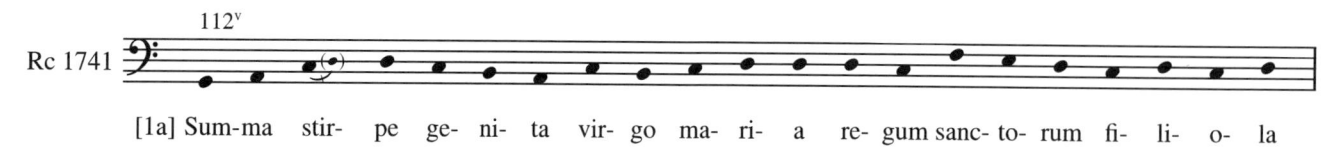

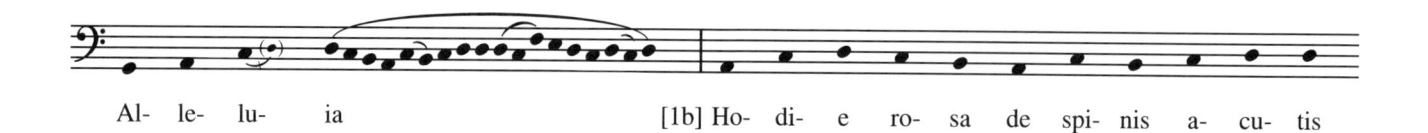

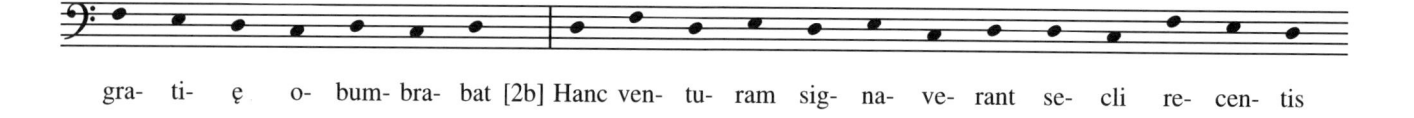

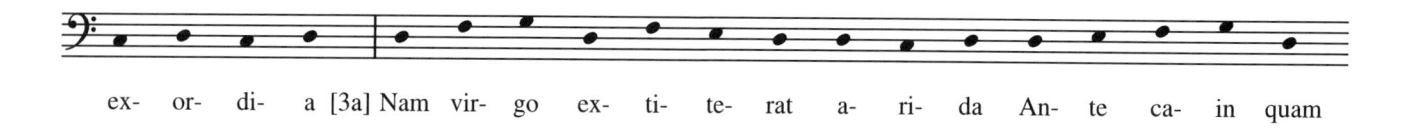

Rc 1741

[1a] Sum-ma stir-pe ge-ni-ta vir-go ma-ri-a re-gum sanc-to-rum fi-li-o-la

Al- le- lu- ia [1b] Ho- di- e ro- sa de spi- nis a- cu- tis

ev- ę or- ta est mol- lis- si- ma [2a] Quę sti- pi- tem ve- tu- stę nox- ę flo- re

gra- ti- ę o- bum- bra- bat [2b] Hanc ven- tu- ram sig- na- ve- rant se- cli re- cen- tis

ex- or- di- a [3a] Nam vir- go ex- ti- te- rat a- ri- da An- te ca- in quam

pol- lu- is- set e- an- dem hu- mo- re fra- ter- ni san- gui- nis li- be- ra li- vo- ris

flam- ma nec ca- lens li- bi- di- nis ma- cu- la [3b] Te vi- ri et fe- mi- nę prę- di- cant

Ca- sti- ta- tem se- quen- tes cę- li re- gi- nam seu cho- rus sub le- ge

princ- ci- pum vel no- vo- rum stem- ma pa- trum in- ter quos tu ru- ti- las ma- xi- ma

[4a] Te sic- ca vir- gu- la a- a- ron mon- strat si- ti- bun- do cor- ti- ce tru- dens

gem- mu- las [4b] Sic cas- to cor- po- re fi- li- um gi- gens pro- tu- li- sti cę- lis

ac ter- ris ger- mi- na [5a] Hie- ru- sa- lem fi- li- a tu ge- ni- trix de- i

simp- pli- ci- bus co- lum- ba- rum o- cu- lis splen- des ni- ti- da [5b] So- la ex- em- plo

si- ne nec pri- us si- mi- lem vi- sa es nec ha- be- re se- quen- tem al- ma

ma- ri- a [6a] Quam fre- quen- tes ce- le- brant an- ge- li in tu- o na- ta- li

hunc di- em sol- lem- nen stel- la lu- ci- da [6b] Nos gre- ga- tos fra- gi- les

ho- mi- nes sub tu- a vi- sce- ra iu- gi- ter tu- e- re pi- a ma- ri- a

29. Alma fulgens crux praeclara

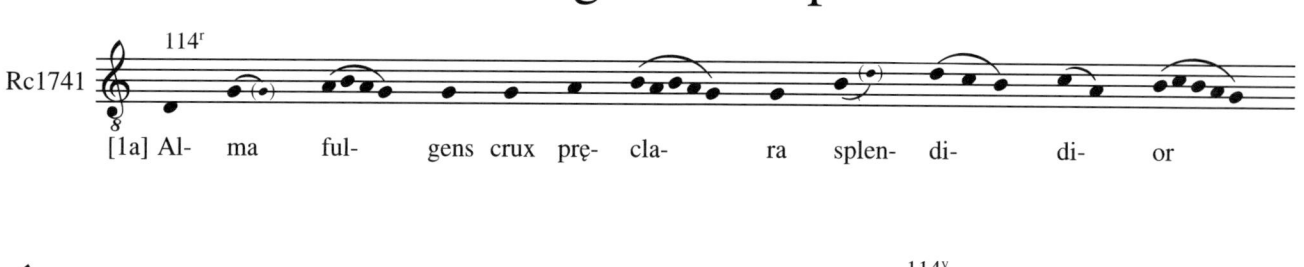

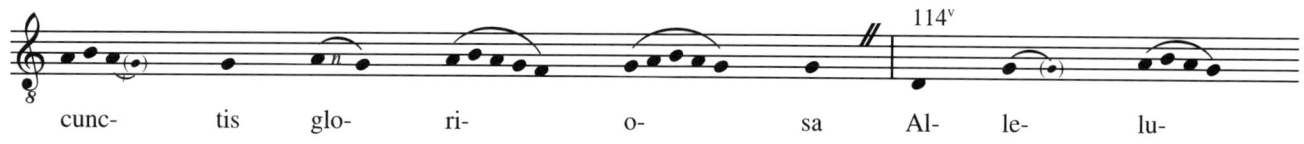

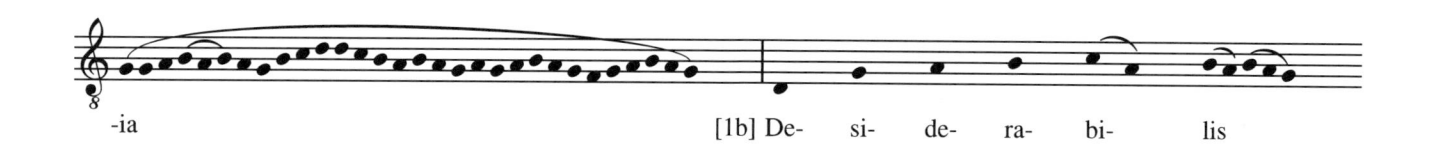

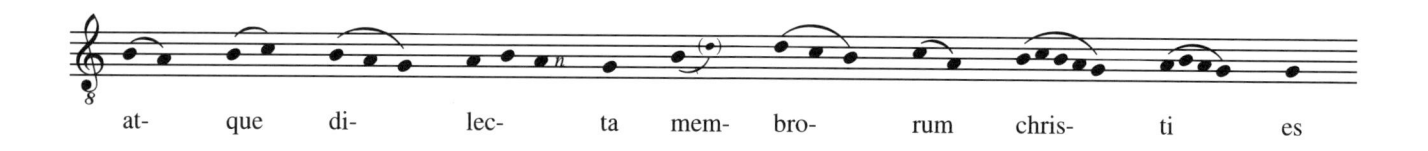

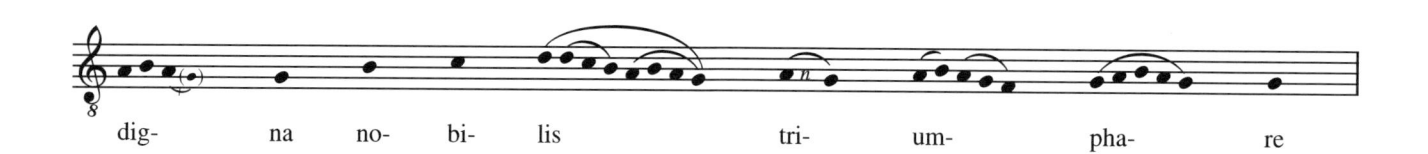

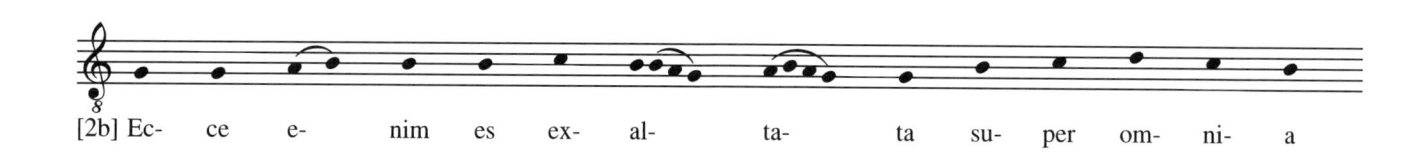

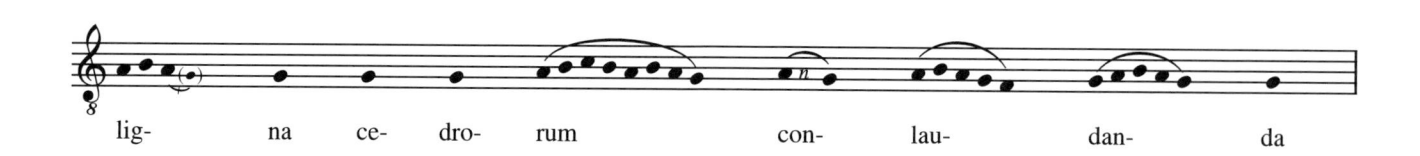

Rc1741

[1a] Al- ma ful- gens crux prę- cla- ra splen- di- di- or cunc- tis glo- ri- o- sa Al- le- lu- -ia [1b] De- si- de- ra- bi- lis at- que di- lec- ta mem- bro- rum chris- ti es a- dor- na- ta [2a] Tu so- la fu- i- sti dig- na no- bi- lis tri- um- pha- re [2b] Ec- ce e- nim es ex- al- ta- ta su- per om- ni- a lig- na ce- dro- rum con- lau- dan- da

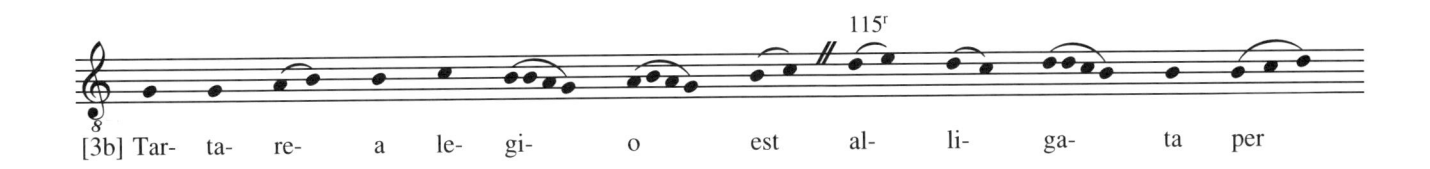

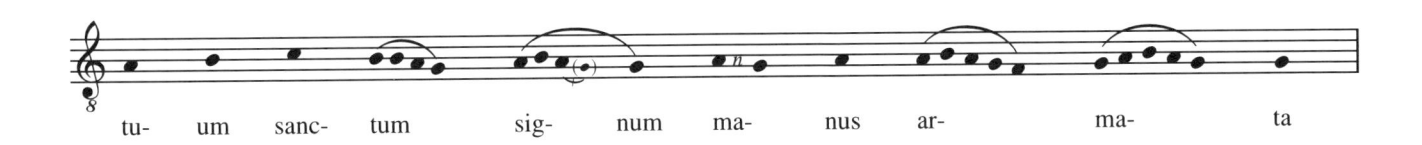

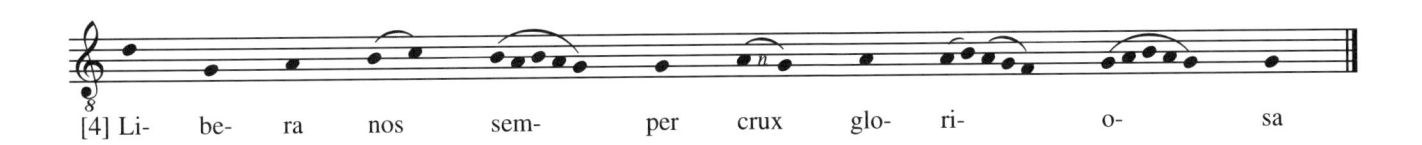

[3a] Ca- te- nę in- fer- no- rum per te sunt de- struc- tę

a- ni- mę sanc- to- rum sunt ab- so- lu- tę

[3b] Tar- ta- re- a le- gi- o est al- li- ga- ta per

tu- um sanc- tum sig- num ma- nus ar- ma- ta

[4] Li- be- ra nos sem- per crux glo- ri- o- sa

30. Summi regis

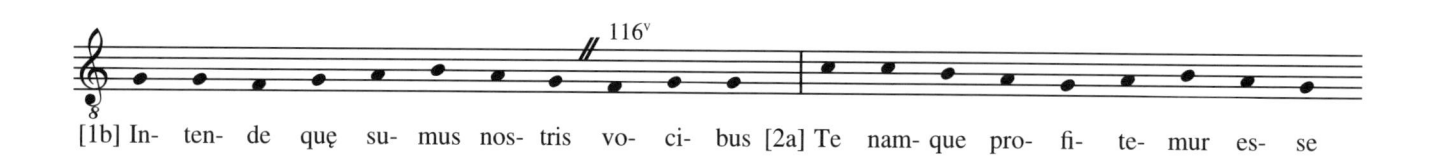

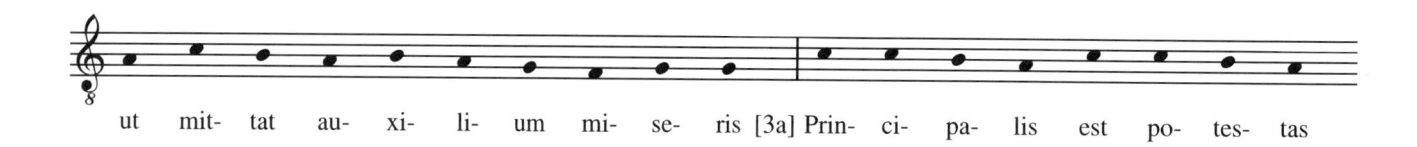

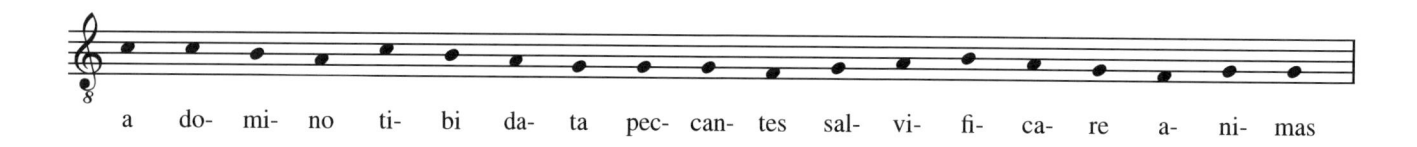

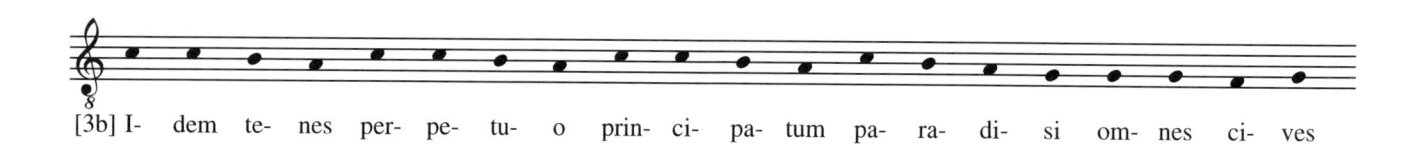

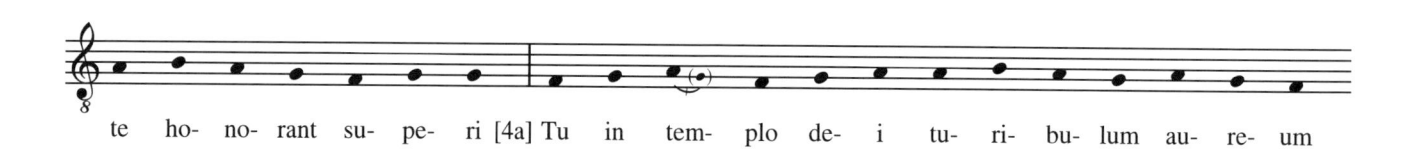

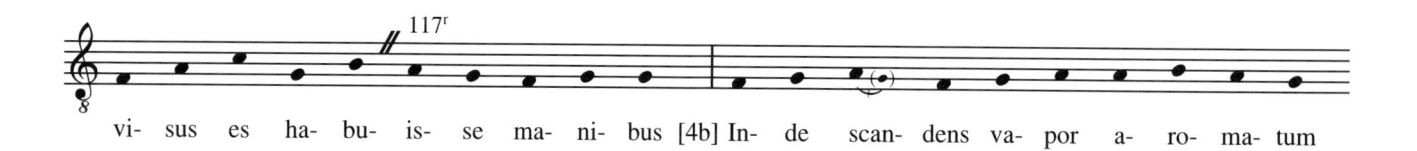

Rc 1741

[1a] Sum- mi re- gis arch- an- ge- le mi- cha- hel Al- le- lu- ia

[1b] In- ten- de quę su- mus nos- tris vo- ci- bus [2a] Te nam- que pro- fi- te- mur es- se

su- per- no- rum prin- ci- pem ci- vi- um [2b] Tu de- um ob- se- cra pro no- bis

ut mit- tat au- xi- li- um mi- se- ris [3a] Prin- ci- pa- lis est po- tes- tas

a do- mi- no ti- bi da- ta pec- can- tes sal- vi- fi- ca- re a- ni- mas

[3b] I- dem te- nes per- pe- tu- o prin- ci- pa- tum pa- ra- di- si om- nes ci- ves

te ho- no- rant su- pe- ri [4a] Tu in tem- plo de- i tu- ri- bu- lum au- re- um

vi- sus es ha- bu- is- se ma- ni- bus [4b] In- de scan- dens va- por a- ro- ma- tum plu- ri- mus per- ve- nit an- te con- spec- tum de- i [5a] Quan- do cum dra- co- ne mag- num

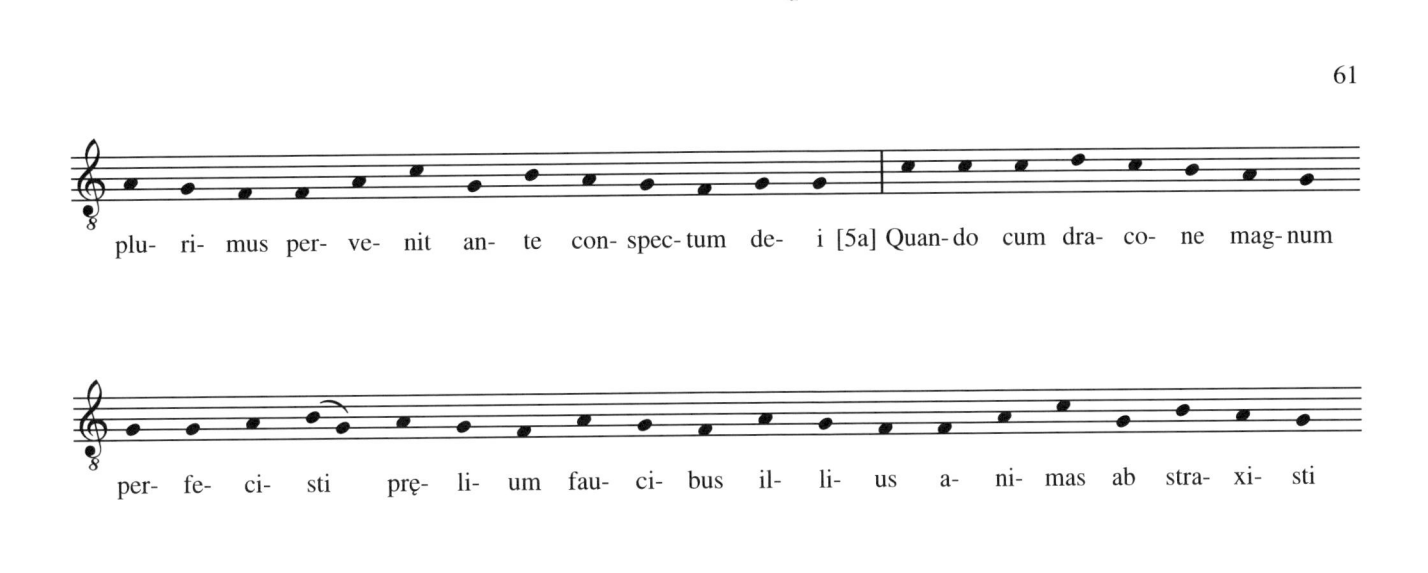

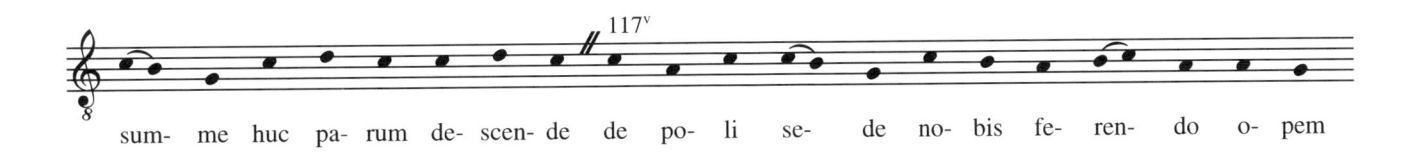

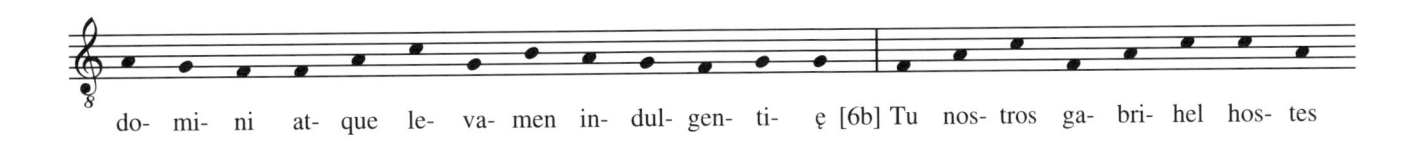

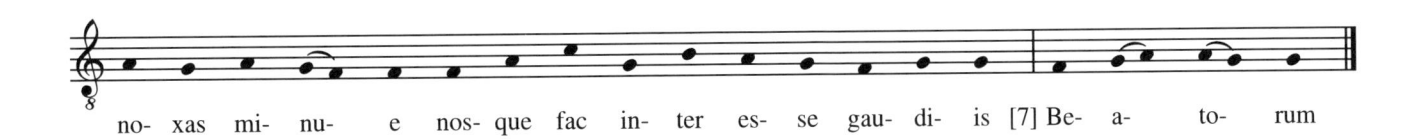

per- fe- ci- sti pre- li- um fau- ci- bus il- li- us a- ni- mas ab stra- xi- sti

plu- ri- mas [5b] Hinc ma- xi- mum a- ge- ba- tur in ce- lo si- len- ti- um mi- li- a

mi- li- um di- ce- bant sa- lus re- gi do- mi- no [6a] Au- di nos mi- cha- hel an- ge- le

sum- me huc pa- rum de- scen- de de po- li se- de no- bis fe- ren- do o- pem

do- mi- ni at- que le- va- men in- dul- gen- ti- ę [6b] Tu nos- tros ga- bri- hel hos- tes

pro- ster- ne tu ra- pha- hel e- gris af- fer me- de- lam mor- bos ab- ster- ge

no- xas mi- nu- e nos- que fac in- ter es- se gau- di- is [7] Be- a- to- rum

31. Clare sanctorum senatus

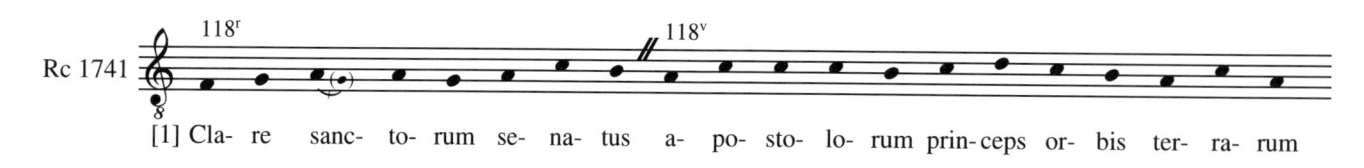

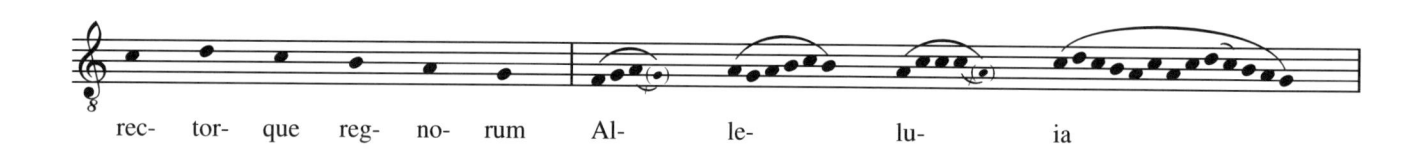

Rc 1741

[1] Clare sanctorum senatus apostolorum princeps orbis terrarum rectorque regnorum Alleluia

[2a] Aecclesiarum mores et vitam moderare [2b] Quę per doctrinam tuam fideles sunt ubique [3a] Antiochus et romus concedunt tibi petre regni solium [3b] Tirannidis tu paule alexandria invasisti greciam [4a] Ethiopes orridos mathee agnelli vellere [4b] Qui maculas nesciant aliquas vestisti candido [5] Thomas bartholomee [6a] Iohannes philippe simon iacobique pariles [6b] Andreas taddee dei

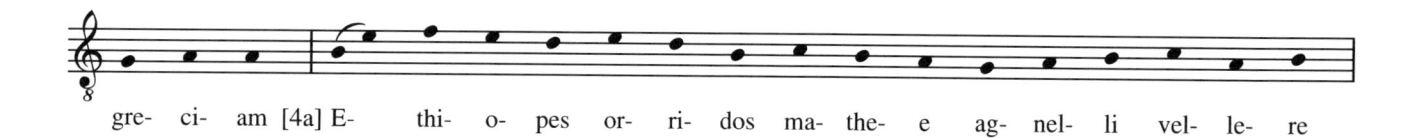

bel- la- to- res in- cli- ti [7a] En vos oc- ci- dens et o- ri- ens [7b] Im- mo- te- res mun- di

cir- cu- lus se pa- tres ha- be- re gau- det et ex- pec- tat iu- di- ces [8] Et id- cir- co

mun- dus om- nis lau- des vo- bis et ho- no- res sa- tis de- bi- tas sup- plex im- pen- dit

32. Omnes sancti seraphin

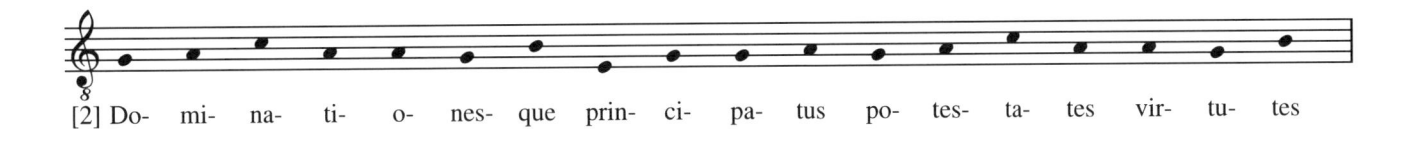

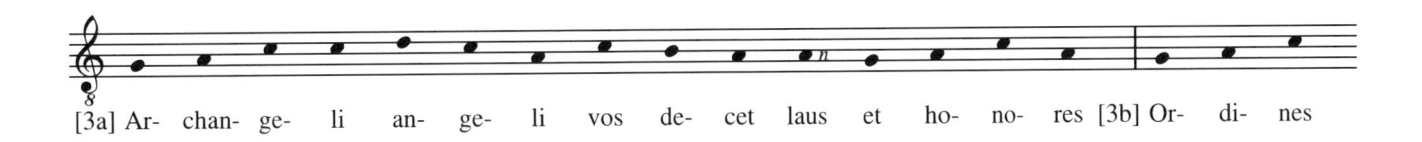

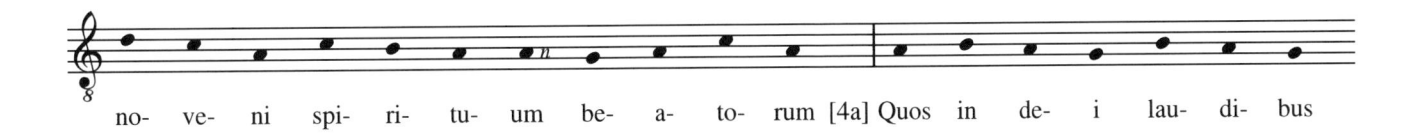

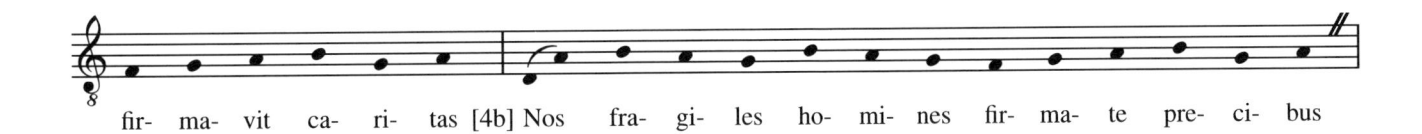

Rc 1741

Om- nes sanc- ti se- ra- phin che- ru- bin thro- ni quo- que Al- le- lu- ia

[2] Do- mi- na- ti- o- nes- que prin- ci- pa- tus po- tes- ta- tes vir- tutes

[3a] Ar- chan- ge- li an- ge- li vos de- cet laus et ho- no- res [3b] Or- di- nes

no- ve- ni spi- ri- tu- um be- a- to- rum [4a] Quos in de- i lau- di- bus

fir- ma- vit ca- ri- tas [4b] Nos fra- gi- les ho- mi- nes fir- ma- te pre- ci- bus

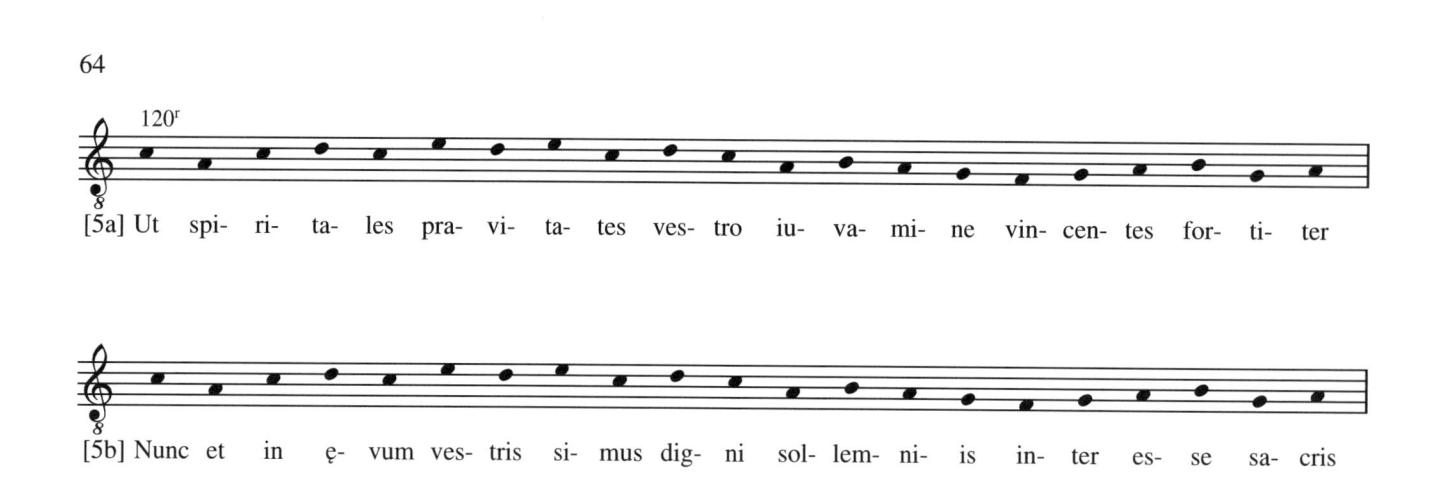

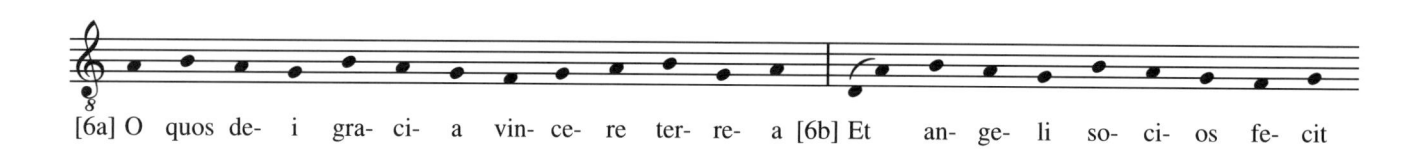

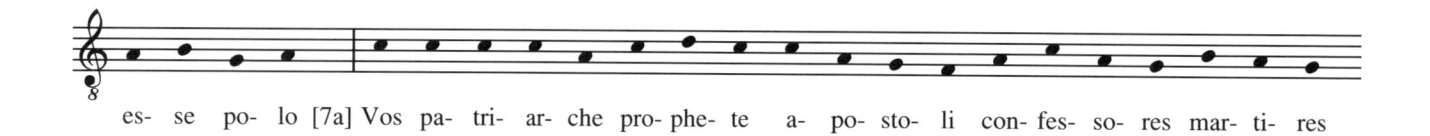

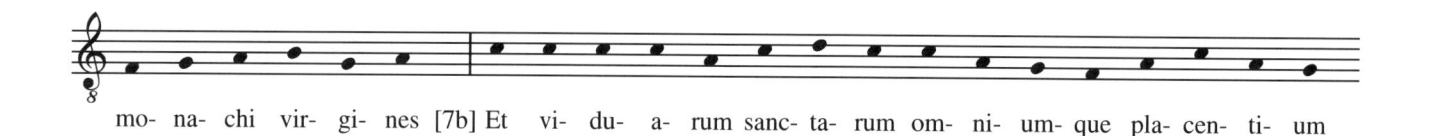

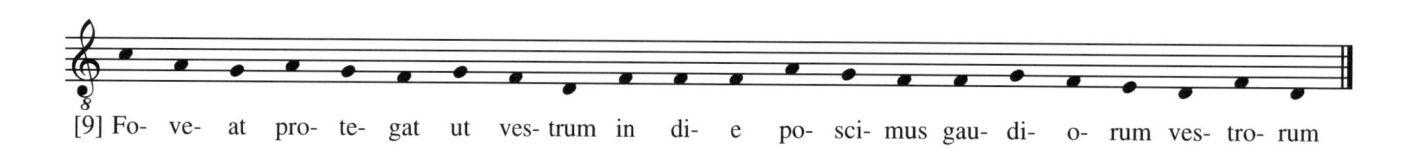

[5a] Ut spiritales pravitates vestro iuvamine vincentes fortiter

[5b] Nunc et in ęvum vestris simus digni sollemniis interesse sacris

[6a] O quos dei gracia vincere terrea [6b] Et angeli socios fecit esse polo [7a] Vos patriarche prophete apostoli confessores martires monachi virgines [7b] Et viduarum sanctarum omniumque placentium populus supremo domino [8a] Nos adiutorium [8b] Nunc et perhenniter

[9] Foveat protegat ut vestrum in die poscimus gaudiorum vestrorum

33. Sacerdotem Christi Martinum

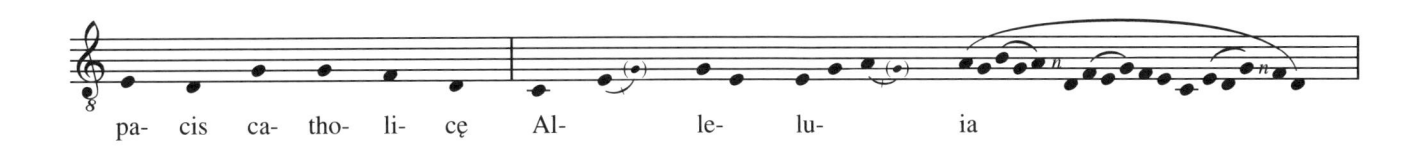

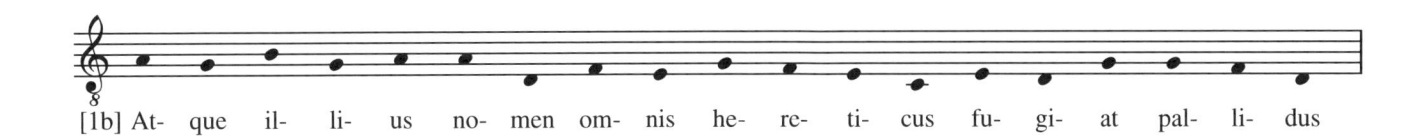

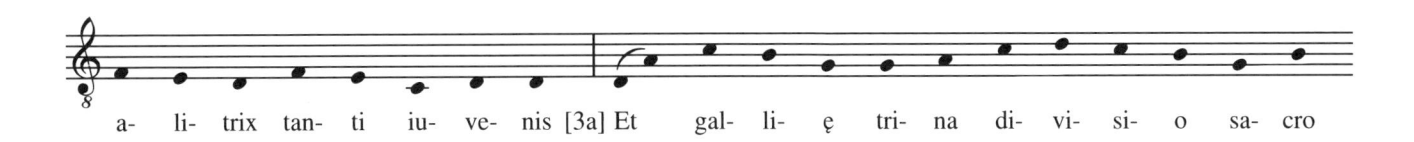

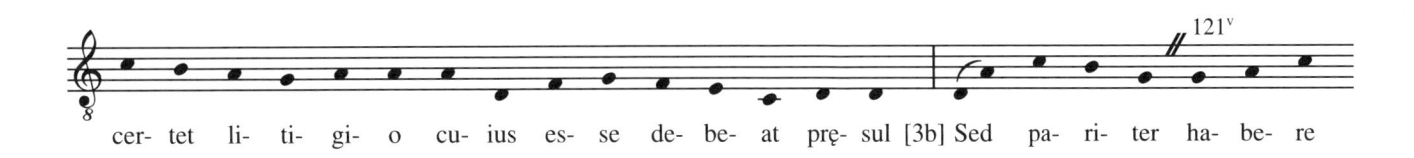

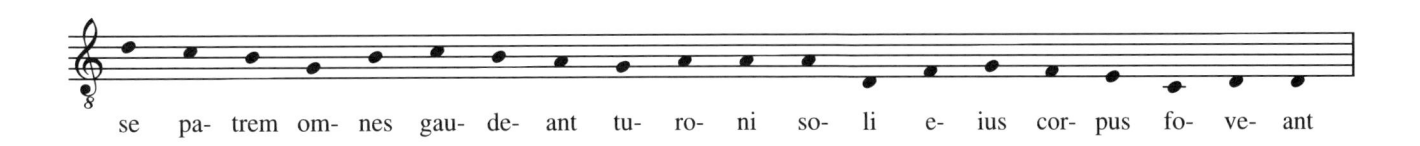

Rc 1741

[1] Sa- cer- do- tem chris- ti mar- ti- num cunc- ta per or- bem ca- nat ęc- cle- si- a pa- cis ca- tho- li- cę Al- le- lu- ia

[1b] At- que il- li- us no- men om- nis he- re- ti- cus fu- gi- at pal- li- dus

[2a] Pan- no- ni- a lę- te- tur ge- ni- trix ta- lis fi- li- i [2b] I- ta- li- a ex- ul- tet a- li- trix tan- ti iu- ve- nis [3a] Et gal- li- ę tri- na di- vi- si- o sa- cro cer- tet li- ti- gi- o cu- ius es- se de- be- at prę- sul [3b] Sed pa- ri- ter ha- be- re se pa- trem om- nes gau- de- ant tu- ro- ni so- li e- ius cor- pus fo- ve- ant

[4a] Hu- ic fran- co- rum at- que ger- ma- ni- ę plebs om- nis plau- dat [4b] Qui- bus vi- den- dum

invexit dominum in sua veste [5a] Hic celebris est egypti patribus greciae quoque cunctis sapientibus [5b] Qui impares se martini meritis sentiunt atque eius medicamini [6a] Nam febres sedat demonesque fugat paralitica membra glutinat [6b] Et mortuorum sua prece trium reddit corpora vite pristine [7a] Hic ritus sacrilegos destruit et ad christi gloriam dat ignibus idola [7b] Hic nudis misteria brachiis conficiens preditus est celesti lumine [8a] Hic oculis ac manibus in celum et totis viribus suspensus terrena cuncta respuit [8b] Eius ori numquam christus abfuit sive iu- sti- ti- a vel quic-quid ad ve- ram vi- tam per- ti- net [9a] I- gi- tur te cunc- ti

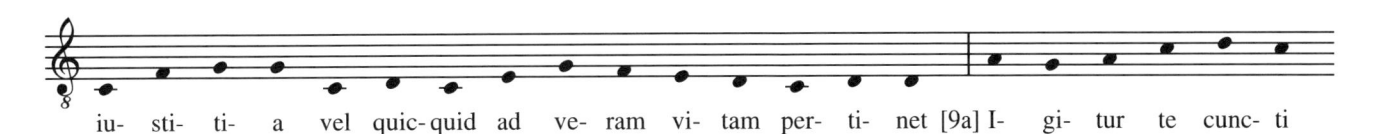

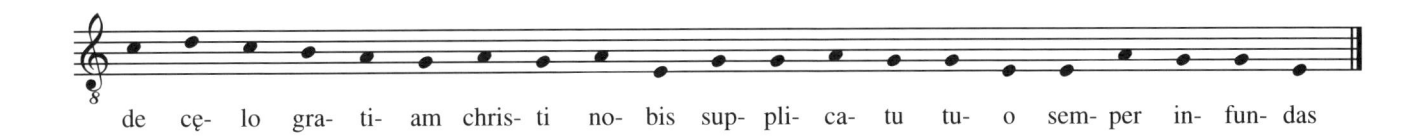

po- sci- mus o mar- ti- ne ut qui mul- ta mi- ra hic o- sten- di- sti [9b] E- ti- am

de cę- lo gra- ti- am chris- ti no- bis sup- pli- ca- tu tu- o sem- per in- fun- das

34. Deus in tua virtute

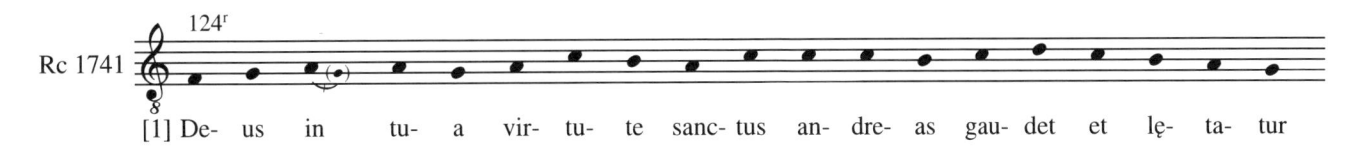

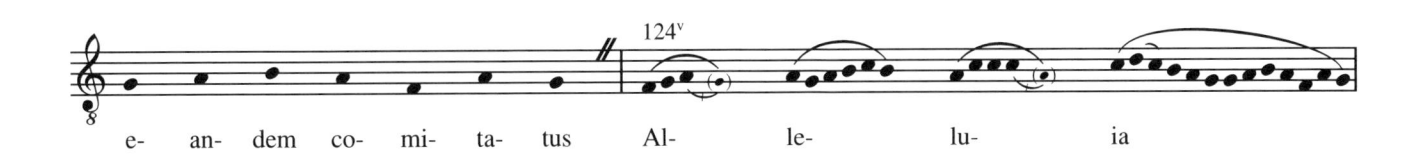

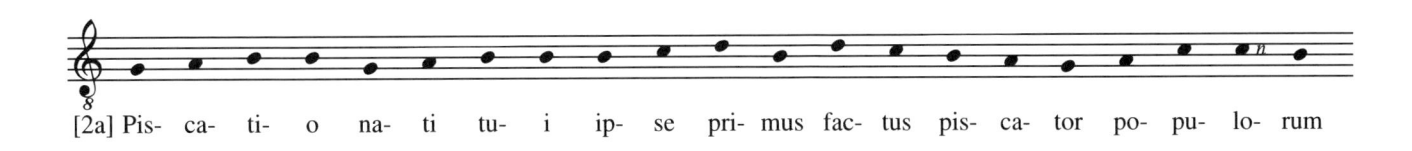

Rc 1741

[1] De- us in tu- a vir- tu- te sanc- tus an- dre- as gau- det et lę- ta- tur

e- an- dem co- mi- ta- tus Al- le- lu- ia

[2a] Pis- ca- ti- o na- ti tu- i ip- se pri- mus fac- tus pis- ca- tor po- pu- lo- rum

Mir- mi- do- nes i- do- la- tras di- u fluc- ti- va- gos re- ti cę- pit fi- de- i

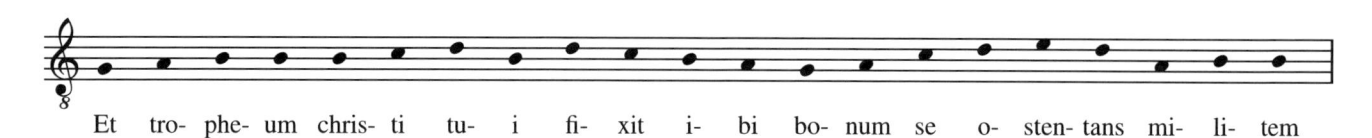

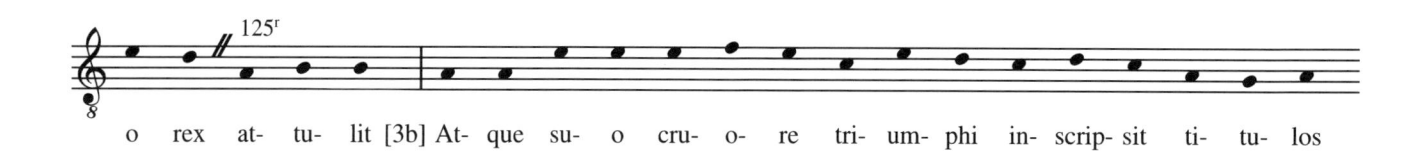

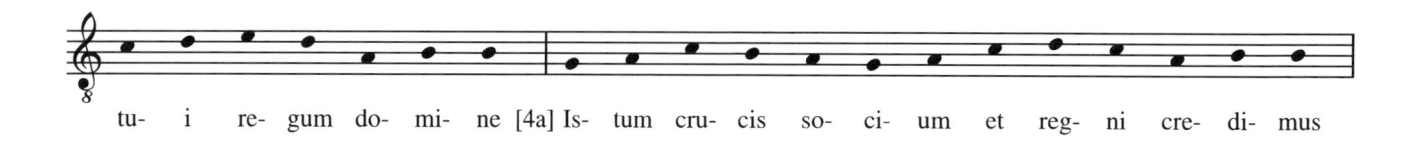

[2b] Is legibus achaiam tuis deus victor illius subiugavit

Et tropheum christi tui fixit ibi bonum se ostentans militem

[3a] Miraculis virtutibus doctrinis quacumque quęsita spolia tibi o rex attulit

[3b] Atque suo cruore triumphi inscripsit titulos tui regum domine

[4a] Istum crucis socium et regni credimus [4b] Christi filii tui atque fraterculum

[5a] Nos igitur peccatis nostris gravati te deus poscimus

[5b] Ut illius quod tua semper sectatus pręcepta tibi placet

[6] Nos intercessione tuearis in ęternum

35. Ad templi huius limina

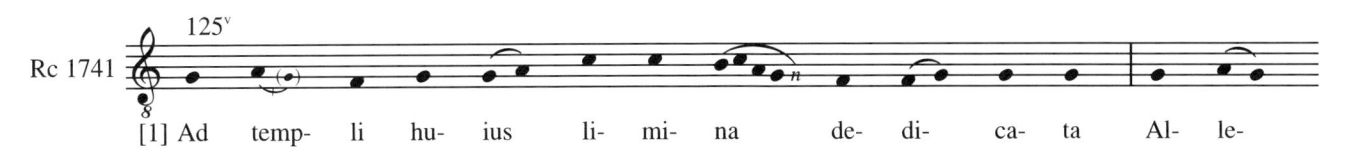

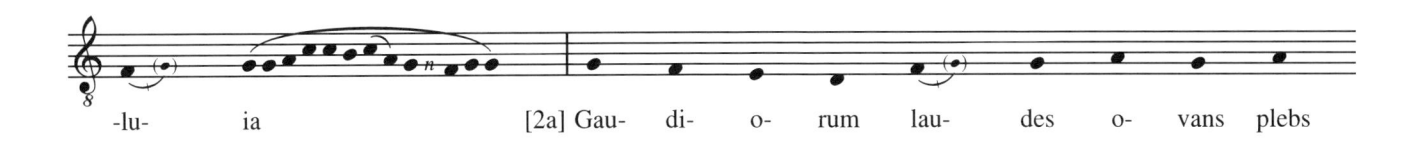

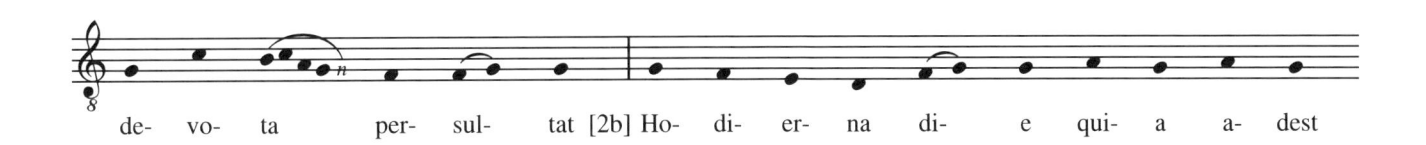

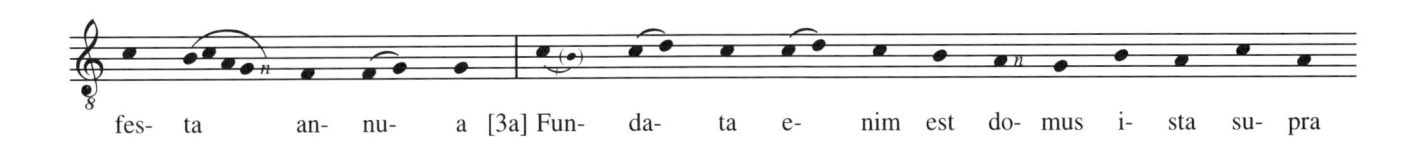

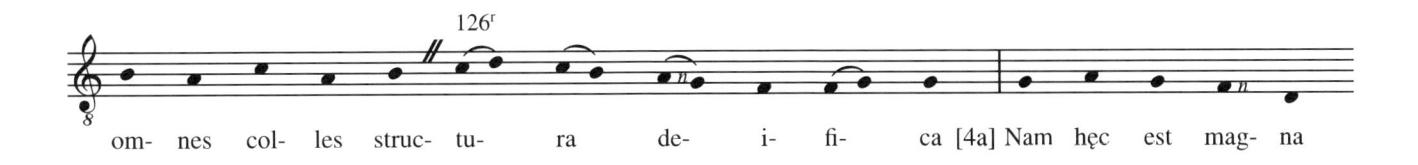

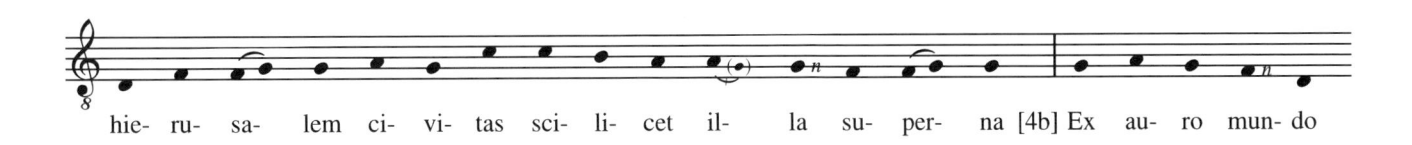

Rc 1741

[1] Ad templi huius limina dedicata Alleluia

[2a] Gaudiorum laudes ovans plebs devota persultat

[2b] Hodierna die qui adest festa annua

[3a] Fundata enim est domus ista supra montium cacumina

[3b] Et exaltata est supra omnes colles structura deifica

[4a] Nam hec est magna hierusalem civitas scilicet illa superna

[4b] Ex auro mundo circumtectis gemmis ac rutilans muris per ampla

[5a] Hec est illa cęlestis

au- la an- ge- lo- rum pa- tri- a [5b] Aec- cle- si- a fir- ma quę pe- tra e- ter- na- que re- gi- a [6a] Dic- ta est quę pa- cis vi- si- o urbs hie- ru- sa- lem cel- sa

[6b] Ex vi- vis quę pe- tris stru- i- tur be- a- to- rum a- ni- mae [7a] Qua de- us quo- que sum- mus rex su- per om- nes u- nus cel- si- o- ra in se- de pre- si- det

il- la [7b] Sunt ma- ies- ta- tes co- ram vir- tu- tes at- que pre- stant fe- li- ci- que qui- e- te mu- ne- ra ple- na [8a] In de- fes- sa vo- ce lau- des per- sul- tant ag- mi- na

[8b] Glo- ri- a et reg- num il- li de- pro- munt per sec- la [9a] Ve- ne- ran- da est er- go au- la no- sci- tu- ra u- bi pre- es- se nu- mi- na ta- li- a

[9b] A- do- ran- da est per- so- na sum- ma im- pe- rans cę- lum et ter- ram

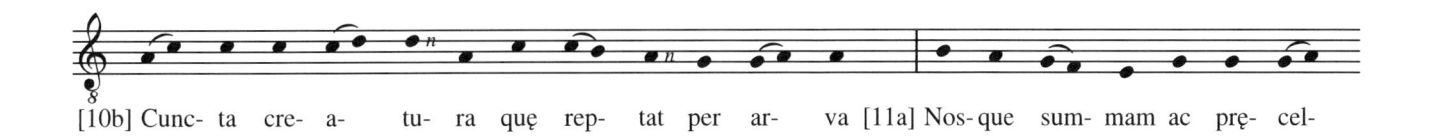

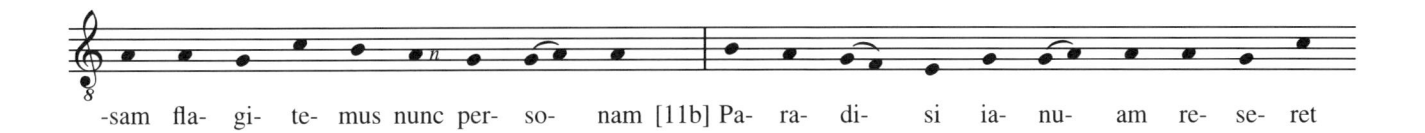

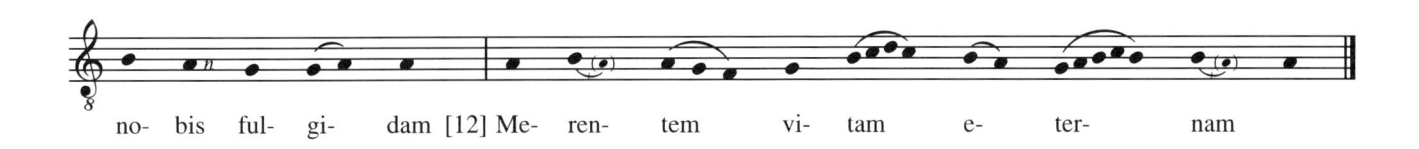

cunc- ta- que ma- ri- a [10a] Sol lu- na et stel- lę il- li dant glo- ri- am

[10b] Cunc- ta cre- a- tu- ra quę rep- tat per ar- va [11a] Nos- que sum- mam ac prę- cel-

-sam fla- gi- te- mus nunc per- so- nam [11b] Pa- ra- di- si ia- nu- am re- se- ret

no- bis ful- gi- dam [12] Me- ren- tem vi- tam e- ter- nam

36. Benedicta semper sancta

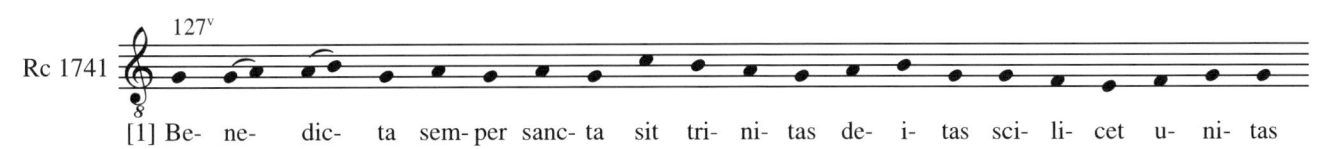

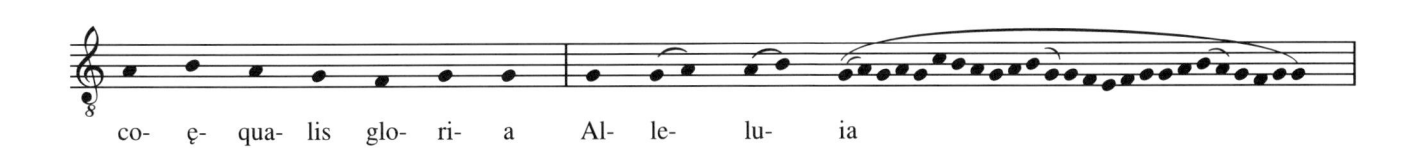

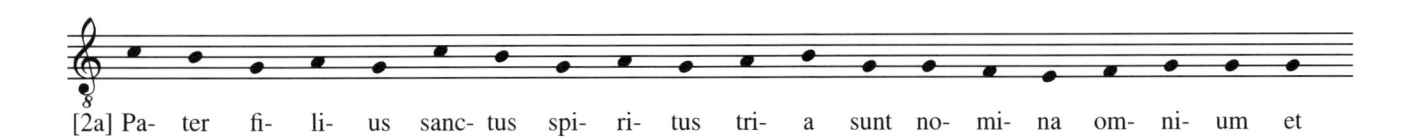

Rc 1741

[1] Be- ne- dic- ta sem- per sanc- ta sit tri- ni- tas de- i- tas sci- li- cet u- ni- tas

co- ę- qua- lis glo- ri- a Al- le- lu- ia

[2a] Pa- ter fi- li- us sanc- tus spi- ri- tus tri- a sunt no- mi- na om- ni- um et

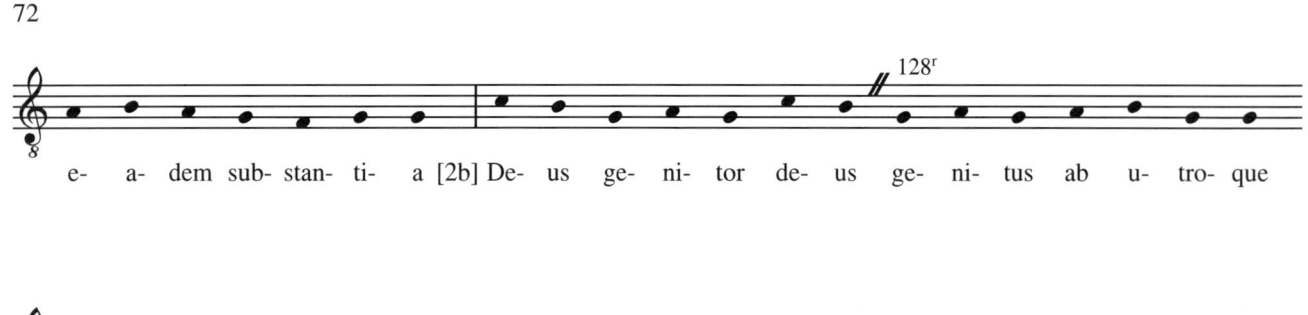

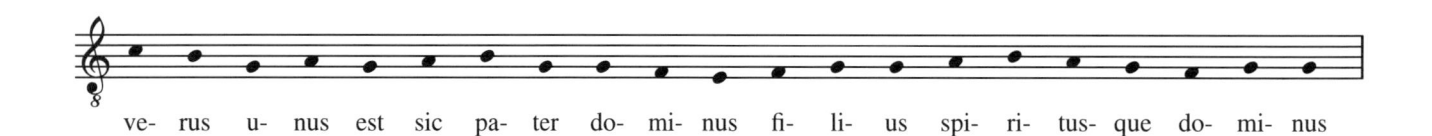

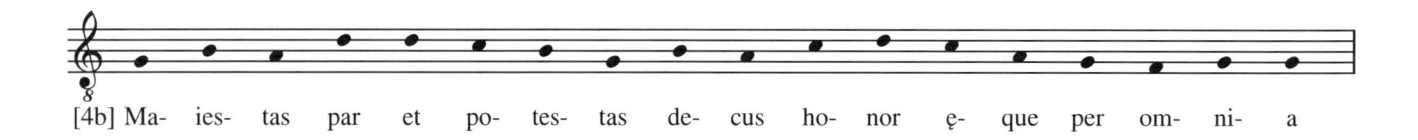

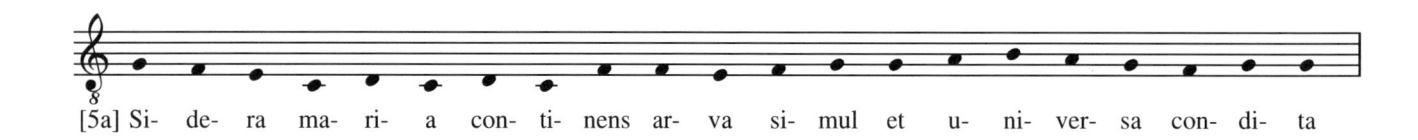

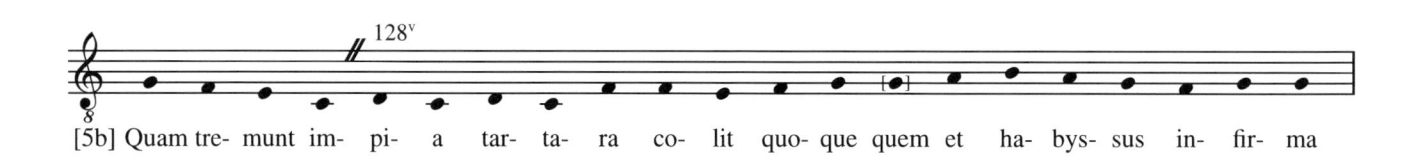

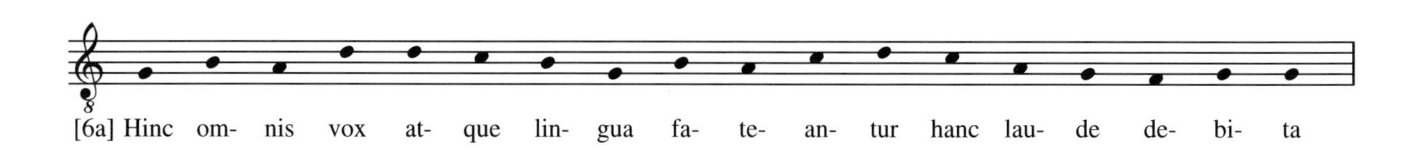

e- a- dem sub- stan- ti- a [2b] De- us ge- ni- tor de- us ge- ni- tus ab u- tro- que

sa- cer de- us spi- ri- tus que do- mi- nus [3] Non tres ta- men di- i sunt de- us

ve- rus u- nus est sic pa- ter do- mi- nus fi- li- us spi- ri- tus- que do- mi- nus

[4a] Pro- pri- e- tas in per- son- is u- ni- tas est et in es- sen- ti- a

[4b] Ma- ies- tas par et po- tes- tas de- cus ho- nor ę- que per om- ni- a

[5a] Si- de- ra ma- ri- a con- ti- nens ar- va si- mul et u- ni- ver- sa con- di- ta

[5b] Quam tre- munt im- pi- a tar- ta- ra co- lit quo- que quem et ha- bys- sus in- fir- ma

[6a] Hinc om- nis vox at- que lin- gua fa- te- an- tur hanc lau- de de- bi- ta

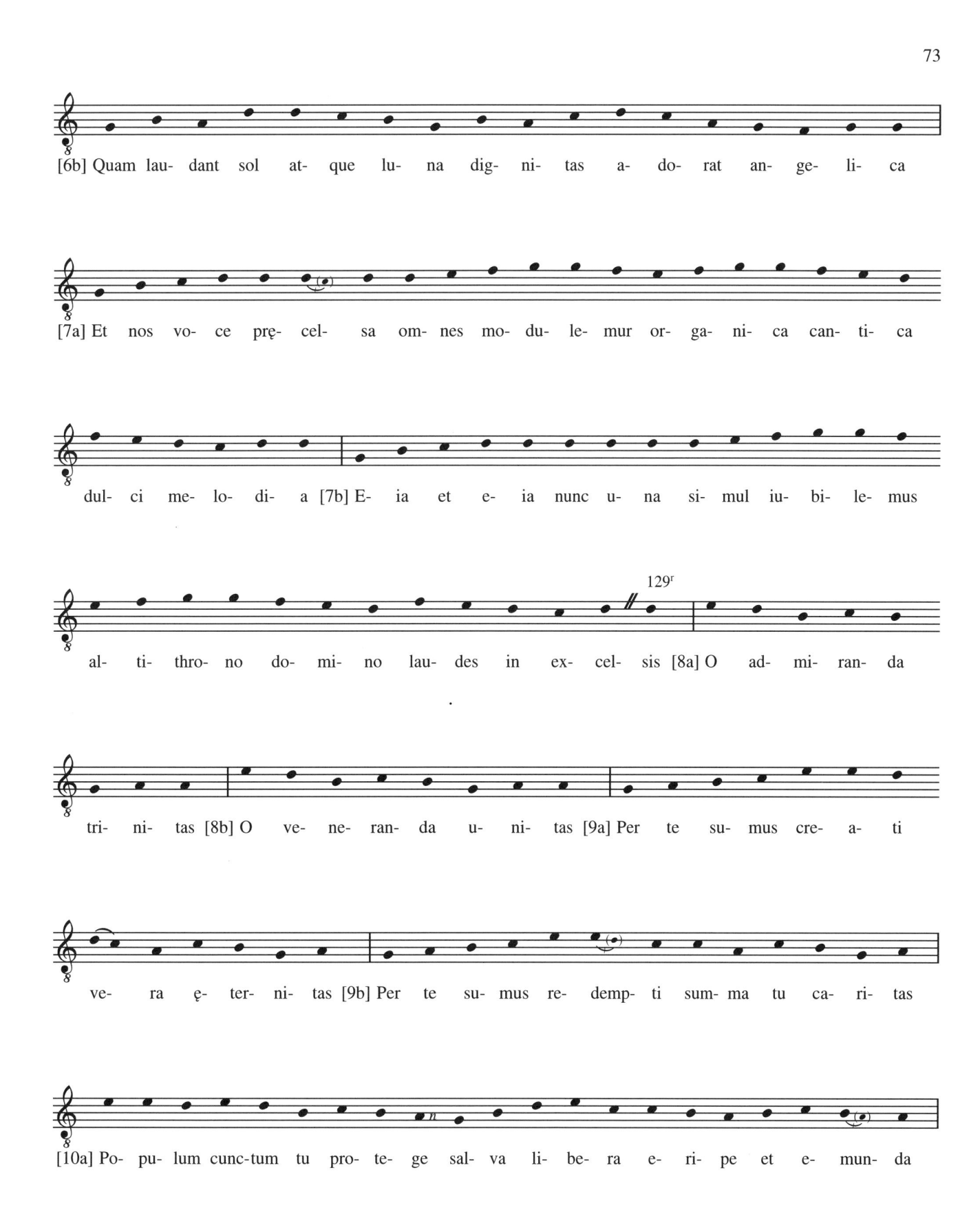

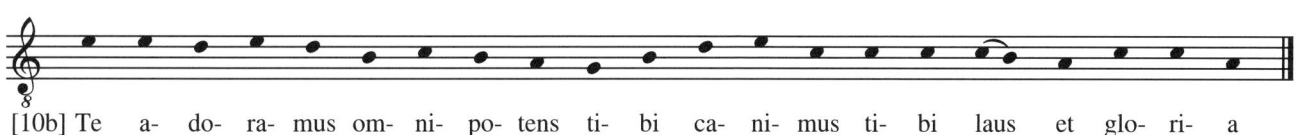

[6b] Quam laudant sol atque luna dignitas adorat angelica

[7a] Et nos voce prę-celsa omnes modulemur organica cantica

dulci melodia [7b] Eia et eia nunc una simul iubilemus

altithrono domino laudes in excelsis [8a] O admiranda

trinitas [8b] O veneranda unitas [9a] Per te sumus creati

vera ęternitas [9b] Per te sumus redempti summa tu caritas

[10a] Populum cunctum tu protege salva libera eripe et emunda

[10b] Te adoramus omnipotens tibi canimus tibi laus et gloria

37. Stans a longe

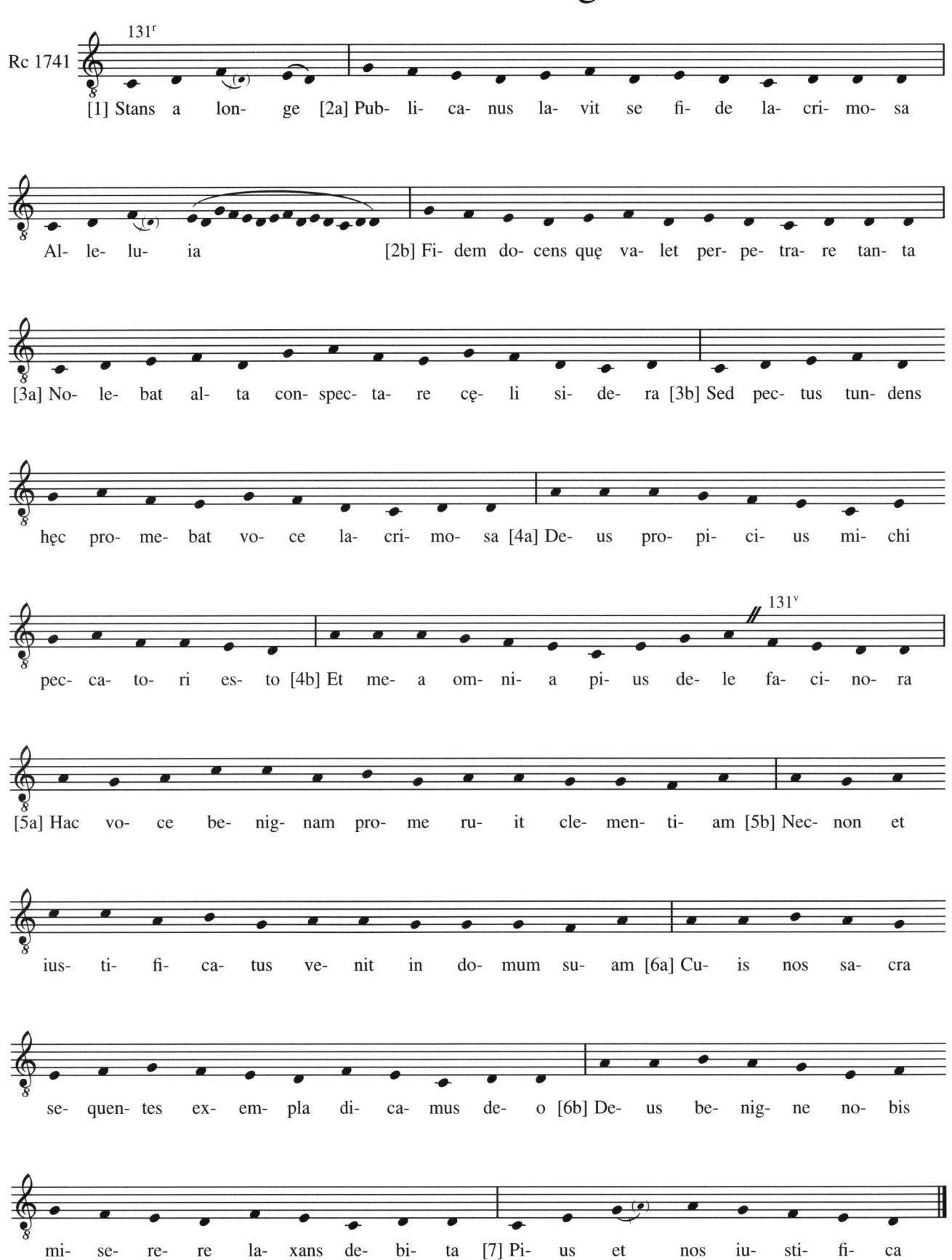

Rc 1741

[1] Stans a longe [2a] Publicanus lavit se fide lacrimosa Alleluia [2b] Fidem docens quę valet perpetrare tanta [3a] Nolebat alta conspectare cęli sidera [3b] Sed pectus tundens hęc promebat voce lacrimosa [4a] Deus propicius michi peccatori esto [4b] Et mea omnia pius dele facinora [5a] Hac voce benignam promeruit clementiam [5b] Necnon et iustificatus venit in domum suam [6a] Cuis nos sacra sequentes exempla dicamus deo [6b] Deus benigne nobis miserere laxans debita [7] Pius et nos iustifica

38. Laeta mente

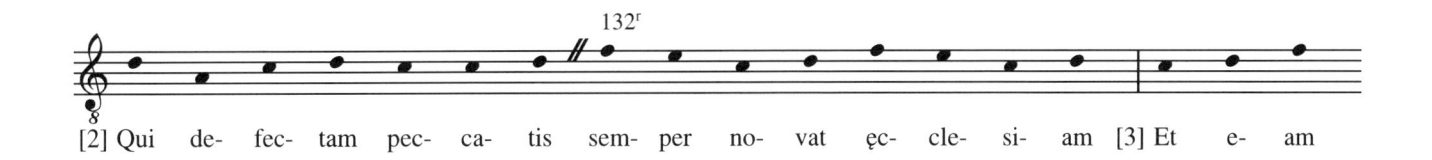

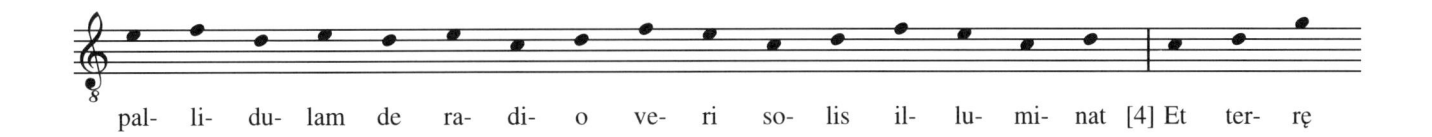

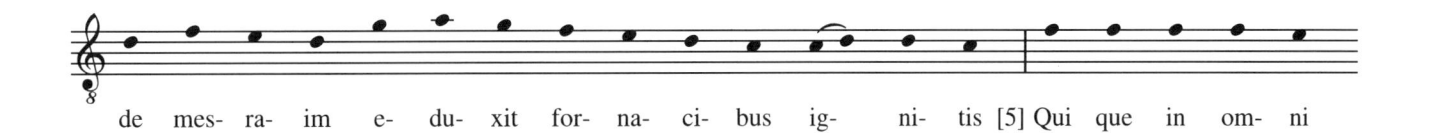

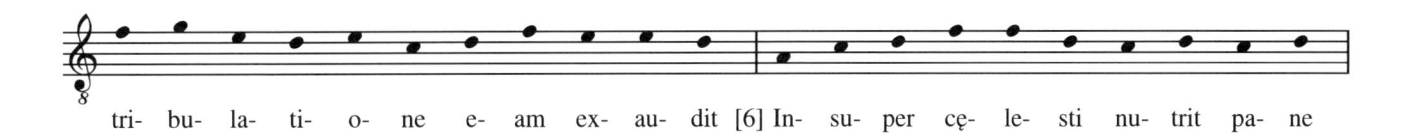

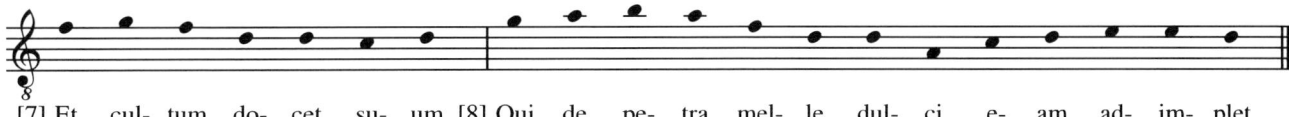

Rc 1741

[1] Le- ta men- te ca- na- mus de- o no- stro Al- le- lu- ia

[2] Qui de- fec- tam pec- ca- tis sem- per no- vat ęc- cle- si- am [3] Et e- am pal- li- du- lam de ra- di- o ve- ri so- lis il- lu- mi- nat [4] Et ter- rę de mes- ra- im e- du- xit for- na- ci- bus ig- ni- tis [5] Qui que in om- ni tri- bu- la- ti- o- ne e- am ex- au- dit [6] In- su- per cę- le- sti nu- trit pa- ne [7] Et cul- tum do- cet su- um [8] Qui de pe- tra mel- le dul- ci e- am ad- im- plet

39. O quam mira

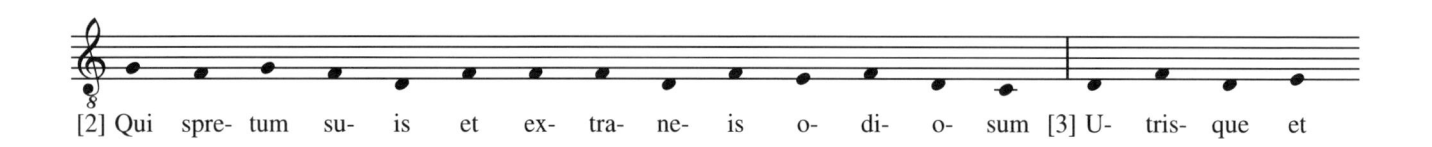

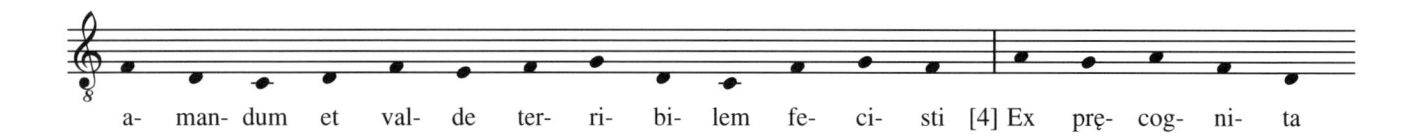

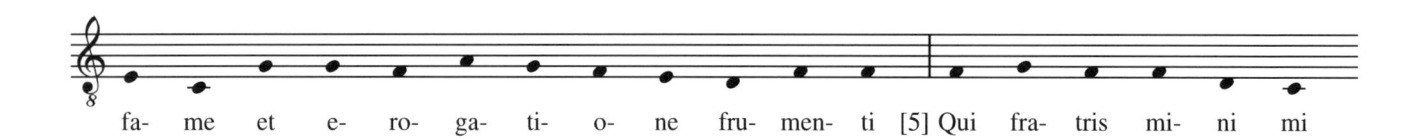

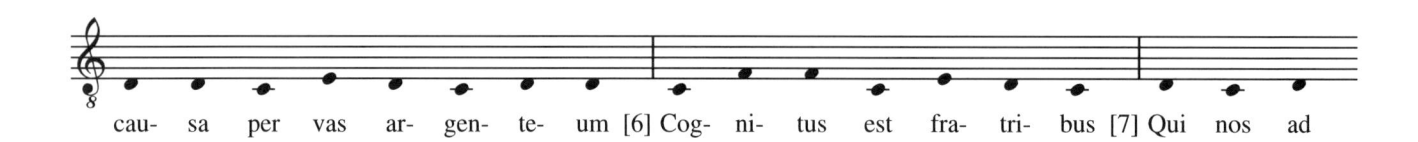

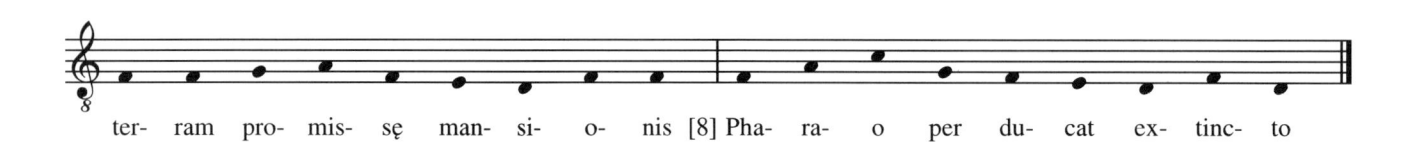

Rc 1741

[1] O quam mi- ra sunt de- us tu- a por- ten- ta Al- le- lu- ia

[2] Qui spre- tum su- is et ex- tra- ne- is o- di- o- sum [3] U- tris- que et a- man- dum et val- de ter- ri- bi- lem fe- ci- sti [4] Ex prę- cog- ni- ta fa- me et e- ro- ga- ti- o- ne fru- men- ti [5] Qui fra- tris mi- ni- mi cau- sa per vas ar- gen- te- um [6] Cog- ni- tus est fra- tri- bus [7] Qui nos ad ter- ram pro- mis- sę man- si- o- nis [8] Pha- ra- o per du- cat ex- tinc- to

40. Almiflua caelorum

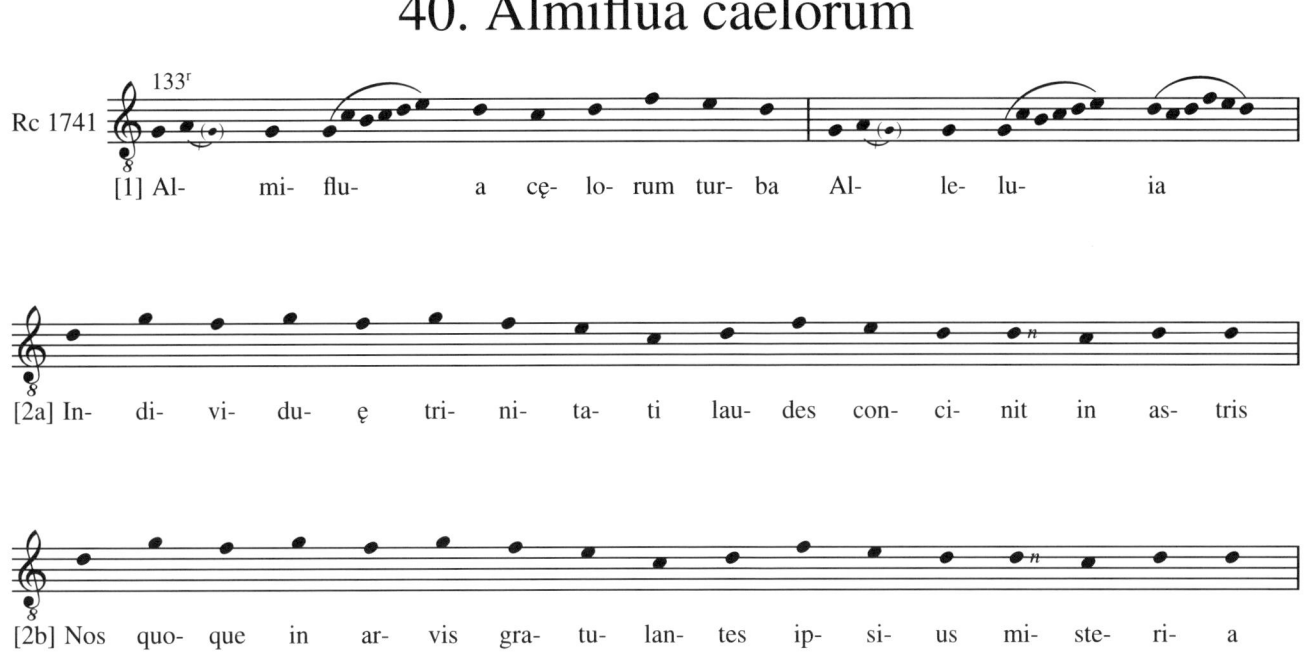

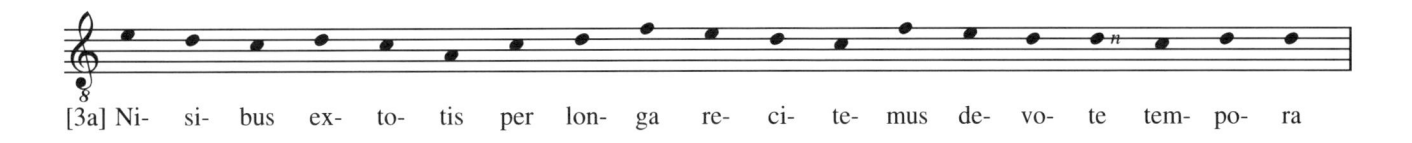

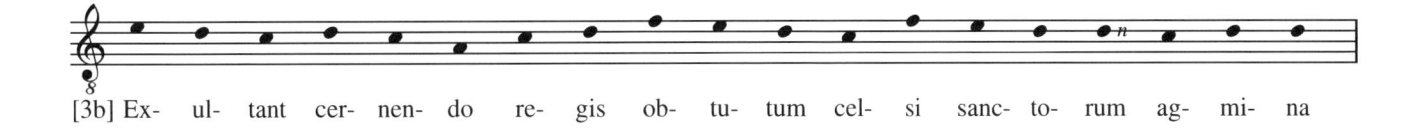

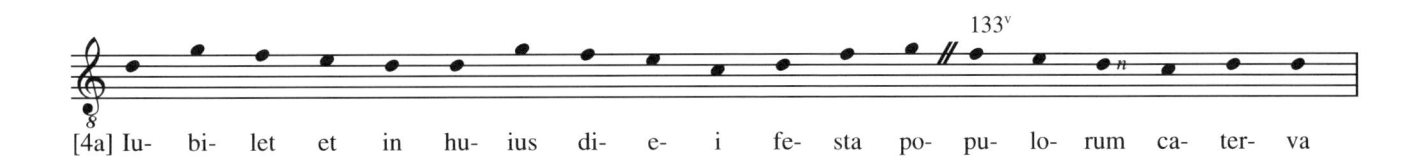

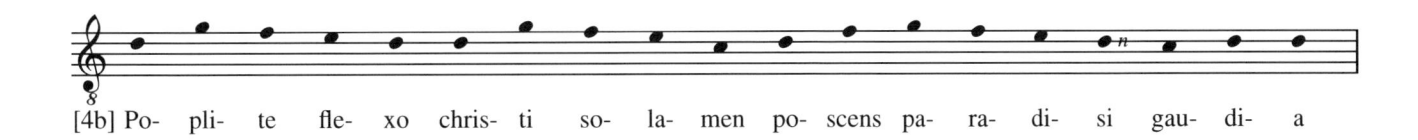

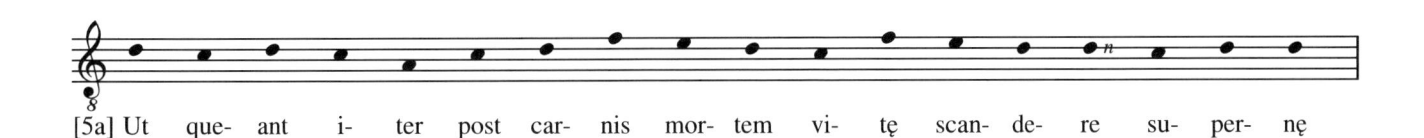

Rc 1741

[1] Al- mi- flu- a cę- lo- rum tur- ba Al- le- lu- ia

[2a] In- di- vi- du- ę tri- ni- ta- ti lau- des con- ci- nit in as- tris

[2b] Nos quo- que in ar- vis gra- tu- lan- tes ip- si- us mi- ste- ri- a

[3a] Ni- si- bus ex- to- tis per lon- ga re- ci- te- mus de- vo- te tem- po- ra

[3b] Ex- ul- tant cer- nen- do re- gis ob- tu- tum cel- si sanc- to- rum ag- mi- na

[4a] Iu- bi- let et in hu- ius di- e- i fe- sta po- pu- lo- rum ca- ter- va

[4b] Po- pli- te fle- xo chris- ti so- la- men pos- cens pa- ra- di- si gau- di- a

[5a] Ut que- ant i- ter post car- nis mor- tem vi- tę scan- de- re su- per- nę

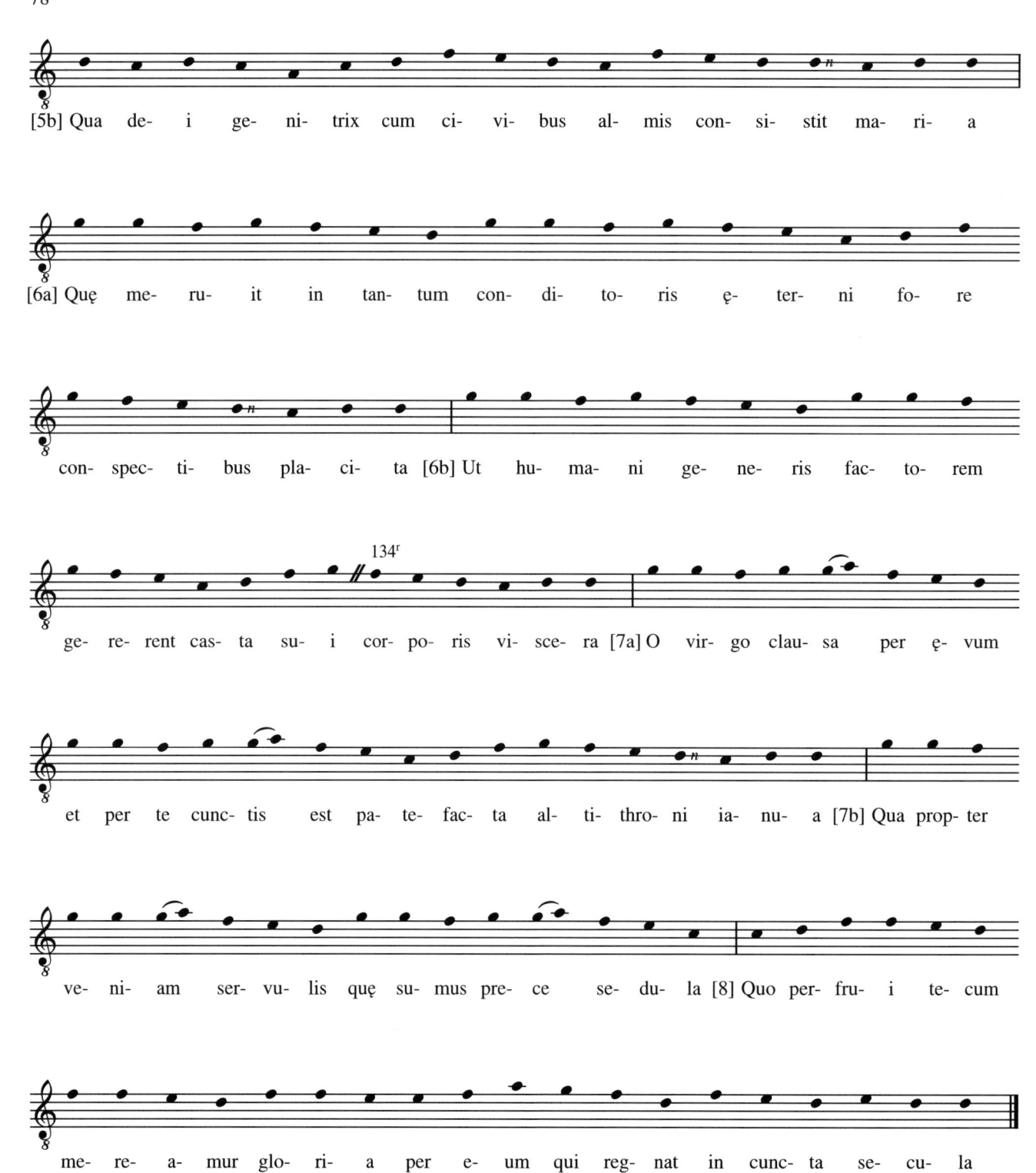

[5b] Qua dei genitrix cum civibus almis consistit maria

[6a] Quę meruit in tantum conditoris ęterni fore conspectibus placita [6b] Ut humani generis factorem gererent casta sui corporis viscera [7a] O virgo clausa per ęvum et per te cunctis est patefacta altithroni ianua [7b] Qua propter veniam servulis quę sumus prece sedula [8] Quo perfrui tecum mereamur gloria per eum qui regnat in cuncta secula